Trauma Theory As an Approach to Analyzing Literary Texts

Other Books by Ted Morrissey

Scholarship
The 'Beowulf' Poet and His Real Monsters
Trauma Theory As a Method for Understanding Literary Texts
A Concise Summary and Analysis of The Mueller Report

Fiction
Men of Winter
Figures in Blue
An Untimely Frost
Weeping with an Ancient God
Crowsong for the Stricken
Mrs Saville
The Artist Spoke
First Kings and Other Stories

Trauma Theory As an Approach to Analyzing Literary Texts

An Updated and Expanded Edition, With Readings

Foreword by Robert L. McLaughlin

New Introduction, Notes & Selected Readings by the Author

Ted Morrissey

Twelve Winters Press

Acknowledgments

My original manuscript benefited from commentary by Curtis White, Susan M. Kim, and (especially) Robert L. McLaughlin, who generously wrote the Foreword for the 2016 edition of the book and allowed me to reprint it in this edition. Brittany Sievers provided valuable assistance in updating the references to posttraumatic stress disorder as currently discussed in *DSM-5*.

To Bob McLaughlin—
my last and greatest teacher

CONTENTS

Chapter 7

Foreword

This book sheds new light on a problem that has bedeviled scholars of contemporary literature for many years. While struggling through the 1970s and 1980s to define a cultural movement that by its own terms resisted definitions of any kind and then in the 1990s and twenty-first century arguing whether the movement was over and, if so, when it ended, we have been flummoxed by the persistent, annoying, but very good question: If postmodern literature is a manifestation of the cultural anxieties of the second half of the twentieth century, then why do so many earlier texts, some of them hundreds of years earlier, look so darn postmodern? If the intertextual deconstructions of Kathy Acker's *Empire of the Senseless* are postmodern, why shouldn't those of *The Canterbury Tales* be? If the carnivalesque excesses of Thomas Pynchon's *Gravity's Rainbow* are postmodern, why shouldn't those of *Gargantua and Pantagruel* be? If the self-referentiality of John Barth's *Coming Soon!!!* is postmodern, why shouldn't that of *Tristram Shandy* be? If the blurring of fact and fiction in Robert Coover's *The Public Burning* is postmodern, why shouldn't that in *Don Quixote* be? Put another way, what's special about the literature of the second half of the twentieth century that its postmodernism is different from what's manifested in the earlier texts I mentioned? Put yet another way, what common cause, existing across centuries, inspired authors to write in similar intertextual, carnivalesque, self-referential, and boundary-blurring ways?

i

In this book, Ted Morrissey has chosen to pursue the last question, looking for the causes of postmodern literature. What was in the air, so to speak, at the specific times when authors produced literature that looked postmodern? Is there some way in which we can say they were the products of a similar zeitgeist? In pursuit of these questions, Dr. Morrissey conducts a liminal analysis, nimbly working the lines between present and past, psychology and art, unconscious and conscious, individual consciousness and collective consciousness, and instinct and craft. His argument begins with the similarity between certain narrative characteristics we associate with postmodern literature and characteristics that are often found in the stories of people suffering from Post-Traumatic Stress Disorder. Is it possible, he asks, that entire cultures can suffer from PTSD, the result of a societally shared traumatic experience? Could the literature that we recognize as seemingly postmodern be a manifestation of a culture's attempting to articulate its trauma, to restore some kind of order to a shattered collective consciousness? It is and it could, according to Dr. Morrissey, and in what follows you will see the careful case he makes, using *Beowulf* and the fiction of William H. Gass as his main case studies. The results are revelatory.

I have spent less time with psychological theory than Dr. Morrissey, but my own ideas on these questions resonate with his. My work on postmodern literature, indeed on literature in general, has been greatly influenced by the work of Mikhail Bakhtin, the eccentric but brilliant Russian theorist of the novel. Bakhtin argues that language, on the micro level, and society, on the macro level, exist in the tension between centripetal and centrifugal forces. Centripetal forces are connected with unity, centrality, contained totality. Centrifugal forces are connected with diversity, plurality, multiplicity. When centripetal forces are dominant, art is limited to the single-voiced expression of the culture's official discourse and ideology is totalitarian. When centrifugal forces are dominant, art is expressed through multiple voices in dialogue and ideology is pluralized and consensus-based. It is in such times that the novel as a genre flourishes: Bakhtin defines the novel by its multivoicedness, what he calls polyglossia and heteroglossia. That is, the novel's ability to mean comes from the many voices, discourses, each of which represents an ideological belief system, that it brings together in dialogue. The multiple discourses each claims to represent the truth, but, by the very act of entering into dialogue, finds its truth claims subverted, and must rally to defend them. Thus the novel's language as language, discourses as discourse, and narratives as narrative are self-referentially foregrounded. In other words, the novel is always about itself and its attempts to represent the world through language. This self-referentialty is, to me, central to anything we call postmodern.

For me, this theory resonates with Dr. Morrissey's argument in that it sees postmodern literature arising from corresponding social conditions. The differences lie in their attitudes. Trauma culture arises from horrific historical moments and the social anxieties they produce. To see postmodern literature as the product of trauma culture is to see its purpose as attempting to represent that culture in an effort to heal it. Art seeks to make us whole. For Bakhtin, heteroglottal culture subverts the dangerous impulse toward totalitarianism by challenging all truth claims. To see postmodern literature as the product of heteroglottal culture is to see its purpose as liberating. Art seeks to free us from enforced homogeneity. Two different ways of looking at postmodern literature, both providing useful frames through which to examine the questions of what exactly postmodern literature is and whence it comes.

Putting aside Bakhtin, I find that Dr. Morrissey's arguments both fascinate and raise further questions for us all to consider. What makes an age traumatic? Are some more traumatic than others? Surely, the perpetual violence of the British medieval period and the nuclear-apocalyptic anxiety of the United States' cold war period justify our seeing them as trauma cultures. But was Georgian England sufficiently traumatized by the succession controversy to produce *Tristram Shandy*? If so, are the standards for trauma such that any culture could be considered a trauma culture?

The way PTSD sufferers present their narratives is to a great extent involuntary in the sense that it is driven by their disorder. When authors' works display the characteristics of trauma narrative, to what extent are they driven by the trauma culture and to what extent are they the products of the authors' craft? Are such postmodern and proto-postmodern works examples of trauma narratives, are they artful representations of trauma narratives, or are they some mixture of the two?

Why do writers in a given traumatic age produce different kinds of work, some postmodern, some not? *Tristram Shandy* is a rather odd duck in the lineup of eighteenth-century English novels defined, according to Ian Watt, by their realism. Writing under the same nuclear shadow of the 1950s, 1960s, and 1970s, William Gaddis, John Barth, Robert Coover, and Thomas Pynchon wrote postmodern masterpieces while Saul Bellow, Philip Roth, Bernard Malamud, and Walker Percy wrote brilliant novels that were nonetheless more conventionally realistic in style. More recently, both Bradford Morrow and Richard Powers, from the second-generation of nuclear anxiety, have written novels about the Trinity explosion of the first A-Bomb, but Powers's *Prisoners' Dilemma* is experimental in form and style, while Morrow's *Trinity Fields* is essentially realistic. Certainly, the Holocaust ranks among the most traumatic events of the twentieth century, yet most of the Holocaust narratives I can think of are composed with realism of style. Colonialism, the Industrial Revolution, slavery, and the American Civil War all introduced upheaval and trauma into culture; there is much work to be done to understand how that trauma became reflected in the literature of the time and thereafter.

In short, this is the best kind of scholarly book: Dr. Morrissey's arguments open our eyes to ideas about literature, its production and reception, its connection to its historical moment, and its history; they also raise questions for us to engage, to up the ante on what we think about when we think about postmodern literature.

Robert L. McLaughlin
Illinois State University
June 30, 2016

Introduction
New to This Edition

Since the publication of *Trauma Theory As a Method for Understanding Literary Texts* in 2016, the interest in an analytical approach based on trauma has only increased—if traffic at the book's webpage and emails and messages from scholars around the world offer anything like a reliable indication. However, the book has been difficult to acquire, and therefore access by scholars and more casual readers has been severely limited. My hope is that this book's publication will help to remedy the situation.

What is more, after the events of 2020 and the first weeks of 2021, it would seem the sources of cultural trauma are only increasing: the Covid-19 pandemic, of course; the rise of Trumpism culminating in the attempted overthrow of the United States government; the uptick in nationalistic movements across the globe; the persistent assassinations of people of color, especially young Black men, at the hands of police; the ever more harrowing effects of climate change; and the dystopic impact of our web-connected world via social media. Sadly, the previous sentence represents only an abridged list of the potential sources of trauma.

There is no doubt that these traumatic events will manifest themselves in the work of writers, poets, artists, and every sort of creative person for years and even decades to come. Literary trauma theory, as discussed here, seeks to recognize the characteristics of the traumatized psyche in, especially, works of fiction. As the book explains, my original interest was the phenomenon of postmodernism as it seemed to ubiquitously emerge in the years following the Second World War. Therefore, I mainly focused on the work of writers in the second half of the twentieth century, especially William H. Gass (who has since become my primary scholarly interest). In short, I theorize that the nuclear annihilation of Nagasaki and Hiroshima in 1945, as the work of the United States, triggered mass posttraumatic stress among Americans, whose psyches were divided by the relief of having achieved The Bomb before their enemies and by the horror of having unleashed its terrible destructive force on the world, especially the civilian populations of two Japanese cities.

Yet, while the literal destruction of the world was a new *achievement* mid-twentieth century, the concept of whole-world annihilation has been one of humankind's greatest fears seemingly forever. To bolster my argument that cultural trauma results in the type of literary production that came to be called postmodern, I looked to older texts that exhibit the telltale signs of postmodernism and an examination of the cultures that produced them to determine if they, too, were *trauma cultures*. In particular, I analyzed the Anglo-Saxon poem *Beowulf* (a study that resulted in another book, *The 'Beowulf' Poet and His Real Monsters* [2013]). In the process, I discovered a rich vein. It appears valid that mass cultural trauma has a tendency to result in literary works with similar narrative characteristics—characteristics which in recent centuries we have labeled *postmodern*: traits such as nonlinear storytelling, repetition, intertextuality, and striving for specialized (even *magical*) language; that is, narrative traits that mimic the struggles the traumatized face when trying to articulate the source of their trauma.

As I said, *Beowulf* and other Old English works demonstrate these postmodern narrative traits—with the Anglo-Saxon Period (c. 410-1066) being marked by decades of continuous warfare, shifting power dynamics, and a host of physical as well as psychological deprivations. The works of Shakespeare have also become a fertile field for literary trauma theorists, as the Bard was writing during a time of great religious upheaval, continual wars or at least threat of war, fear of demonic forces, attempted regicide, and reoccurring bouts of plague (to list a few sources of cultural trauma). Also, we think of James Joyce as a modernist writer, but his greatest works—*Ulysses* and *Finnegans Wake*—clearly demonstrate the narrative traits we have attached to postmodernism; and, indeed, both are interbellum works (published in 1922 and 1937, respectively), responding to the horrors of the First World War and to the inevitability of the Second—in addition to Joyce's own personal horrors, like the very real possibility of his going blind, combined with his beloved daughter, Lucia, slipping toward mental illness, beginning around 1930 and eventually becoming institutionalized after her father's death in 1937. In 1934 she was given the diagnosis of schizophrenia.

These are only a few examples. It seems that wherever there is cultural trauma, *postmodern* narrative techniques are likely to follow. This correlation may help us to understand the psychic origins of creativity, which was part of my original goal.

The full text of *Trauma Theory As a Method for Understanding Literary Texts: The Psychological Basis of Postmodern Hermeneutics* is contained here, including a Foreword by my mentor, Bob McLaughlin, a complete bibliography, and a detailed index. That book, published in

2016, was a mildly updated version of my doctoral dissertation—"Zeitgeist and the Zone: The Psychic Correlation between Cultural Trauma and 'Postmodern' Literaure" (2010)—for the Ph.D. in English studies at Illinois State University. For this new (and retitled) edition, I have added an introduction, updated the text here and there (primarily through the addition of chapter endnotes), and added four readings that, I hope, help to demonstrate how to put literary trauma theory to good use. The fourth reading deals more with trauma writing than literary analysis.

Much of this book's contents are static, meaning that they present a theoretical framework for literary trauma theory (by examining pioneers in the field, like Freud and Lacan, as well as contemporary trauma theorists, like Caruth, Di Prete and Whitehead); therefore, very little updating was required. Here and there, however, are statistics and analyses drawn from the sciences (especially neuropsychology) that beg for revision. For the most part I have resisted: first, scientific data quickly become outdated, so keeping up with new research is all but impossible; and second, for practical purposes I have elected to keep the formatting of the 2016 edition so that the index would not require a substantial (and time-consuming) makeover. I trust that out-of-date information can be easily brought up to speed by anyone who is interested. Perhaps, then, my more venerable data, from around 2009 and 2010, suggest the sorts of issues one may wish to investigate.

There is one scientific area, though, of particular concern because it is so central to my investigation: posttraumatic stress disorder (PTSD). For my original manuscript, I drew from the American Psychiatric Association's (APA) *Diagnostic and Statistical Manual of*

Mental Disorders, fourth edition (1994; reissued 2000), i.e., *DSM-IV*. *DSM-5* was published in 2013, and its revision of the section on PTSD soon became a flashpoint of controversy in the psychiatric community. From a clinician's perspective, the changes regarding posttraumatic stress disorder were significant, potentially leading to a substantial drop in diagnoses of PTSD.

For my purposes, however, the revisions have little to no effect. There were noteworthy rewordings of PTSD's symptomology, but they do not meaningfully alter my discussion here. One change that could be seen to impact my analysis has to do with the subject's direct versus indirect exposure to the stress-inducing event, especially as regards to the event's being experienced second-hand via television or the Internet. In essence, *DSM-5* requires *direct* witnessing of the traumatic event for it to be a source of PTSD for the subject, unless the electronic representation closely parallels the subject's real-life situation.

All in all, the revisions to *DSM-5* were intended to reverse the "criterion creep" that *DSM-IV* seemed to encourage when it came to the diagnosis and treatment of posttraumatic stress disorder, according to some clinicians.

Again, though, these changes to the profession's consideration of PTSD have been quite controversial, and there is no question that the APA will continue to study the phenomenon of trauma and make changes when a new manual is eventually published. In the meantime, I think it is fair to say my discussion of trauma and PTSD remains valid and supported by the psychiatric community by and large.

To come full circle, my hope is that this updated and expanded edition, with readings, of my original dissertation will be of use to both scholars and casual readers who are interested in the production of literary texts, and, more broadly, what I call the psychic origins of creativity.

Ted Morrissey
Sherman, Illinois
15 February 2021

Chapter 1

The Correlation Between
Trauma and Literature

In Chapter 2 I will lay out the parameters and objectives of my argument in greater detail, but at the beginning it is important to know that, broadly speaking, I am interested in the production of literature and its psychic origins: *Why do writers write what they write? Why do writers choose certain narrative techniques over others? And conversely, what can topic and technique tell us about the culture in which that writer is producing text?* In particular I am interested in trauma, its effects on the psyche, and how these effects manifest themselves in narrative style. The first step in exploring these complex issues is looking at the correlation between psychoanalysis (especially Freudian psychoanalysis) and literary analysis—a synthesis of disciplines that has generated increased interest in scholars from various arenas since the attacks of September 11, 2001. Some may argue, though, that referring to a synthesis in the studies of the human psyche and of literature is something of a redundancy because to consider a work of literature *is* to consider the psyche that produced it; in other words, one cannot think about a work of literature without at some level also thinking about the mind that created it. In the following chapter I will look in particular at the psychic link between trauma and postmodern literary style. The focus of Chapter 3 is the pervasive trauma culture that developed almost spontaneously at the conclusion of the Second World War. To validate that this psychic link was not unique to the twentieth century, in the fourth and fifth chapters I will discuss traumatic stress in Anglo-Saxon England and how that stress was manifested in the epic *Beowulf*. Then I will turn my attention to twentieth-century postmodernism, examining in particular the fiction of William H. Gass. Finally, I will discuss the pedagogical implications of my research, and what those implications may mean within the context of an English studies paradigm.

Trauma and Psychoanalysis

To begin, then, an increasing number of theorists, in a wide range of disciplines, have become interested in the psychic correlations between trauma and literature. Cathy Caruth[1], one of the best-known voices in the branch of literary analysis that is making particular use of psychoanalysis and trauma, maintains that such study has been going on virtually since the birth of psychoanalysis, as Freud himself turned to literature for illustrations of symptomology he was seeing in his patients. And for Caruth, the pairing of psychoanalysis and literary study is a natural one. She writes,

> If Freud turns to literature to describe traumatic experience, it is because literature, like psychoanalysis, is interested in the complex relations between knowing and not knowing. And it is at the specific point at which knowing and not knowing intersect that the language of literature and the psychoanalytic theory of traumatic experience precisely meet. (*Unclaimed Experience* 3)

It must be noted that within the social sciences some scholars feel that other disciplines, especially in the humanities, have consistently misrepresented or at least oversimplified Freud's views on trauma. Sociologist Jeffrey C. Alexander, for example, cites Caruth in particular as someone who has promoted what he calls "lay trauma theory" (Alexander et al. 6). Critics like Alexander feel that scholars in the humanities have paid little attention to Freud's views on trauma as they evolved over his lifetime and instead discuss his ideas too narrowly and selectively. Sociologists Michael Lambek and Paul Antze agree, writing, "It is impossible to refer to contemporary debates about memory without speaking about Freud. But it is not so easy to do so in a manner that does justice to Freud or to psychoanalytic thought. [. . .] We should not allow the popular misrepresentations of Freud to substitute for Freudian thought itself" (Antze and Lambek xxvi, xxvii).

At the risk of committing an oversimplification myself, it seems the social sciences' primary issue is that Freud, especially in his early writings, believed that for a traumatic event to have a profound impact on someone in adulthood, he or she must already be repressing and incubating an earlier (childhood) sexual trauma. However, as Neil J. Smelser points out, "[t]his formulation soon proved limited and inadequate for Freud himself [. . . and s]ubsequently, he developed two separate models of trauma" (Alexander et al. 55). One model accounted for adult neuroses, due to a traumatic event, in the absence of childhood sexual trauma; the other model continued to connect neuroses to a sexual experience in childhood. According to Smelser, who is also from the field of sociology, Freud's two-part concept regarding neurosis—that is, an earlier trauma must be (1) repressed and incubated prior to (2) an adult trauma leading to neurosis—has evolved into the contemporary psychoanalytic community's general acceptance that traumatic stress disorders develop in part

3

because of the causal event, but also because there was a context in place that precipitated the event being interpreted as traumatic: "It is part of the human condition that life is a continuous struggle, in the sense that any individual is forever experiencing, defending against, capitalizing on, and coming to terms with both external and internal dangers and threats of danger" (47). (In fairness, I should point out that Alexander's criticism of Caruth's use of Freudian theory, mild as it is, appears in the introductory chapter of *Cultural Trauma and Collective Identity* [2004], and his co-authors, also from the social sciences, cite Caruth unreservedly in other chapters.)

Therefore, as we proceed we must be mindful that Freud's theories continued to evolve throughout his lifetime—a testament to the complexity of our subject at hand. Even before the First World War provided Freud with untold numbers of young men suffering from "war neuroses" (what the profession of psychology has recognized as posttraumatic stress disorder, PTSD, since 1980) with which to develop his theories regarding traumatized psyches, he understood the interfacing of literature and psychology. He begins *Totem and Taboo* (1913) with this recognition, stating that our understanding of primitive man is via "his art, his religion and his attitude toward life, which we have received either directly or through the medium of legends, myths and fairy-tales" (1). Moreover, Freud writes, "[A] comparison of the 'Psychology of Primitive Races' as taught by folklore, with the psychology of the neurotic as it has become known through psychoanalysis, will reveal numerous points of correspondences and throw new light on subjects that are more or less familiar to us" (1). In other words, the workings of the mind—perhaps especially the neurotic mind—are

4

reflected in a culture's literature; and by studying the literature of times past, even past our recording of it, we can come to know the minds of the peoples who produced that literature. Let me underscore several points that relate directly to my interests here: First, Freud suggests a causal relationship between mental state and the sort of narrative that it produces. Second, we can draw conclusions about the mental states of peoples long dead by analyzing the literary record they left behind. Third, such an analysis can also yield insights into contemporary psychology. Finally, Freud is suggesting that the literature of the past tells us about entire cultures, and not just the individual authors who produced the works.

The Power of Language

Freud theorizes that primitive man (to continue the convention of Freud's sexist terminology) recognized the power of language, and, therefore, of naming. In *Totem and Taboo*, he discusses at length what he calls "the savage's dread of incest" and the impediments that societies place on their members to avoid inappropriate "social intercourse" (10). He chooses to illustrate such important impediments by focusing especially on "[t]he most widespread and strictest avoidance [. . . namely] that which restricts the social relations between a man and his mother-in-law" (10). Moreover, in these illustrations he makes particular note of language prohibitions. Using modern examples as reflective of primitive peoples, Freud points out that in Vanna Lava "[i]t is quite out of the question that [a man] should ever pronounce the name of his mother-in-law, or she his." On the Solomon Islands, meanwhile, "a man must neither see nor speak with his mother-in-law" once he is married.

5

Furthermore, "[a]mong the Zulu Kaffirs custom demands that a man should be ashamed of his mother-in-law and that he should do everything to avoid her company. [. . .] Communication among them must either be made through a third person or else they may shout at each other at a considerable distance if they have some barrier between them[. . . .] Neither may utter the other's name" (11). In these examples we see human beings' belief that the use of words, in particular the *wrong* words at the *wrong* times, can result in dire consequences for the speaker; and great pains must be undertaken to avoid these linguistic dangers.

The power of language, which can be traced back to primitive man, is also seen in his totemic practices. Freud writes, "The tribal totem (clan totem) is the object of veneration of a group of men and women who take their name from the totem and consider themselves consanguinous offspring of a common ancestor, and who are firmly associated with each other through common obligations towards each other as well as by the belief in their totem" (89). For primitive man the totem was most often an animal but could be any natural entity found in his world. Freud further explains, "On the solemn occasions of birth, initiation into manhood or funeral obsequies this identification with the totem is carried out in deeds and words" (90). Here we see that all the perceived benefits of totemism, including things like plentiful food supplies and protection from harm, are generated through language—by the initial naming of the animal, for example, as the totem, and by crucial rites that consecrate the bond between the totem and the clan under its protection. It is important to note that this belief in the power of language is universal, implying that it derives from the substructure of the human mind; it does not grow out of a specific cultural environment. This aspect will be discussed in detail in Chapter 2.

Associated with linguistic power is the cultural practice of mythmaking, that is, of using language to construct potent personas with which an entire people can identify. In *Moses and Monotheism* (1939), Freud calls on the work of his contemporary Otto Frank to discuss the importance and the universality of mythmaking. He quotes Frank's *Mythus von der Geburt des Helden* (1909),

> "[A]lmost all important civilized people have early woven myths around and glorified in poetry their heroes, mythical kings and princes, founders of religions, of dynasties, empires and cities—in short, their national heroes. [. . . T]he amazing similarity, nay, literal identity, of those tales, even if they refer to different, completely independent peoples, sometimes geographically far removed from one another, is well known and has struck many an investigator." (7)

Indeed, the stories from various cultures are so similar that they constitute what Freud terms an "average myth," and he sites the oldest such myth as that of Sargon of Agade, who founded Babylon about 2800 B.C.E. (8). Some of the common elements of this average myth include the hero's being descended from the top stratum of society; his conception's being hampered in various ways; during pregnancy the father's learning via supernatural means that the coming child will be a danger to him; as such, the father's orchestrating the death of the newborn, who is saved by either animals or common folk; and ultimately the mythic hero's finding out about his nobility, seeking revenge on his father, and ascending to be a leader of his natural people (7-

8). Among the figures reflecting this average myth are Moses, Cyrus, Romulus, Oedipus, Paris, Perseus, Heracles, and Gilgamesh (9). For my purposes, it is worth pointing out that Freud uses the phrase "the imagination of a people" (9) as the genesis of a regional myth that conforms to the plot details of the "average myth" as it implies that myths are cultural constructs, and not the product of an individual's creativity. What is more, these cultural constructs must be rooted in the substructure of the human psyche since the average myth is found around the globe with only minor variations.

Freud's ideas regarding the power of language and the genesis of mythmaking are supported by a host of theorists, including those from other scientific disciplines besides psychology. For example, Alex Argyros has brought together research in biogenetic anthropology, information theory, and chaos theory to reach conclusions that very much support Freud's thinking. Argyros's interests lie in explaining what he terms "the ubiquity of narrative," that is, the phenomenon that people all over the world organize their perceptions of reality via the same narrative patterns. Argyros writes, "The universality of narrative implies that it reflects an underlying neural substrate or a set of epigenetic rules predisposing human beings to organize experience in a narratival manner. [. . . T]he mind will automatically cast into a narrative mold even the most random and unconnected information" (667). He goes on to say that "narrative is perhaps best conceptualized as a hypothesis about the nature of an existing slice of reality or about the potential consequences of certain variations on a model of the world" (667). That is to say, the human mind is hard-wired to respond to its environment by organizing it into a narrative structure, with sequences of events dependent on cause-and-effect relationships. Turning back to Freud, the Viennese doctor suggests, in *Civilization and Its Discontents* (1930), that all civilizations have grown out of the same human need and have faced the same central obstacle: "Necessity alone, the advantages of work in common, will not hold [men] together. But man's natural aggressive instinct, the hostility of each against all and of all against each, opposes the programme of civilization" (82). In other words, in order to survive, man had to be territorial and ego-centric; yet he recognized the value of working with other men to supply his needs and wants. Therefore, the program of civilization (of men working together for the common good) has always been at odds with human nature (man working for himself). Freud describes these opposing instincts as Eros (life) and Death (destruction).

If both Freud and Argyros are correct, then all men everywhere have faced the same fundamental Eros/Death conflict, and their identical mental substrate have responded with the same narratival representations of that conflict. Argyros writes that the mind, regardless of a situation's level of complexity, "tends to plug such information into simple, linear, and deterministic default narratives" (671). The notion of "deterministic default narratives" is reminiscent of Freud's "average myth" that can be identified in so many cultures in spite of the fact that the cultures had no contact with each other, that is, no physical way for the myth to spread and be synthesized anew elsewhere. What is more, Argyros suggests that "narrative offers an elegant solution to the problem of human information management" (665). It must be noted, too, that human information management, while crucial in every epoch, has become even more vital over time. Writes Argyros:

> If narrative indeed proves to borrow its resources from those dynamical configurations which nature has chosen to enable the delicate dance between innovation and conservation, then it should be possible to claim that it is especially in the contemporary world, with its exponential growth of information, that the narratival techniques which humans have developed in the course of their evolution are most desperately needed. (665)

Argyros's assertion concerning the heightened need for narratival cognitive processing in contemporary culture is especially germane to our discussion of postmodern literature as its most-celebrated practitioners (e.g., Gaddis, Pynchon, DeLillo, and Gass) tend to concern themselves with the modern world's dizzying complexities. This connection will be discussed in detail in Chapter 6.

Group Psychology

For now, however, more must be said regarding group psychology, especially group neuroses. From the beginning of the field that would become known as psychoanalysis, Freud was concerned not only with individual neuroses but with group neuroses as well. His works that primarily focus on cultural psyche development and neuroses began to appear around 1920. In fact, Freud translator/editor James Strachey, who oversaw the Standard Edition of Freud's collected works, identified a letter in the spring of 1919 as the first reference to the "'simple idea' of an explanation of group psychology" (vii); however, as early as 1912-13's *Totem and Taboo*, Freud was beginning to

10

develop the notions that culminated in *Group Psychology and the Analysis of the Ego* (1921). In *Totem and Taboo*, Freud posits that the beginning of civilization was rooted in the same primeval event, which Freud eventually labeled the Oedipus complex. Freud theorized that the same basic scenario played out all over the world in prehistoric times, when humans lived in what Freud terms "primal hordes," which were essentially isolated from other such hordes. In brief, these hordes were dominated by an aggressive male who maintained possession and control of all the females in his horde; other males, as the off-spring of the aggressive leader, were dominated by their father and prevented from any sexual contact with the horde's females, that is, the sons' mothers and sisters. The dominated sons were ultimately forced from the horde or castrated, but eventually they banded together to murder and eat the father who brutalized them. The killing and cannibal consumption of the father, said Freud, evolved into a totemic practice whereby the sons honored the father and attempted to expiate the guilt they felt for having participated in his violent death. "Thus totemism helped to gloss over the real state of affairs," writes Freud in *Totem and Taboo*, "and to make one forget the event to which it owed its origin. In this connection some features were formed which henceforth determined the character of every religion" (124). Going further, he says, "Society is now based on complicity in the common crime, religion on the sense of guilt and consequent remorse, while morality is based partly on the necessities of society and partly on the expiation which this sense of guilt demands" (125).

Thinking through more completely this "original sin" of murdering the father, Freud opens *Group Psychology and the Analysis of Ego* with the statement that "[t]he contrast

11

between individual psychology and social or group psychology, which at first glance may seem to be full of significance, loses a great deal of sharpness when it is examined more closely" (1). Because an individual's mental state is affected by those around him, and because, meanwhile, his mental state impacts others in his sphere, there is no clear distinction between individual and group psychologies:

> Group psychology is therefore concerned with the individual man as a member of a race, of a nation, of a caste, or a profession, of an institution, or as a component part of a crowd of people who have been organized into a group at some particular time for some definite purpose. (2)

Freud makes it clear that, first, groups form easily, and, second, the group's collective conscious is established almost immediately. "In a group," he writes, "every sentiment and act is contagious, and contagious to such a degree that an individual readily sacrifices his personal interest to the collective interest" (7). Every formed group is a reconstitution, at the subconscious level, of the original primal horde; as such, "[w]e must conclude that the psychology of groups is the oldest human psychology" (55).

Freud conjectured that groups form so easily and that individuals so readily give up their personal interests in favor of the group's interests due to biomechanical processes at the cellular level. Citing the herding-mentality work of Wilfred Trotter, Freud writes in *Group Psychology*, "If we thus recognize that the aim is to equip the group with the attributes of the individual, we shall be reminded of a valuable remark of Trotter's, to the effect that the tendency towards the formation of groups is biologically a

12

continuation of the multicellular character of all higher organisms" (19). That is to say, human beings (and all complex life forms) consist of millions of individual cells, each hailing from a specific biological function, that voluntarily subordinate their specific function to the greater service of the organism's overall longevity. In this way, the group is akin to the organism, and each individual in the group is akin to each cell in the organism. Freud quotes the work of Gustave Le Bon (1895): "'The psychological group is a provisional being formed of heterogeneous elements, which for a moment are combined, exactly as the cells which constitute a living body form by their reunion a new being which displays characteristics very different from those possessed by each of the cells singly'" (5). Because of individuals' voluntary subordination to the group, writes Le Bon, a "'collective mind'" is formed that "'makes them feel, think, and act in a manner quite different from that in which each individual of them would feel, think, and act'" (5).

The critical faculties of this newly formed collective mind are greatly reduced, says Freud, and therefore a "group is extraordinarily credulous and open to influence [. . .] and the improbable does not exist for it" (*Group Psychology* 10). Because of the group mind's inability to engage its environment critically, "[i]t thinks in images, which call one another up by association, [. . .] and whose agreement with reality is never checked by any reasonable agency" (10). To be clear, by *images* Freud does not mean strictly *pictures*. In fact, he writes that groups are "subject to the truly magical power of words; they can evoke the most formidable tempests in the group mind, and are also capable of stilling them" (12). Here he alludes to the magic associated with names and words found among primitive peoples, discussed

13

in *Totem and Taboo*, the sort of magic, for example, that requires men to avoid speaking with their mother-in-law or even saying her name. Again citing Le Bon, Freud concludes,

> [G]roups have never thirsted after truth. They demand illusions, and cannot do without them. They constantly give what is unreal precedence over what is real; they are almost as strongly influenced by what is untrue as by what is true. They have an evident tendency not to distinguish between the two. (12)

With this point regarding the group consciousness, we come full circle and return to the power of language and the average myth (e.g., Moses) created by that language.

The Development of Civilization

Most of the aforementioned was offered in the service of establishing that groups behave as individuals behave, or, said differently, group psychology operates as individual psychology does. Indeed, in *Civilization and Its Discontents* (1930), one of Freud's last works, published less than a decade before his death, he says that "the development of civilization is a special process, comparable to the normal maturation of the individual" (52). Given my overarching interest in cultural trauma and literary production, I must look to Freud for two other crucial factors, namely the development of widespread melancholia or anxiety; and the process by which such feelings (moods) spread not only from one group to another, but from one generation to another. Once I have explored Freud's ideas on these phenomena, I will return to Cathy Caruth and other contemporary theorists, including sociologists and psychologists who specialize in studying the correlation between individual and group mentalities.

Freud speculates in *Civilization and Its Discontents* that primitive man must have come to understand that there were advantages in laying aside his aggressive, ego-centric impulses in order to live in harmony with others and thereby achieve greater happiness and security. The first of these groups was the family wherein the father did not drive out and/or castrate his sons—no doubt, said Freud, the father of a primal horde established by an avenging son who did not want to continue the cycle that would lead to his own usurpation. That is, the father allowed Eros to dominate his psyche, and this love of family evolved further into whole communities:

> The love which founded the family continues to operate in civilization both in its original form, in which it does not renounce direct sexual satisfaction, and in its modified form as aim-inhibited affection. In each, it continues to carry on its function of binding together considerable numbers of people, and it does so in a more intensive fashion than can be effected through the interest of work in common. (57)

The fact that civilization development is rooted in libidinal love (the sort of love = sex that drove the primal horde father to dominate or drive out his male offspring in order to keep his wives/daughters purely for his own pleasure) is evidenced by the pervasive use of the word *love* in modern times. That is, in order to establish, first, families, then communities, then whole civilizations, man had to diffuse libidinal *love* into myriad related forms. Freud writes, "People give the name 'love' to the relation between a man and a woman whose genital needs have led them to found a family; but they also give the name 'love' to the positive feelings between parents and children, and between brothers and sisters of a family, although we are obliged to describe this as 'aim-inhibited love' or 'affection'" (57-58). Because all civilizations are descended from the primal father's sexual love of his mates, today people describe as *love* the feelings they have for their spouse, their children, their neighbor, their pet, their favorite sports team, but also their job, their car, pizza, and cozy fires on rainy days. The linguistic ubiquity of *love* is due to the fact that civilization can be traced to the libidinal love that was the nucleus of the primal horde.

Unfortunately, said Freud, the diffusion and spread of love have not been enough to overcome another relic of the primal horde: man's inherent aggression toward others. "As a result," he writes, "[men's] neighbour is for them not only a potential helper or sexual object, but also someone who tempts them to satisfy their aggressiveness on him, to exploit his capacity for work without compensation, to use him sexually without his consent, to seize his possessions, to humiliate him, to cause him pain, to torture and to kill him" (*Civilization* 68-69). Man's aggressiveness Freud attributed to an instinct for Death that is the counterforce to Eros: "This aggressive instinct is the derivative and the main representative of the death instinct which we have found alongside of Eros and which shares world-dominion with it." Moreover, this "struggle between Eros and Death" is "the meaning of the evolution of civilization" (82). This struggle affects both individuals and societies in the same way, by producing a profound sense of guilt. In short, we love our neighbors (instinctive Eros) but cannot help doing harm to them nevertheless (instinctive Death). What is more, our

16

doing harm to our neighbors (or at least our wanting to do harm, even if we can resist the instinct) leads to anxiety because we both fear our neighbor's retribution (symbolically, the primal father's casting us out or castrating us) and we fear our neighbor's loss of love for us (symbolically, the brotherly love that allowed us to band together and overcome the primal father's aggression). Freud writes, "A threatened external unhappiness—loss of love or punishment on the part of the external authority—has been exchanged for a permanent internal unhappiness, for the tension of the sense of guilt" (89). Freud further speculates that "the sense of guilt produced by civilization is not perceived as such either, and remains to a large extent unconscious, or appears as a sort of *malaise*, a dissatisfaction, for which people seek other motivations" (99).

Transmission of Mood

The previous discussion seems to imply that people have always been and will always be unhappy (or, more accurately, the only truly happy people were those primal fathers who were having their unencumbered way with every wife/daughter in the horde). While it seems accurate to state that unhappiness is always easier to achieve than happiness, according to Freud, the guilt/anxiety at the root of the unhappiness can be repressed until circumstances call it forth. I must leave this notion (of calling forth) for the time being and concentrate on another crucial phenomenon of cultural psychology, namely the passing of a feeling (mood) from one generation to another, or even one time period to another. Freud identifies two (related) mechanisms to account for this phenomenon and discusses them at length in

17

Moses and Monotheism. The first mechanism is oral communication. The description of an event or a person can be passed from one generation to the next, for several generations. Over time, the description will be modified as it moves from the eyewitnesses and actual participants to those who know it only via communication. For his example, Freud points to Moses, who, he asserts, was actually Egyptian and who taught the Jews a monotheistic religion (centered on the god Aton) that was practiced for a time in Egypt. Over the centuries, the account of Moses and his teachings was transformed so that Moses became a Jew and the worship of Aton became Judaism. Freud writes that "such a tradition was maintained by conscious memory of oral communications which had been passed on from forebears of only two or three generations before. The latter had been participants and eyewitnesses of the events in question" (119). In this case, then, an enduring Mosaic tradition was based on storytelling and mythmaking over centuries.

However, oral communication alone does not account for the Mosaic tradition surviving to the present day. Here Freud introduces a more radical mechanism: "retain[ing] an impression of the past in unconscious memory traces" (*Moses* 120). He writes that "there probably exists in the mental life of the individual not only what he has experienced himself, but also what he brought with him at birth, fragments of phylogenetic origin, an archaic heritage" (125). One concrete example of archaic heritage (that is, knowledge that an individual acquires through genetic transmission and not from an individual's own experiences, which includes the experience of being taught by someone else) is the use of language, specifically "the universality of

18

speech symbolism" (126). That is, the use of language is far too complex to not only be learned from scratch, so to speak, by every human being, but to be virtually mastered by the age of five or six. Rather, the knowledge of speech symbolism is passed genetically from generation to generation. Freud goes further and asserts that "the archaic heritage of mankind includes not only dispositions, but also ideational contents, memory traces of the experiences of former generations" (127). Indeed, Freud suggests that a people's "national character" can be passed on via archaic heritage "and not carried on by word of mouth" (127). Archaic heritage is the human manifestation of animal instinct, he says:

> [Animals] carry over into their new existence the experience of their kind; that is to say, that they have preserved in their minds memories of what their ancestors experienced. In the human animal things should not be fundamentally different. His own archaic heritage, though different in extent and character, corresponds to the instincts of animals. (129)

Here we will recall Alex Argyros's claim that humans' use of narratival constructs is a survival tool passed on through evolution. He writes, "Traditional narrative, and its most ambitious subset, grand narrative, can be understood in the light of chaos theory as an evolutionary adaptation[. . . .] Narrative is indeed mimetic. It imitates nature" (672).

It is worth noting that many of the psychoanalytic theories that are often associated with Freud in fact originated, at least in part, with Otto Rank, who was a protégé of Freud but whose theories eventually evolved in such a way as to put him at severe odds with Freud and his inner circle. Stephen Khamsi says that Rank was "excommunicated" from the circle in the 1920s: "Though largely unacknowledged, Rank is a forerunner of ego psychology, object-relations theory, interpersonal psychotherapy, existential psychology, and [Carl Rogers's] client-centered approach." In addition to his disfavor in the psychoanalytic community, Rank's "notoriously difficult" writings have contributed to his relative obscurity, compared to Freud and other theorists. Freud's theory of archaic heritage, especially germane to our interests here, owes much to Rank's work with "[i]ntrauterine ecstacy [which] is interrupted by the agony of biological birth," writes Khamsi. According to Rank's theory, "our unconscious perpetually pushes us in a lifelong desire to return to primal paradise lost." Regarding the significance of group psychology, Rank's therapeutic techniques strived to reunite the individual neurotic with "the other, with the self, and with the Cosmos."

Jacques Lacan and "imago"

In support of these notions (the pervasiveness of melancholia and archaic heritage) that are foundational to my overarching argument, I would point in particular to Freud devotee Jacques Lacan, who did not always agree with Freud point for point but who nevertheless expanded on and refined these two concepts in particular. Lacan's theory of the imago (idealized mental picture) is associated with the pervasiveness of depression or melancholia. In Lacan's "Presentation of Psychical Causality" (1946), he identifies "the marked prevalence of visual structure in recognition of the human form" as the root of humans' "suicidal tendency," or what Freud tried to account for with his terms "'death

20

instinct' and 'primary masochism.'" Lacan writes, "[M]an's death, long before it is reflected [. . .] in his thinking, is experienced by him in the earliest phase of misery that he goes through from *the trauma of birth* until the end of the first six months of *physiological prematurity*, and that echoes later in the *trauma of weaning* [*sic*]" (*Écrits* 152, translator's italics). That is, the trauma of birth—of being separated (*alienated*, in Lacanian thinking) from the maternal place of safety we had always known—constitutes a miserable experience that prefigures the terror of death, and, in so doing, lays the groundwork for the onset of neuroses: "At the beginning of this development we see the primordial ego, as essentially alienated, linked to the first sacrifice as essentially suicidal. In other words, we see here the fundamental structure of madness" (152). This trauma of birth is of course universal, as it is the maternal alienation that is key, and it matters not whether someone is born naturally or surgically (setting aside Macduff's equivocation that he was not born of woman but rather "was from his mother's womb / Untimely ripp'd" when facing Macbeth on the field of battle before Castle Dunsinane).

Lacan's concept of *physiological prematurity* or *prematurity at birth* is associated with Freud's *archaic heritage*. By *prematurity at birth*, Lacan means humans' "incompleteness and 'delay' in the development of the central nervous system during the first six months of life" (*Écrits* 152). In essence, humans are born too soon, even when gestation reaches a point that is described as full term. Lacan pointed out that anatomists had long acknowledged that human infants enter the world underdeveloped physically, emerging virtually helpless at birth. During the six months or so of physiological prematurity, infants' vision

21

is key to their psychological development, specifically to the development of the imago that will have such a profound impact on the formation of their individual psyches. Because of the importance of the imago in psychic formation, gregariousness is crucial, as individuals become the people they see around them, accounting for the close connection between—the *mirroring* of, if you will—individual psychology and group psychology. Like Freud, Lacan alludes to the animal kingdom for evidence of the imago, that is, evidence that psychical phenomena are rooted in biological structures. In particular, he cites the phrase "*psychophysiolgical* mechanism" coined by physiologist Rémy Chauvin as a result of his study of "gregarious" versus "isolated" species of locusts, published in 1941 (155-56, translator's italics). Clearly Chauvin's "psychophysiological mechanism" is unconsciously evocative of Freud's "archaic heritage" concept.

The power of language to shape, even create, *reality* is not a concept unique to psychoanalysis, but it is worth underscoring the importance that Lacan placed on the patient's (the subject's) speech during psychoanalytic sessions. Addressing a group of largely younger analysts in 1953, Lacan says that "[w]hether it wishes to be an agent of healing, training, or sounding the depths, psychoanalysis has but one medium: the patient's speech" (*Écrits* 206). He derides his younger colleagues for not honing their skills of linguistic analysis, saying, "[H]owever empty [the subject's] discourse may seem, it is so only if taken at face value" (209). Lacan emphasizes that the subject's speech must be considered a metaphor, even using the word "scansion"—a term most often associated with poetic analysis—to describe the psychoanalyst's work in finding meaning in the subject's discourse. Moreover, Lacan was interested in the performative nature of speech, comparing the subject's discourse to the lines of an actor on the stage, saying that the

> recitation [. . .] may even be carried out in the present with all the vivacity of an actor; but it is like indirect speech, isolated in quotation marks in the thread of the narrative, and, if the speech is performed, it is on a stage implying the presence not only of a chorus, but of spectators as well. (212)

In other words, to be fully understood the subject's discourse must be evaluated in full context, taking into account the larger framework of the subject's totalizing experiences and the intended recipients of the discourse—only then can the metaphoric import of the subject's language be grasped by the critically engaged analysist.

PTSD and Collective Trauma

Now to return to more contemporary theorists and the specific neurosis of PTSD, which, says Caruth, "seems to provide the most direct link between the psyche and external violence and to be the most destructive psychic disorder" (*Unclaimed Experience* 58). As a working definition of PTSD, Caruth offers that it "reflects the direct imposition on the mind of the unavoidable reality of horrific events, the taking over of the mind, psychically and neurobiologically, by an event that it cannot control" (58). At the center of the disorder is trauma, a term which has evolved over time to mean a variety of related things. Originally from the Greek, *trauma* referred to a wound that was inflicted on the body. For Freud and other medical/psychiatric specialists, *trauma* became thought of as a wound of the mind. According to Caruth, Freud specifically came to consider trauma as "the breach in the mind's experience of time, self, and the world [. . . as] an event that [. . .] is experienced too soon, too unexpectedly, to be fully known and is therefore not available to consciousness until it imposes itself again, repeatedly, in the nightmares and repetitive actions of the survivor" (3-4). Kai Erikson examines the contemporary use of the term further and writes that *trauma* can also reference "the *event* that provoked" the traumatized state of mind (184, Erikson's italics). Moreover, in current usage trauma does not necessarily refer to a specific event but rather to a state of mind "resulting from a *constellation of life experiences* as well as from a discrete happening, from a *persisting condition* as well as from an acute event" (185). As such, the distinctions between *trauma* and *stress* become blurred, acknowledges Erikson, who writes,

> [I]t only makes sense to insist that trauma can issue from a sustained exposure to battle as well as from a moment of numbing shock, from a continuing pattern of abuse as well as from a single searing assault, from a period of severe attenuation and erosion as well as from a sudden flash of fear. The effects are the same, and that, after all, should be our focus. [. . .] The moment becomes a season, the event becomes a condition. (185)

Erikson offers the example of the battered wife. Is her traumatized state of mind due to a single beating, or from the daily stress of anticipating the next brutalization? The question is moot, he says; what matters to the clinician is that she is traumatized. Smelser, too, has traced what he calls "the scientific evolution and devolution" of trauma, from the shell-shocked soldiers of the First World War to ever-expanding categories of symptoms and victims. He writes,

24

"The overall result is an enormous gain in recognition of comprehension and complexity, but a loss of formal scientific precision [. . . which has] created a jungle that defies attempts at scientific formulation and understanding" (Alexander et al. 58, 59).

Concurring with Freud's and Lacan's assertions that individual psyches develop and operate essentially the same as group psyches, Erikson suggests, "Sometimes the tissues of community can be damaged in the same way as the tissues of mind and body." What is more, "traumatic wounds inflicted on individuals can combine to create a mood, an ethos—a group culture, almost—that is different from (and more than) the sum of the private wounds that make it up. Trauma, that is, has a social dimension" (185). Drawing on his professional experiences of working with communities that have suffered profound disasters, Erikson has developed the notion of *collective trauma* (versus *individual trauma*), which he describes as "a blow to the basic tissues of social life that damages the bonds attaching people together and impairs the prevailing sense of communality" (187). He says further that traumatic events have "both centripetal and centrifugal tendencies," meaning that victims are simultaneously driven from the group while also drawn back, thus creating "a ghetto for the unattached" (186). Flood victims are a good example. Through the physical destruction of their homes and property, they lose what connects them to others in their community; there is no longer anything tangible that binds them. Yet, their shared sense of loss provides them an empathic connection unique to their community's disaster. In such a case, writes Erikson, "the sense of community is so palpable that it is easy to think of it as tissue capable of being injured" (187).

Collective trauma can be far-reaching, both temporally and geographically. A location can become so indelibly associated with a traumatic event (e.g., Love Canal) that the place itself generates the trauma. "[T]raumatic experiences work their way so thoroughly into the grain of the affected community," writes Erikson, "that they come to supply its prevailing mood and temper, dominate its imagery and its sense of self, govern the way its members relate to one another." He adds that this phenomenon can "happen to whole regions, even whole countries," creating "social climates, communal moods, that come to dominate a group's spirit" (190). As such, people moving into an area after a traumatic event has transpired, or children being born into it, are still traumatized by the social climate, by the affected place's zeitgeist. We will recall that Freud referred to this effect as contagion within the group. Furthermore, because of the speed and ubiquity of modern media, disasters can be shared across the globe instantaneously—"broadcast so quickly and so widely that it becomes a moment in everyone's history, a datum in everyone's store of knowledge" (191). Erikson offers Chernobyl as such an example; today most adults would add 9/11. In Chapter 3 I will look in particular at the atomic bombings of Hiroshima and Nagasaki, and their effects on the American cultural psyche.

One of the long-term effects of trauma is a dramatically altered worldview. "Traumatized people calculate life's chances differently," writes Erikson. "They look out at the world through a different lens. [. . . T]hey also come to feel that they have lost a natural immunity to misfortune and that something awful is almost *bound* to happen" (194, Erikson's italics). It is worth noting that trauma resulting from human-made disasters is even more profound than that caused by natural events, like a flood:

> Technological catastrophes [. . .] are never understood by those who suffer from them as the way the world of chance sorts itself out. They provoke outrage rather than resignation. They generate a feeling that the thing ought not to have happened, that someone is at fault, that victims deserve not only compassion and compensation but something similar to what lawyers call punitive damages. Most significant, they bring in their wake feelings of injury and of vulnerability from which it is difficult to recover easily. (192)

With the increasingly sophisticated technologies of post-Second World War American culture and the corresponding increase in confidence in the sciences, the aftermath of technological catastrophes can be especially devastating. "When one begins to doubt the findings of scientists and the calculations of engineers," writes Erikson, "one can begin to lose confidence in the use of logic and reason as ways to discern what is going on." As a result, "a cultural mood [is created] in which dark but familiar old exuberances flourish—millennial movements, witchcraft, the occult, and a thousand other systems of explanation that seem to make sense of bewildering events" (196).

Narrative Memory and Traumatic Memory

At the core of Erikson's assertions regarding an altered worldview for victims and survivors of trauma is a degraded perception of *truth*. The traumatized no longer *know what is true* (setting aside for the moment the inherently subjective nature of truth). This aspect, the

27

question of truth, is key to understanding PTSD, says Caruth: "[T]he dreams, hallucinations and thoughts are absolutely literal, unassimilable to associative chains of meaning" (*Trauma* 5). Associative chains of meaning, of course, would be another way of describing narrative. In fact, psychoanalysts have identified two distinct types of memory: narrative memory and traumatic memory. Bessel A. van der Kolk and Onno van der Hart explain that "[h]ealthy psychological functioning depends on the proper operation of the memory system, which consists of a unified memory of all psychological facets related to particular experiences" (159). Narrative memory, then, "consists of mental constructs, which people use to make sense out of experience" (160). On the other hand, traumatic experience "causes the memory [. . .] to be stored differently and not be available for retrieval under ordinary conditions" (160). Narrative memory allows whoever is communicating the narrative to be selective as to which details to include, which to exclude, which to emphasize, and which to play down— depending on the social situation of the narration. With traumatic memory, however, "[w]hen one element of a traumatic experience is evoked, all other elements follow automatically" (163). They follow automatically, but not sequentially or logically, rather in haphazard fragmentary form. From this perspective, one of the main goals of psychotherapy is to assist the traumatized victim to move the event from traumatic memory to narrative memory.

What is more, traumatic memory, if left unreconciled, can impact the storage and retrieval of later nontraumatic experiences. Van der Kolk and van der Hart write, "It is now widely accepted that memory is an active and constructive process and that remembering depends on

28

existing mental schemas[. . . .] In other words, preexisting schemes determine to what extent new information is absorbed and integrated" (170). Therefore, a traumatic experience can prevent new experiences from being processed normally, which can in turn generate anxiety about a mundane event because of the inability to properly store it as narrative memory: "Previously traumatized people are vulnerable to experience current stress as a return of the trauma" (174). As such, "[m]emories easily become inaccurate when new ideas and pieces of information are constantly combined with old knowledge to form flexible mental schemas" (171). Flexible mental schemas are the untrue "memories" or fantasies/delusions that PTSD sufferers generate unbidden. The authors quote Edward O. Wilson (1978), who writes that "'the brain is an enchanted loom where millions of flashing shuttles weave a dissolving pattern. [. . .] The brain invents stories and runs imagined and remembered events back and forth through time'" (171). Thus, the perception of truth is degraded as the result of trauma.

The Unreliability of Traumatic Memory

A final point that is crucial to our interests is that traumatic memory is very erratic, meaning that victims of traumatic stress often repress or dissociate their recollection of the source event itself. Repression and dissociation, though similar, have important distinctions. To *repress* a memory means, of course, to force it from the conscious mind altogether, while to *dissociate* a memory means to replace it with a memory that is less troubling to one's conscious perception of the world. For example, a victim of child sexual abuse may repress the abusive event and have

29

no conscious recollection of it whatsoever, or a victim may dissociate the event by recalling the attack of a vicious dog in lieu of a close relative's molestation. In either case, the traumatic event is still at work on the victim's traumatized psyche. According to Chris R. Brewin, neuropsychologists studying the PTSD phenomenon of flashbacks believe that they "[involve] a breakdown in the everyday process responsible for binding together individual sensory features to form a stable object, episodic memory, or action sequence. Insufficient binding means that objects or memories will be fragmented or incomplete" (Vasterling and Brewin 135). He explains further:

> During traumatic events attention tends to be restricted and focused on the main source of danger, so that sensory elements from the wider scene will be less effectively bound together. Laboratory research has shown that such unattended patterns or events, provided they are sufficiently novel, produce long-lasting memory traces whose existence can be detected even though they cannot be deliberately retrieved. (135-36)

Victims of PTSD can even suffer "amnesia for the details of the event." In other words, it is quite common for trauma victims to have only partial recollection of the source event, or no recollection whatsoever—yet they still suffer the symptoms of PTSD. Some neuropsychologists have turned to the "dual-representation theory" to account for the phenomenon. In brief, they point to two memory systems: "verbally accessible memory" (VAM) and "situationally accessible memory" (SAM). The theory suggests that during a traumatic event, some aspects of it can be "integrated with other autobiographical memories and [. . . therefore] can be deliberately retrieved as and when required" (139). Such aspects are *recorded* if you will by the VAM, and can be discussed, or verbalized, by the trauma victim. However, other aspects do not fit within the paradigm of previous experiences and are only retrieved via SAM in the form of flashbacks "triggered involuntarily by situational reminders of the trauma (encountered either in the external environment or in the internal environment of a person's mental processes)" (140). Marian Mesrobian MacCurdy sums up this aspect of PTSD by saying that "traumatic memories appear both indelible and forgettable" (27).

Specializing in cultural trauma and its correlation to individual trauma, Smelser posits that not all national crises automatically become culturally traumatic, and he has identified characteristics of cultural trauma. He says that "full-blown cultural traumas" are exemplified by "constant, recurrent struggle—moments of quiescence perhaps, when some convincing formula for coming to terms with it takes root, but flarings-up when new constellations of new social forces and agents stir up the troubling memory again" (42). As such, he believes that true cultural trauma is never "cured" per se, as we might say an individual's is. Nevertheless, there are close associations between individual and group psyches. For example, just as an individual may "deny" or "become numb" to a traumatic memory, "[t]he counterpart of these reactions at the collective level is collective denial or collective forgetting" (42, 43). Later, I will reference the work of Smelser and other sociologists who are specializing in the dynamics of cultural trauma, but for now I will offer Alexander et al.'s "formal definition of cultural trauma":

a memory accepted and publicly given credence by a relevant membership group and evoking an event or situation which is a) laden with negative affect, b) represented as indelible, and c) regarded as threatening a society's existence or violating one or more of its fundamental cultural presuppositions. (44)

Allow me to extract from the preceding some of the concepts that are most germane to my interests. First, development of the human psyche is so intertwined with language development that a linguistic record is, in essence, a psychological record as well. As such, linguistic analysis can unlock our understanding of the psyche. Second, the psyche is genetically predisposed to develop in particular biomechanical ways, regardless of factors like culture and time period. Third, group psychology operates in much the same way as individual psychology. Moreover, individuals easily adopt the mindset of the group, so that members of a group—even an entire nation—can be said to share a common psychological posture: a zeitgeist. Fourth, communal moods (zeitgeists) can be passed from one generation to the next, and from one geographical region to another. The modes of transmission are numerous, from simple word of mouth, to knowledge that is passed genetically via archaic heritage; and in contemporary times electronic media have assisted the contagion of a mood. A place, in fact, can generate its own mood of trauma and high anxiety. Fifth, PTSD appears to be the most damaging psychic disorder; and trauma, both physical and emotional, constitutes not only a single violent event but also a continuing series of oppressive events—so that, in contemporary usage, *trauma* is virtually synonymous with prolonged *stress* and *anxiety*. Sixth, psychologists have identified two types of memory: narrative memory (normal) and traumatic memory (abnormal). And it seems that in order for a neurosis to be discontinued, the traumatic memory—which is characterized by illogical and fragmentary recall of details—must be transformed to narrative memory. Finally, trauma victims often suffer the symptomology of PTSD without having a clear recollection of the source event; in fact, they often have no conscious recollection whatsoever.

1. As of this writing, Cathy Caruth has published two additional books related to trauma and literary trauma theory: *Literature in the Ashes of History* (2013) and *Listening to Trauma: Conversations in the Theory & Treatment of Catastrophic Experience* (2014), both with Johns Hopkins UP.

Chapter 2

The Postmodern Voice

Literary postmodernism is largely associated with the latter half of the twentieth century, with the end of the Second World War being regarded as a de facto starting point. The term *postmodernism* itself and its origin are, however, less easily pinpointed. Steven Best and Douglas Kellner, citing among others British historian Arnold Toynbee, offer the year 1875 as a reasonable starting point for postmodernism. They write, "On this account, Western civilization had entered a new transitional period beginning around 1875 which Toynbee termed the 'post-Modern age'. This period constituted a dramatic mutation and rupture from the previous modern age and was characterized by wars, social turmoil and revolution" (6). The term "postmodern" first appeared around 1870, according to Best and Kellner, as it was applied to painting by Englishman John Watkins Chapman (5). And the term cropped up sparingly here and there over the next seventy years or so until Toynbee's study was published in 1947; thereafter, more and more scholars adopted the term "postmodern" and explored ideas of postmodernism and postmodernity, especially in the decade after the Second World War. Thus, the end of the war in 1945 is often cited as the beginning of postmodernism, especially as the concept is applied to literature. For example, Robert L. McLaughlin, in his introduction to *Innovations: An Anthology of Modern & Contemporary Fiction* (1998), writes, "[W]e tie the production of postmodern literature to historical and social developments arising after the end of the Second World War. This approach is valid [. . .]" (xii).

Literary Postmodernism

In a moment I will get to the business of defining the characteristics of literary postmodernism, that is, of highlighting those traits that make a literary text *postmodern*; but first a few words about my study's primary concern. It is generally accepted that, even though we associate postmodern literature with the second half of the twentieth century, one can name numerous examples of pre-twentieth-century texts (very *pre-* in several cases), that demonstrate telltale signs of postmodernism. A short list would include the works of writers like François Rabelais (sixteenth century), William Shakespeare (seventeenth century), Laurence Sterne (eighteenth), Herman Melville (nineteenth)—and the work, earlier still than these others, that is my particular interest in this regard, *Beowulf* (dating sometime, probably, from the eighth to eleventh century). While the "postmodernness" of these texts is widely accepted, no one has tried to account for the phenomenon. That is to say, no one has asked the question, *If we associate postmodernism with the latter half of the twentieth century, how do we account for the fact that literary texts which clearly bear marks of postmodernity can be identified hundreds of years before the Second World War?* My purpose is to answer this question precisely and at length. But for now I will offer the short version: *The historical and cultural factors that resulted in the production of the twentieth-century literature we call "postmodern" were manifest in these other time periods as well.*

36

Now let me return to defining postmodernism, or more specifically, identifying the traits of postmodern texts. Many scholars have worked to define postmodernism and have spoken to the inherent challenge of the task. Best and Kellner write that "there is no unified postmodern theory, or even a coherent set of positions. Rather, one is struck by the diversities between theories often lumped together as 'postmodern' and the plurality—often conflictual—of postmodern positions" (2). Similarly, discussing the plasticity of the term *postmodern*—and how terms like *experimental*, *avant-garde* and *innovative* share common features—McLaughlin writes that tales of this ilk "seek to expand our notions of what fiction can be, of how narratives can be organized (or whether there can be fiction without narrative), or how characters are presented (or whether they're needed at all), of what language can do, of what fiction can mean" (xi). Meanwhile, F. W. Fawkner, in his examination of Immanuel Kant and Jean-François Lyotard, explains, "[T]he postmodernist artist writes a text that is not in principle governed by preestablished rules: hence the application of familiar categories of judgement is not relevant" (101). As such, the postmodernist forces a fresh examination of the subject. Indeed, McLaughlin says of work labeled postmodern that it "seeks to challenge its readers to think or to see the world in new ways" (xvii).

The elusiveness of "postmodernism" is taken up in detail by the editors of Norton's *Postmodern American Fiction* (1998), who write in their introduction:

> For many observers, the term "postmodern" refers to "postmodernity," a historical period stretching from the 1960s to the present, marked by such phenomena as upheavals in the international economic system,

the Cold War and its decline, the increasing ethnic heterogeneity of the American population, the growth of the suburbs as a cultural force, the predominance of television as a cultural medium, and the rise of the computer. For others, however, the term "postmodern" connotes "postmodernism," a tentative grouping of ideas, stylistic traits, and thematic preoccupations that set the last four decades apart from earlier eras. (x)

One thing we notice is that the editors—Paula Geyh, Fred G. Leebron, and Andrew Levy—identify the 1960s, not 1945, as the starting point for American postmodernism. They are of course not alone; Marianne DeKoven is another scholar who shares the editors' thinking, as evidenced by the title of her book *Utopia Limited: The Sixties and the Emergence of the Postmodern* (2004). We also note the word "tentative" in the editors' remarks, meaning that the "grouping of ideas, stylistic traits, and thematic preoccupations" is fluid and flexible. Underscoring this point, they write, "The history of postmodern American fiction belongs to those authors who, in any idiom and for any audience, for brief passages or for entire careers, shared a new cultural sensibility as a response to an altered world" (xi). Here I call attention to two points: first, an artist might produce a single work that is "postmodern" in a career that is marked by works that are decidedly "un-postmodern"; and second, the literary style is in "response to an altered world"—this latter point being key to my study, that "postmodern" techniques are reflective of an artist's re-conceptualized worldview.

Due to the extreme elusiveness of the concept of postmodernism, and to the extreme plasticity of using it as a label, the term "postmodern" itself runs the risk of meaning almost everything and, as such, almost nothing. Umberto Eco writes,

> Unfortunately, "postmodern" is a term *bon à tout faire* ["good to use everywhere"]. I have the impression that it is applied today to anything the user of the term happens to like. Further, there seems to be an attempt to make it increasingly retroactive: first it was apparently applied to certain writers or artists active in the last twenty years, then gradually it reached the beginning of the century, then still further back. And this reverse procedure continues; soon the postmodern category will include Homer. (44)

Given my interest in identifying older texts as "postmodern," Eco's remarks are particularly germane—and cautionary! That is, if one does not practice restraint, one could find a way to call virtually any text postmodern. But Eco goes on to assume a posture that is useful to my interests. He believes that "postmodernism is not a trend to be chronologically defined, but, rather, an ideal category—or, better still, a *Kunstwollen*, a way of operating. We could say that every period has its own postmodernism, just as every period would have its own mannerism" (44). Here Eco's language—"way of operating" and "mannerism"—suggests that any age can produce a "postmodern" way of operating (of viewing the world, of crafting text); and, moreover, "mannerism" is evocative of *zeitgeist* (of an entire culture adopting a particular mood).

Defining a "Postmodern Text"

To avoid the trap of making "postmodernism" into such an enormous net that, when cast into literary history, it ensnares virtually everything, I will turn to the work of

39

contemporary trauma theorists and limit, quite definitively, what it means to say that a text is *postmodern*. As has been noted, Cathy Caruth and others have turned to psychoanalysts such as Freud and Lacan to illustrate the close connections between trauma and literature. Caruth writes,

> If PTSD must be understood as a pathological symptom, then it is not so much a symptom of the unconscious, as it is a symptom of history. The traumatized, we might say, carry an impossible history within them, or they become themselves the symptom of a history that they cannot entirely possess. (*Trauma* 5)

I want to call particular attention to Caruth's statement that the traumatized "become themselves the symptom of a history that they cannot entirely possess" as it implies a duality. The traumatized usually have a conscious awareness of the causal event, but it also colonizes their subconscious in a way that is beyond their control and quite possibly even their awareness (a common phenomenon, we recall, according to neuropsychologists). As a result of the trauma, points out Anne Whitehead, there are "[u]nsettling temporal structures and disturbing relations between the individual and the world" (5). That is, the victim of trauma is unable to perceive time and space *normally*. And, as Bessel A. van der Kolk and Onno van der Hart explain, the impediment to processing time and space perceptions normally are not limited to the traumatic event itself (if, indeed, there was a specific and singular event), but rather affect non-traumatic events as well (until such time that the PTSD can be effectively treated). Here, too, we must recall that the group psyche operates much the same as the individual psyche.

Whitehead reiterates, "[Traumatic] crisis extends beyond the individual to affect the ways in which historical experience can be accessed at a cultural level" (7). Ronald Granofsky is among critics who have studied the close ties between the traumatic events of the Second World War and the literature that emerged in its aftermath, with Granofsky coining the term "the trauma novel" to refer to the work of writers like Kurt Vonnegut, Jr., and Thomas Pynchon. Moreover, Laura Di Prete explains that "all of these writers tackle the issue of trauma by depicting imagined collective disasters that only indirectly relate to real historical or personal traumas" (5).

Indeed, the emergence of postmodernism seems a direct reflection of cultural PTSD. Writes Whitehead,

> [Postmodernism's] innovative forms and techniques critique the notion of history as grand narratives, and it calls attention to the complexity of memory. Trauma fiction emerges out of postmodernist fiction and shares its tendency to bring conventional narrative techniques to their limit. In testing formal boundaries, trauma fiction seeks to foreground the nature and limitations of narrative and to convey the damaging and distorting impact of the traumatic event. (82)

Professionals working with victims of trauma in an attempt to help them articulate and come to terms with their traumatizing event(s)—to relocate their "traumatic memory" to "narrative memory"—note that the traumatized voice mirrors narrative techniques of postmodern writers. "[T]raumatic knowledge cannot be fully communicated or retrieved without distortion," says Whitehead, who has identified key features of postmodern texts that reflect aspects of the traumatized voice: "intertextuality, repetition and a dispersed or fragmented narrative voice" (84). Here, then, is the vehicle for limiting my examination of "postmodern" texts. Or, said differently, the intersection of trauma and postmodern literature is at these key points: 1) intertextuality, that is, the use of various "texts" to create meanings when contextualized together that are somehow different from the meanings of those same texts when read independently; 2) repetition, that is, the compulsion to return to images and events, particularly ones that at first blush may seem relatively insignificant but that gain significance(s) with each return, with each echo; and 3) a dispersed or fragmented narrative voice, that is, a style of narration that employs multiple authorial voices/perspectives, and/or a decidedly nonlinear emplotment (or even a decidedly "non-plotted" emplotment). Whitehead explicitly names these three aspects of postmodern technique that mirror the traumatized voice, but I would augment the list with a fourth (implied) aspect: a search for language—if you will, for powerful, indeed, almost magical words—that will uncouple the traumatized from the traumatizing event. One significant aspect of this language-power is the act of testimony; in fact, some trauma theorists have dubbed the end of the twentieth century and the beginning of the twenty-first the Age of Testimony. Shoshana Felman writes, "It has been suggested that testimony is the literary—or discursive—mode par excellence of our times, and that our era can precisely be defined as the age of testimony" (17). She goes on to compare writing about trauma in a testimonial mode as akin to psychoanalysis, in which patients confide to their therapist.

Characteristics of the Traumatized Voice

Each of these characteristics of the traumatized voice/postmodern technique obviously needs much more fleshing out. I shall begin with intertextuality, a term I suppose that seems straightforward enough on the surface: that which occurs when there is connectivity between texts. The "inter" part is reasonably simple but not the "text" part, because *text* can mean so many things, including written or verbal language, pictorial images, musical or ambient noises . . . even fabrics (bringing "text" full circle, back to its cousins "texture" and "textiles"). More abstractly, physical spaces can be perceived as texts to be "read" or interpreted, as a politician may read a crowd before delivering a speech, or as an actor may read an audience before performing a play. For trauma theorists, the traumatizing event is a text. Caruth writes, "In its most general definition, trauma describes an overwhelming experience of sudden or catastrophic events in which the response to the event occurs in the often delayed, uncontrolled repetitive appearance of hallucinations and other intrusive phenomena" (*Unclaimed Experience* 11). In this definition of trauma, then, the "hallucinations and other intrusive phenomena" are texts which assert themselves into the *text of the present*. We recall van der Kolk and van der Hart's observation that "[w]hen one element of a traumatic experience is evoked, all other elements follow automatically [. . . and m]emories easily become inaccurate when new ideas and pieces of information are constantly combined with old knowledge to form flexible mental schemas" (163, 171). Their description of the process of traumatic memory impairing narrative memory evokes a *textual* sense as "pieces" are "combined" and "form flexible mental schemas," as if memories and

43

thoughts are tangible objects that can be (almost) physically manipulated.

Caruth develops the idea of intertextuality further in her discussion of the French film *Hiroshima mon amour* (by Alain Resnais and Marguerite Duras, 1959): "[T]he film dramatizes something that happens when two different experiences, absolutely alien to one another, are brought together" (34). It is a story of a French actress who comes to Hiroshima more than a decade after the bombing and begins a relationship with a Japanese man, to whom she confesses that during the Occupation she had an affair with a German soldier; the soldier was killed on the day of the liberation, the same day they had planned to run away together. Her family and the townspeople discovered the affair, and she was punished so cruelly—on top of the grief over her German lover—that she was driven mad. In Japan, the woman is haunted by images of her pre-war affair and of her lover's death, a death that she knows to be true but cannot accept because she did not witness it herself. In *Hiroshima mon amour* what is missing, so to speak, is the text of the lover's death. I stray a bit from Caruth's analysis, but I will suggest that the Frenchwoman's efforts to darn the textual hole are not dissimilar to a fiction writer's work to create text. She knows the circumstances of the German soldier's death and is haunted by "visions" of it even though she did not actually witness it. In a sense she is testifying to an imagined event— *imagined* in that it is her imagination that provides the killing's text, not *imagined* in that it is "untrue." Indeed, Freud acknowledged the attractiveness of incomplete histories to creative minds. In *Moses and Monotheism*, he writes,

Incomplete and dim memories of the past, which we call tradition, are a great incentive to the artist, for he is free to fill in the gaps in the memories according to the behests of his imagination and to form after his own purpose the image of the time he has undertaken to reproduce. One might almost say that the more shadowy tradition has become, the more meet is it for the poet's use. (89-90)

I would go further and suggest that it is not only the shadowy *tradition* that compels the creative mind to invent narrative but *any* shadowy (that is, fragmentary) episode, including an episode whose recollection is incomplete due to trauma.

Intertextuality and Postmodern Literature

Intertextuality is so fundamental to postmodern literature that many theorists have explored it at length. Indeed, intertextuality has many faces in literary works. For now I will discuss a face that is most closely connected to my topic's sociohistorical interests. Linda Hutcheon spends a great deal of her study *A Poetics of Postmodernism* (1988) on issues of intertextuality, and she argues that the "accessibility" of history is "entirely conditioned on textuality." In particular, Hutcheon writes, "We cannot know the past except through its texts: its documents, its evidence, even its eye-witness accounts are *texts*. Even the institutions of the past, its social structures and practices, could be seen, in one sense, as social texts" (16). She further asserts that postmodern novels, because of their emphasis on intertextuality, "teach us about both this fact and its consequences." Later, Hutcheon quotes historian Dominick LaCapra "who argue[s] that 'the past arrives in the form of texts and textualized remainders—memories, reports, published writings, archives, monuments, and so forth'" (129). In this sense, then, fiction writers connect sociohistorical texts with their fictive narratives. Theorist Brian McHale also devotes a significant number of pages to sociohistorical intertextuality in *Postmodernist Fiction* (1987). In way of contrast, he first looks at classic historical novels (by writers like James Fennimore Cooper and Leo Tolstoy) that take great pains to *be true* to recorded history: "[T]he logic and physics of the fictional world must be compatible with those of reality if historical [realms] are to be transferred from one realm to the other; otherwise, the text will be at radical variance with the norms of 'classic' historical fiction" (88). That is, historical figures must behave as historians tell us they behaved, they must be where historians tell us they were, and their worlds must operate in the ways that historians tell us they operated (Napoleon cannot order his submarine commander to launch his nukes). Meanwhile, the postmodernist historical novel revises the past in two ways. Writes McHale, "First, it revises the *content* of the historical record, reinterpreting the historical record, often demystifying or debunking the orthodox version of the past. Secondly, it revises, indeed transforms, the conventions and norms of historical fiction itself" (90, McHale's emphasis).

Specific literary examples are in order to fully elucidate this sociohistorical sense of intertextuality, and I will provide those examples (mainly in Chapter 6)—but for the time being I want to continue in a theoretical vein. Another significant face of intertextuality occurs when postmodern writers make use of other literary texts within their own fictive narratives. McHale borrows Umberto Eco's term "transworld identity" in his discussion of "intertextual

46

space," which "is constituted whenever we recognize the relations among two or more texts, or between specific texts and larger categories such as genre, school, period" (56-57). McHale claims that "the transmigration of characters from one fictional universe to another" is the most "effective [. . .] device" of "foregrounding this intertextual space and integrating it in the text's structure" (57). He further points out that this postmodern technique is rooted in the tradition of novel-writing. Robert L. McLaughlin concurs, saying that "the novel [. . .] is intertextual, or built on, adapted from, or made up of previously existing texts" (xxii). He cites a number of pre-postmodern examples, including *The Arabian Nights*, *The Canterbury Tales*, and the works of Shakespeare: "This repetition of and transformation of previously heard stories—the practice of texts speaking through other texts—occurs throughout the history of literature" (xxii). On the one hand, McLaughlin's remarks appear especially supportive of my interests—the notion that one can readily find the "postmodern" trait of intertextuality in pre-twentieth-century texts—but, on the other, I must be mindful of Eco's warnings about being too liberal with the label *postmodern*. Clearly, not all intertextual references are the result of cultural trauma. According to Whitehead, intertextuality is just *one* feature of the traumatized voice; for my purposes, literary texts must reflect more than a single traumatic characteristic to be considered a likely "trauma-culture" text.

Before leaving intertextuality (for the moment) to pursue other aspects of the traumatized voice, it must be noted that there are many more textual sources besides history and literature. In fact, Hutcheon suggests that perhaps the term *intertextuality* is too narrow. She writes,

47

> In many cases, intertextuality may well be too limited a term to describe this process [of writing working through other writing]; interdiscursivity would perhaps be a more accurate term for the collective modes of discourse from which the postmodern parodically draws: literature, the visual arts, history, biography, theory, philosophy, psychoanalysis, sociology, and the list could go on. (129-30)

That is, postmodernists place no limits on the sources of their discursive references. One of the effects of this textual eccentricity, says Hutcheon, is that the "[m]argins and edges gain new value. The 'ex-centric'—as both off-center and de-centered—gets attention" (130). It is perhaps postmodernism's tendency toward interdiscursivity that allows it to achieve its most important societal function, according to McLaughlin, who writes that postmodern fiction "seeks to challenge its readers to think or to see the world in new ways [. . .] to defamiliarize the world through language [. . . and] to shake us out of the overly habitual perceptions that keep us from seeing the world around us" (xvi-xvii). Similarly, Italo Calvino says that "the real revolutionary value of philosophy [as revealed through postmodern literature . . . is] in its power to upset common sense and sentiments and to outrage every 'natural' manner of thinking" (43). Of course, intertextuality/discursivity is not the only technique employed by postmodernists that achieves this "outrage," but by most accounts it is an important one.

Repetition and Its Many Forms

In *Trauma Fiction*, Whitehead discusses the correlation between literary intertextuality and the traumatized voice at length. Quoting the work of Peter Middleton and Tim Woods, she writes that "the relation of the text to its intertexts resonates with the way 'traces of the past emerge in the present as textual echoes, determinations and directions.' Intertextuality can suggest the surfacing to consciousness of forgotten or repressed memories" (85). Whitehead finds the novel an especially rich form when exploring the connections between postmodern technique and trauma:

> The intertextual novelist can enact through a return to the source text an attempt to grasp what was not fully known or realised in the first instance, and thereby to depart from it or pass beyond it. [. . .] The novelist's return to the source text can enable us to grasp a latent aspect of the text, and at the same time to depart from it into an alternative narrative construction. (90-91)

Intertextuality often coincides with another postmodern technique that is mimetic of the traumatized voice: repetition. Whitehead says, "One of the key literary strategies in trauma fiction is the device of repetition, which can act at the levels of language, imagery or plot" (86). That is, a writer may repeat specific words or phrases throughout the work, or return time and again to the same or nearly the same symbolic element, or characters may find themselves in emplotted loops. "Repetition mimics the effects of trauma," writes Whitehead, "for it suggests the insistent return of the event and the disruption of narrative chronology or progression" (86). As such, "[i]ntertextuality can gain powerful effects through repetition [. . . and] is profoundly disruptive of temporality" (90, 91). What is more, the readers of postmodern literature often find themselves in a similar

49

role to psychoanalysts who are trying to reconstruct the events of a patient's traumatic episode: "The intertextual novel constructs itself around the gap between the source text and its rewriting, and depends on the reader to assemble the pieces and complete the story" (93). In sum, writes Whitehead, "In stylistic terms, intertextuality allows the novelist to mirror the symptomatology of trauma by disrupting temporality or chronology [. . .]" (94).

Indeed, the involuntary reliving of the traumatic event may be the most telltale sign of PTSD. As van der Kolk and van der Hart explain, "[o]ne of the hallmarks of Post-Traumatic Stress Disorder is the intrusive reexperiencing of elements of the trauma in nightmares, flashbacks, or somatic reactions" (173). They say that cognitive psychologists attribute these symptoms to the fact that the "[traumatic] experience cannot be organized on a linguistic level, and this failure to arrange the memory in words and symbols leaves it to be organized on a somatosensory or iconic level" (172). Freud noted that the traumatized endeavor "to revive the trauma, to remember the forgotten experience, or, better still, to make it real—to live once more a repetition of it" (*Moses* 95). Caruth pays special attention to repetition in *Unclaimed Experience*, writing, "[T]he repetition at the heart of catastrophe—the experience that Freud will call 'traumatic neurosis'—emerges as the unwitting reenactment of an event that one cannot simply leave behind" (2). Moreover, "[w]hat returns to haunt the victim [. . .] is not only the reality of the violent event but also the reality of the way that its violence has not yet been fully known" (6). This aspect of repetition is the subject of *Hiroshima mon amour* as the Frenchwoman is traumatized, in part, by the fact she did not witness (experience) the death

50

of her German lover firsthand. McHale, meanwhile, devotes a significant portion of his postmodern study to the French concept of *mise-en-abyme*: in essence, an endless succession of internal duplications (i.e., repetitions). *Mise-en-abyme* may take various forms in a postmodern literary work—a repeated image, for example, or a repeated action—but in any event, writes McHale, it "is another form of short-circuit, another disruption of the logic of narrative hierarchy" whose net effect is "disquieting" to the reader (125).

The Dispersed or Fragmented Voice

Both intertextuality and repetition contribute to the third feature of postmodern narrative technique that mirrors the traumatized voice, as identified by Whitehead, and that is a dispersed or fragmented voice, which could manifest itself in various narrative forms. A postmodern text could have multiple narrative voices, or be comprised of multiple genres; details of plot could be related in bits and pieces, often out of logical (especially *chrono*logical) sequence; or the narrative may not relate a complete tale at all. Geyh, Leebron, and Levy point out that many postmodern texts are "[suggestive of] narrative attempts to make order from a world where each bit of information is linked richly and associatively to other bits of information, and meaning seems to multiply the moment one begins to speak or write" (xxi). This sort of fragmentation, they say, is sometimes achieved through pastiche, "the incorporation of fragments of other texts such as newspaper articles, dialogue from films, poems, songs, signs, diary entries, and photographs into the literary text" (xxii). Whitehead believes that such efforts are an attempt "to profoundly rethink the modes of our engagement with the past." She writes further, "History is no longer available as a completed knowledge, but must be conceived as that which perpetually escapes or eludes our understanding" (13). Testimony, too, is reflective of fragmentation in that the "trauma returns in disjointed fragments and the role of the listener is to [. . . make] sense out of the broken fragments that emerge" (34). Moreover, Felman says, "As a relation to events, testimony seems to be composed of bits and pieces of memory that has been overwhelmed by occurrences that have not settled into understanding or remembrance [. . .]" (16).

The Search for Powerful Language

I conclude my discussion of the traumatized voice with an aspect that Whitehead does not expressly identify, but I daresay it is so fundamental to both psychoanalysis and literature study it would be easy to leave if off the list—just as a survivor of shipwreck may inventory his salvaged supplies and neglect to include his still-beating heart—and that is the search for language that is powerful enough to recount the traumatic tale in such a way as to finally move beyond it. Freud obviously understood the power of language, as observed earlier (for example, in *Totem and Taboo*); and Lacan, as noted, stressed the imperativeness of linguistic analysis to budding psychoanalysts. Moreover, postmodern theorists, like Foucault and Derrida, were very much interested in the power of language. In *The Order of Things* (1966/1970), Foucault says that, beginning in the eighteenth century, "[k]nowledge and language are rigorously interwoven. [. . .] It is in one and the same movement that the mind speaks and knows" (86). Regarding written language in particular, Foucault suggests that alphabetic writing provides specific insights into cognition:

52

"So it does not matter that letters do not represent ideas [as "tropal hieroglyphics" do], since they can be combined together in the same way as ideas, and ideas can be linked together and disjoined just like the letters of the alphabet" (112). Because of this profound connection, "the progress of writing and that of thought [. . .] provide each other with mutual support." Derrida, too, believed that language evolution is reflective of deep cognitive connections. In *Of Grammatology* (1967/1976), he also discusses the movement from pictographic to phonetic writing: "Going beyond this real consciousness, the structure of the signifier may continue to operate not only on the fringes of the potential consciousness but according to the causality of the unconscious" (89). In other words, as people moved from picture representation to alphabetic writing, they selected *sounds* to signify ideas for reasons they themselves did not consciously grasp. In short, writes Derrida, "Metaphor shapes and undermines the proper name." Derrida's point about unconscious causality is especially meaningful to my purpose, which is to suggest that cultural trauma has affected artists at the subconscious level in such a way as to cause them to unwittingly mimic a traumatized voice in their "postmodern" narrative techniques.

Indeed, Foucault speaks even more specifically to my overarching agenda in *The Order of Things* when he writes,

> [T]rue ideas have in them the indelible mark of an order that chance on its own could never have created. What civilizations and peoples leave us as the monuments of their thought is not so much their texts as their vocabularies, their syntaxes, the sounds of their languages rather than the words they speak;

not so much their discourse as the element that made
it possible, the discursivity of their language. (87)

Here, then, he posits that through careful language analysis
we can come to know past cultures, to determine their
zeitgeist if you will. What is more, his assertion that chance
on its own could never have created a particular idea speaks
to the causality that Derrida underscores; so, again, my
purpose in citing a cause—cultural trauma—is especially
relevant. Taking up a related discussion in *The Discourse on
Language* (1971/1971), Foucault writes that since the 1600s
"the author's function has become steadily more important
[in literature . . . as t]he author is he who implants, into the
troublesome language of fiction, its coherence, its links with
reality" (222). Foucault again supports the notion that via an
analysis of literature—of aesthetic language—we can
reconstruct the *reality* of a given time period, at least as
presented to us by a specific author and a specific text. It is
worth keeping in mind that that specific author—though
unique as an artist—is part of a whole culture and his work
(or the mindset as demonstrated through his work) can be
emblematic of the whole culture (as discussed earlier via
Freud, Lacan, Caruth, Erikson, and so forth).

Language and Trauma

Turning more specifically to the correspondence
between language and trauma, I begin by revisiting van der
Kolk and van der Hart's ideas about narrative memory
(normal) and traumatic memory (abnormal). They write,
"Traumatic memories are the unassimilated scraps of
overwhelming experiences, which need to be integrated with
existing mental schemas, and be transformed into narrative
language" (176). This transformation is achieved by "the

54

traumatized person [. . .] return[ing] to the memory often in order to complete it." When the traumatic memory has become narrative memory, the subject's recovery is complete: "Instead [of flashbacks and involuntary reenactments] the story can be told, the person can look back at what happened; he has given it a place in his life history, his autobiography, and thereby in the whole of his personality" (176). Finding a way to tell the story is paramount to trauma theorists. Laura Di Prete writes, "[T]he representation of any traumatic experience involves the complex articulation of a narrative voice in response to the demands of objectivity and truthfulness, however problematic such desiderata may be" (8). It is worth noting Di Prete's expression "complex articulation" in that postmodern narrative technique is known for its complexity. She goes on to discuss texts that function psychoanalytically. "By performing a function similar to psychoanalysis," says Di Prete, "texts allow the remembering, the telling, and the convergence of unassimilated memories in a way that encourages forms of textual working through or healing." Moreover, such texts encourage "a process of public sharing and exposure" and "can indeed constitute a precious social and ethical service" (8). Another trauma theorist, Lynn Worsham, emphasizes the necessity of precise language in relating traumatic memory. Citing Roberta Culbertson, Worsham writes that "trauma is preeminently rhetorical" as "the traumatized subject is left in profound silence without the motivation or resources to construct a narrative [. . . yet] the traumatized subject is left with an overwhelming need to 'tell what seems untellable'" (176). Worsham also quotes Dori Laub:

"There is in each survivor an imperative need to *tell* and thus to come to know one's story, unimpeded by ghosts from the past against which one has to protect oneself. . . . Yet no amount of telling seems ever to do justice to this inner compulsion. There are never enough words or the right words [. . .]" (176-77; italics and unbracketed ellipsis in Worsham)

Laub's use of the phrase "right words" calls to mind the power of language (the totemic power of words, for example, as discussed by Freud; or the need for psychoanalytic "scansion," as discussed by Lacan). That is to say, the victim of trauma must find the specialized language (the magic words, if you will) to get beyond the traumatizing event; and, furthermore, the listener/reader must be attune to such language in order to fully grasp the traumatic experience—to unearth it from the traumatized psyche.

Postmodern literary theorists have of course paid special attention to innovative and complex language use. For example, Part four of six of Brian McHale's *Postmodernist Fiction* is devoted to "Words." He identifies several "stylistic strategies" whose labels are for the most part self-evident: "lexical exhibitionism, the catalogue, and brokeback and invertebrate sentences." McHale says that such language-play "strew[s] obstacles in the path that leads from text continuum to reconstructed world, making the process of reconstruction more difficult, hence more highly visible" (156). The text continuum refers to the seamless narrative put forth by modernist writers, who wanted to envelop their reader in a fictional dreamworld from first syllable to last. Postmodernists, meanwhile, by using disruptive linguistic practices, alternately hypnotize and awaken their attentive reader. "[T]his determination of world by word is normally [i.e., in modernist prose] kept in the background," writes McHale, "below the threshold of perceptibility, allowing us to efface the text continuum in favor of a world which we may think of as free-standing, independent of the text's language [. . .]" (156). On the other hand, postmodernist texts "foreground the determination of world by word, visibly placing the world at the mercy of the word." The net results:

> The syntactical flow is disturbed, the projected world undermined, collapsing time and again, then reconstituting itself only to collapse once more; it flickers. The reader becomes schizoid, his or her attention divided between the level of world and the level of words. (158)

McHale's use of the word *schizoid* is provocative given my interests in connecting the traumatized voice to postmodern technique.

Furthermore, Ihab Hassan, in *The Postmodern Turn* (1987), cites "[n]ew languages" as one of the hallmarks of postmodern "experimentalism": "Innovation, dissociation, the brilliance of change in all its aesthetic shapes. [. . .] Also, the Word beginning to put its miracle to question in the midst of an artistic miracle" (37). Hassan's focus on the miraculous nature of words is clearly rooted in the primitive, nearly magical, power of language. Italo Calvino, in *The Uses of Literature* (1980/1986), poetically expresses the almost alchemical power of language when he writes, "But words, like crystals, have facets and axes of rotation with different properties, and light is refracted differently according to how these word crystals are placed, and how the polarizing surfaces are cut and superimposed" (40). The aspect of Calvino's metaphor associated with spreading light is noteworthy in that I hope to illuminate the zeitgeist of past cultures via their literature. I will conclude (for now) this discussion of the importance of wordplay in postmodern texts with a workman-like quote from William H. Gass, who, in his 1981 preface to *In the Heart of the Heart of the Country*, lists nine points of his own writing process with number-seven being ". . . the better word . . . the better word . . . the better word . . ." (xl). It is fair to say that by *better* Gass surely means *more powerful*, even *more magical*. The writer's quest for the better word is also reflected in Calvino when he writes, "The struggle of literature is in fact to escape from the confines of language; it stretches out from the utmost limits of what can be said; what stirs literature is the call and attraction of what is not in the dictionary" (18). Again, the postmodernist's challenge mirrors that of trauma victims: to find the crucial words that will allow them to articulate their experience and free themselves of the ensnaring trauma.

Trauma and Postmodernism

It is significant that each of these characteristics of the traumatized voice which coincides with postmodern literary technique—intertextuality, repetition, fragmentation, and the search for empowering language—helps to create an overall correlation between trauma and postmodernism: the merging of reality and unreality, or what McHale refers to as a "zone," after Thomas Pynchon's Zone in *Gravity's Rainbow* (1976), which McHale calls the "paradigm" for such authorially created postmodernist spaces. He writes, "War in our century has forced us to rethink the received categories of space, conceptual as well as geographical space; it has taught us to think in terms of the zone. The

lexicon of war is one of the sources of the term 'zone' [. . .]"
(55). McHale offers several examples of military zones—
including, ironically, the demilitarized zone. If he were
writing today, he would no doubt include Baghdad's "Green
Zone." While there are various manifestations of the
postmodern zone, they generally describe a place where the
real world (whatever *that* may be) collides with or overlaps
an unreal world: "[T]here is a sense in which the worlds of
the zone *do*, in most cases, occupy the same *kind* of space"
(56, McHale's italics). He goes on to posit that "the
ontological confrontation occurs between our world and
some other world or worlds somehow adjacent or parallel to
our own, accessible across some kind of boundary or barrier"
(61). McHale notes that the postmodern zone corresponds
with the wordly-and-otherwordly place Foucault termed a
"heterotopia." Foucault writes in *The Order of Things*,

> [T]here is a worse kind of disorder than that of the
> *incongruous*, the linking together of things that are
> inappropriate; I mean the disorder in which fragments
> of a large number of possible orders glitter separately
> in the dimension, without law or geometry, of the
> *heteroclite*[. . . . . U]topias permit fables and
> discourse; they run with the very grain of language
> and are part of the fundamental dimension of the
> *fabula*; heterotopias [. . .] desiccate speech, stop
> words in their tracks, contest the very possibility of
> grammar at its source; they dissolve our myths and
> sterilize the lyricism of our sentences. (xvii-xviii,
> translator's italics)

Jean Baudrillard has put forward the idea of "implosion,"
which is very much in keeping with Foucault's hetertopia. In
The Ecstasy of Communication (1987/1988), Baudrillard

writes, "Just as we have reached the limits of geographic space and have explored all the confines of the planet, we can only implode into a space which is reduced daily as a result of our increasing mobility [. . .]" (39). This implosion has led to the "erosion of polar structures, and the movement towards a universe that is losing the very dimension of meaning," leaving people "[d]isinvested, disenchanted, and disaffected" (*Seduction* 104).

Each of these characterizations of the same phenomenon—McHale's zone, Foucault's heterotopia, and Baudrillard's implosion—is especially interesting within the context of one's reaction to trauma. For the traumatized, the unreality of the traumatic event collides with or overlaps, unbidden, day-to-day reality. Freud noted that victims of trauma "are not influenced by outer reality [. . . and] they take no notice of real things." He writes, "They are in a state within a state, an inaccessible party, useless to the common weal [. . . and it is possible that] the sovereignty of an inner psychical reality has been established over the reality of the outer world" (*Moses* 86). That is, the traumatic event has colonized the psyche so thoroughly, the victim has difficulty differentiating between the real world and the unreal return of traumatic memory (to use van der Kolk and van der Hart's term). Importantly (for my focus), groups can also have difficulty with the real and unreal, according to Freud: "They constantly give what is unreal precedence over what is real [. . .] They have an evident tendency not to distinguish between the two" (*Group Psychology* 12). Caruth characterizes the returning traumatizing event as "a waking memory [. . .] that appears to work very much like a bodily threat but is in fact a break in the mind's experience of time" (*Unclaimed Experience* 60, 61). We recall that McHale describes a telltale characteristic of the postmodernist zone as when "an ontological confrontation occurs between our world and some other world or worlds somehow adjacent or parallel to our own, accessible across some kind of boundary or barrier." His description sounds very much like the traumatized mind that is having trouble distinguishing between reality and unreality across a porous internal psychic boundary. Moreover, when Foucault remarks that heterotopias "desiccate speech, stop words in their tracks, contest the very possibility of grammar at its source; they dissolve our myths and sterilize the lyricism of our sentences," it is reminiscent of the trauma victim who cannot adequately articulate the originating event—who cannot move the event from traumatic memory to narrative memory. Finally, Baudrillard's analysis of twentieth-century Western culture in general—with its "erosion of polar structures, and the movement towards a universe that is losing the very dimension of meaning"—could be a quote from the *Diagnostic and Statistical Manual of Mental Disorders* (DSM). In other words, what each of these postmodern theorists may be discussing, unawares, is mass posttraumatic stress disorder—a possibility I will take up at greater length in the following chapter.

Chapter 3

Twentieth-Century Trauma Culture

As noted previously, there is no clear beginning of postmodernism—some gesture toward the end of the Second World War, others to the 1960s, still others trace it to before the twentieth century altogether—and even though I am focusing my attention on the literature created after 1945, some attention must be paid to the first half of the century as well, as postmodernism certainly did not spring from nothing. In fact, Niklas Luhmann conjectures that there is no real difference between the modernism of the first half of the century and the postmodernism of the latter. He writes, "Our whole life depends upon technologies, today [1995] more so than ever, and again, we see more problems, but no clear break with the past, no transition from a modern to a postmodern society." Then he asks, "Why do we indulge in a semantic discussion that does not burden itself with realities?" (172). One possible response, Luhmann suggests, is merely a function of memory, that we need labels to keep track of the *system* of human history: "The system will not have an unselected past, nor will it be able to follow linear prospect into the future" (174). This notion may account for our current fuzziness in defining postmodernism: We need for it to become a thing of the past before we can say with authority what exactly it *was*. Nevertheless, Luhmann ultimately offers a functional distinction for postmodern Western culture, as opposed to its predecessor:

> It seems, therefore, that we have to prepare ourselves
> to live with a society that does not provide for
> happiness, nor for solidarity, nor for a desirable

equalization of living conditions. There may be occasions where people can meet and critique society, but to all this "civil society" is pure hypocrisy given the facts we have to endure. (179)

In essence, in the first half of the twentieth century there were catastrophic wars and genocidal pogroms, but by and large Western culture was able to deceive itself into thinking that society was evolving in more or less the *correct* sociopolitical direction. The Holocaust, the mass death and destruction of the Second World War, and, especially, the atomic bombing of Japan—all occurring in a relatively brief time span—ended the self-deception. In short, writes Luhmann, "There are increasing doubts whether society (that is, self-reproducing social operations) can 'control' its environment changed by its own output [. . .]" (182).

Birth of the Atomic Age

Of all the cataclysmic events of the 1930s and '40s, the one that had the most profound impact on the Western (if not global) cultural psyche was the United States' ushering in the nuclear age in August 1945 by detonating uranium and plutonium bombs over Hiroshima and Nagasaki, respectively, thus annihilating hundreds of thousands of men, women and children, and obliterating two major urban centers. "Struggles with the Hiroshima narrative have to do with a sense of meaning in a nuclear age, with our vision of America and our sense of ourselves," write Jay Lifton and Greg Mitchell in *Hiroshima in America: Fifty Years of Denial*. The authors assert that "Hiroshima casts a shadow on every aspect of our personal and collective existence" (xvi). By "the Hiroshima narrative," they mean, in large part, the version of the bombings, their justifications, and their aftermaths as written and revised by the U.S. government and military, starting with Truman's administration and running through Clinton's (the book was published in 1995). In brief, the Hiroshima narrative says that the atomic bombings were necessary to end the war more speedily and thus save the lives of untold American and Allied servicemen; that the achievement proved American resolve and scientific/industrial superiority in the world; that the radioactive aftermath was nominal to humans and the environment; and that continued atomic weapons development was vital for national security. Lifton and Mitchell's research shows that American citizens were deeply conflicted about the bombings almost immediately. In a Gallup survey conducted only days after Nagasaki's destruction, 69 percent of Americans said it was a "good thing" that the atomic bomb was developed, compared to only 17 percent who indicated it was a "bad thing"; but in the same survey more than a quarter of respondents (27 percent) believed that an atomic explosion "will destroy the entire world" (33). Write Lifton and Mitchell, "This reflected the seemingly contradictory emotions of approval and fear the bomb evoked, a combination that has continued to disturb and confuse Americans ever since."

This internal conflict is key to understanding the zeitgeist of twentieth-century America. "Hiroshima marks a powerful psychological turning point in our attitude toward our own science and technology," write Lifton and Mitchell:

> Ordinary people, that is, experience their own post-Hiroshima entrapment—mixtures of nuclearism [in essence worshipping nuclear weapons technology] and nuclear terror, of weapons advocacy and fearful anticipation of death and extinction. The feelings

65

could frequently be suppressed, only to reassert themselves when one is reminded of nuclear danger, or unexpectedly in dreams. And even at the end of the Cold War, when our interviews showed something of a switch from nuclear to environmental fear, those post-Hiroshima anxieties by no means disappeared. (306)

Besides the out and out fear of nuclear war (most likely with the Soviet Union), throughout the century Americans became increasingly aware of the dangers of radiation, to themselves and to the planet; and over time it became clear that the U.S. military-industrial complex was reckless in its handling of atomic material, and—much worse—it deliberately subjected American citizens to various hazards to see what effects they would have on human biology. "The full extent of the experiments—now officially said to be 'in the thousands'—is still not known (as of this writing in early 1995)," report Lifton and Mitchell, "but what has been learned suggest a pattern of planned experimental abuse that is unique in American history" (322). Regarding the covert experimentation on humans and animals, Hugh Gusterson writes in *People of the Bomb* (2004), "Scientists have methodically metamorphosed the mutilated and suffering bodies [. . .] into tidy bodies of data in myriad strategic calculations [. . .]" (69). The elaborate and protracted government cover-up—which began with robust censorship of news reports and photographic evidence coming out of Japan immediately after the bombings—contributed to a mentality of official obfuscation, say Lifton and Mitchell, that led to such scandals as Watergate and Iran-Contra.[1] All of which have contributed to a "sense of the world as deeply absurd and dangerous" (335). One is reminded of the 1963 film—though, ironically *and* appropriately, a comedy—*It's a Mad Mad Mad Mad Mad World* (by Stanley Kramer).

The Measured Self and the Apocalyptic Self

To return specifically to the psychology of living in post-Hiroshima America, Lifton and Mitchell recount numerous studies and anecdotal accounts that speak to people's deep-seated trauma due to the bomb. They attribute the rebelliousness of the Beat movement and the drug experimentation of the Hippies to the belief that nuclear annihilation was just a matter of time, and very little of it. They write, "By the 1960s, Americans were living a nuclear 'double life': aware that any moment each of us and everything around us could be suddenly annihilated, yet at the same time proceeding with our everyday, nitty-gritty lives and conducting 'business as usual'" (351). As such, Americans have been divided in two, with a "measured self" that "deals with everyday living" and tries to achieve "a meaningful life"; but also an "apocalyptic self" that is "preoccupied with the nuclear end [. . .] and haunted by death in general" (352). This double life is another aspect of Americans' simultaneous loving of and loathing of the bomb—loving because of our victory in the Second World War, because of our worldpower superiority, and because of our appreciation of the bomb as a technological leap forward; but loathing because of its destructive capabilities and the fact that we inhumanely unleashed it on thousands of innocents, and because we live in fear of destruction by our own creation. Perhaps the deep-seatedness of this loving/loathing duality is due to its being at the epigenetic level of the human psyche. We recall Freud's theory of the primal father who brutalized his sons, banishing them from

67

the horde and/or castrating them to prevent their copulation with the father's horde-harem of females. The sons ultimately banded together to kill and consume the father, which led to their exultation at having overcome the father but also their simultaneous guilt at having done so. "The feelings of the sons found a natural and appropriate substitute for the father in the animal[. . . .] Thus totemism helped to gloss over the real state of affairs and to make one forget the event to which is owed its origin," writes Freud in *Totem and Taboo*. Moreover, all religions aim "at the same great event with which culture began and which ever since has not let mankind come to rest" (124). Perhaps Americans' conflicted psyche regarding the bombing of Japan is a refiguring of the beyond-ancient loving/loathing of the primal father. Interestingly, President Truman claimed unconditional surrender from Japan, but in fact there was one significant condition: that Japan was allowed to keep its constitutional monarchy and, specifically, that Emperor Hirohito would retain the throne—a symbolic expiation of primal guilt after so much (likely unnecessary) carnage, conjured up from the distant, distant past and deep, deep psychic structures?

As discussed in Chapter 2, the origin of postmodernism, as a term and as a concept, is unclear, and its terminus is even less so (that is, are we still postmodern, or have we moved on to something else?). My purpose is not to examine its (possible) end, but one may be tempted to wonder if the end of the Cold War also *ended* postmodernism per se—as the mindset seemed to arrive, more or less, with the Cold War and be fueled by the atomic tensions between the U.S. and the Soviet Union. In his introduction, Gusterson writes that, by the beginning of the

1990s, antinuclear activists among many others were anticipating a world without the threat of nuclear war and, in fact, one with more global harmony in general. The author points out that U.S. State Department strategist Francis Fukuyama "declared [. . . in 1989] that the end of the cold war was poised to bring about the global triumph of Western democracy"; moreover, Tony Lake, the Clinton administration's original national security adviser, "proclaimed that democracies do not fight one another and foretold an unprecedented era of peace and prosperity as democracy and free trade spread around the world under American tutelage" (xvii). Obviously, such thinking was too hasty, and we know in retrospect that the break up of the Soviet Union gave rise to a potentially less safe world—a phenomenon that Gusterson describes as "a broader mutation of the global nuclear system" (xviii). He writes,

> It has become an increasingly important way of legitimating U.S. military programs in the post-cold war world since the early 1990s, when U.S. military leaders introduced the term *rogue states* into the American lexicon of fear, identifying a new source of danger just as the Soviet threat was declining. (24, Gusterson's italics)

I will return to this discussion, of the continuation of fear into the twenty-first century, in a moment, but it is fair to say that even though the terminus of postmodernism is debatable, it is quite evident that fear of atomic annihilation (the psychic duality of our measured and apocalyptic selves) has not diminished with the dissolution of the Soviet Union as such; if anything, it may have become even more profound.

Post-Hiroshima America

Before saying anything more about the twenty-first century, I want to speak further of the twentieth. In particular, I want to look at factors that seem to have deepened the profundity of cultural trauma throughout the 1900s, especially the post-Hiroshima half. One vital factor was that people of the twentieth century began perceiving warfare and related acts of violence in ways that must have been similar to firsthand traumatic experience because of advances in military technology combined with the burgeoning sciences of photography and, later, videography. Joseph Dewey discusses the spontaneous cultural impact of the atomic bombing in *In a Dark Time: The Apocalyptic Temper in the American Novel of the Nuclear Age* (1990) and writes that the image of "[t]he billowing mushroom cloud represented the last crisis in human history" (7). Moreover, "the Hiroshima blast immediately ushered in a new age that was announced in world headlines, analyzed in political columns of every stripe, splashed across covers of news magazines" (5). Dewey suggests that the image of the mushroom cloud itself has come to represent the discordantly complex ideas that Americans have been grappling with, consciously and unconsciously, since the bombs were detonated. He writes that

> an awesome image entered the cultural mythos: the stout, churning column of the atomic mushroom cloud. Like the dazed citizenry of Hiroshima, Americans (as the first developers of the weaponry and the only culture to use it against another) have been puzzling just what such a terrifying image implies. We have become certain of only one

70

premise: this force demands not only an entirely new
vocabulary, but a new way of thinking. (4)

This "new way of thinking" would eventually be termed *postmodern* of course. Dewey goes on to hypothesize as to why, for the most part, the response of American writers to the bombings was delayed by more than a decade, and I will take up Dewey's hypothesis in Chapter 6.

For now, however, I want to continue with the significance of media and cultural images in the twentieth century. Humans have always responded on an emotional level to visual representation, especially to the visual representation of other humans. This point is probably mere common sense, but to provide some theoretical underpinning: Jacques Lacan was particularly interested in the power of visualization. There is, for example, his well-known theory of "mirroring" in which infants' personality development hinges on their seeing (and mimicking) those around them. In a lecture titled "What Is a Picture?" Lacan discusses the attraction of visual stimuli to adults. Lacan concerns himself primarily with *trompe-l'oeil* painting, a style which tries to achieve photograph-like realism. Lacan suggests that humans' self-image is dependent upon how we believe others see us; that is, upon the image (our "mask") we present to others' gaze (the "screen"): "Man, in effect, knows how to play with the mask as that beyond which there is the gaze. The screen is here the locus of mediation" (*The Seminar* 107). When gazing at realistic pictures (of people presumably), we also sense ourselves being gazed upon, reinforcing the mask that we have created for ourselves, says Lacan. Desirable reinforcement of our self-image (of our ego, as Freud may have characterized it) leads to an insatiable desire to view realistic images, which in turn puts us, at least momentarily, in a dreamlike state. Says Lacan, "This appetite of the eye [on the part of the person looking] that must be fed produces the hypnotic value of painting" (115). Though Lacan does not speak to gruesome images, or images of the dead, one can conjecture that the psychic desire is, if anything, intensified. In the same lecture, Lacan does say that "the painting of a veil [. . .] incites [the viewer] to ask what is behind it" (112). Perhaps the eyes of the dead, as one is likely to find in war pictures, act as a metaphoric veil, thus intensifying the viewer's desire to gaze. In any case, humans have a psychic need to look at pictures, no matter how disturbing the images may be.

Susan Sontag, in her book *Regarding the Pain of Others* (2003), explains that because of easily transportable cameras and 35-mm film, "[p]ictures could now be taken in the thick of battle [. . .] and civilian victims and exhausted, begrimed soldiers studied up close. The Spanish Civil War (1936-39) was the first war to be witnessed ('covered') in the modern sense [. . .]" (21). She goes on to say, "Photojournalism came into its own in the early 1940s—wartime" (34), and "[. . .] since the 1960s, most of the best-known photographers covering wars have thought their role was to show war's 'real' face" (37). Thanks, first, to newspapers, then newsreels, television, and now the Internet, scenes of carnage are commonplace, but very often still disturbing:

> Wars are now also living room sights and sounds. Information about what is happening elsewhere, called "news," features conflict and violence—"If it bleeds, it leads" runs the venerable guideline of tabloids and twenty-four-hour headline news shows—to which the response is compassion, or

indignation, or titillation, or approval, as each misery heaves into view. (18)

The images of war and one's inability to avoid such images in the twentieth-century media culture can only be superseded by someone living in a warzone—someone who has come to understand, as Sontag puts it, that war is not an "aberration," but in fact "[w]ar has been the norm [throughout history] and peace the exception" (74).

Trauma Culture's Otherworldliness

The ubiquity of war and warlike images in the twentieth century—images that we were drawn to, according to Lacan, perhaps in spite of our conscious desire to avoid disturbing imagery—may have contributed to the otherworldliness of the post-Hiroshima trauma culture. We recall that victims of posttraumatic stress disorder have trouble differentiating between reality and unreality, as Caruth characterizes the returning traumatizing event as "a waking memory [. . .] that appears to work very much like a bodily threat but is in fact a break in the mind's experience of time" (*Unclaimed Experience* 60, 61). Psychoanalyst Jerry Kroth, in *Omens and Oracles* (1992), cites a sleep-deprivation study which suggested that for "[n]ormal subjects [. . .] subclinical hallucinating may be occurring [in the daylight hours]." That is, people's normal need for "dream-time" (which is about 82 minutes per night) may be augmented by media imagery during their waking hours because the brain interprets the images as dream*like*. Kroth writes, "The images that greet us in the morning news, for example, may be less descriptive of objective reality and more dream like than we generally are accustomed to admit" (9). As such, "[t]he content of the news can be seen, therefore, as a surrealistic caricature of reality, as dream-residue heavily colored with unconscious influences" (9-10). Media images, then, may amplify the "unreal reality" perspective that haunts PTSD victims. Kroth could only begin to speculate what the study's findings mean in terms of a nation's collective unconscious, but he says, "It is as if the world we have come to know as factual, objective, and real turns out to be just as much a set of collective, mythological epics expressing human needs, wishes, and repressed longings as the tales of Grimm and Disney" (11). Immediately after the atomic bombing of Hiroshima and Nagasaki, many journalists commented on the dreamlike (nightmarish?) *reality* they suddenly found themselves living in. A writer for *Time* magazine said, "Man has been tossed into the vestibule of another millennium. It was wonderful to think of what the Atomic Age might be, if man was strong and honest. But at first it was a strange place, full of weird symbols and the smell of death" (Lifton and Mitchell 36). A *Life* writer said that Americans "are in a strange new land" (39). Australian journalist Wilfred Burchett, the first foreign correspondent to visit Hiroshima after the bombing, described it as a "death-stricken alien planet" (47). The main point here is that the atomic bombing of Japan may have brought on (or may have been the proverbial final straw that brought on) pervasive cultural trauma, and the escalating flow of media images throughout the remainder of the century contributed to society's sense of unreality that is a key symptom of posttraumatic stress disorder.

Daily Reminders of Armageddon

In addition to the saturation of media images that kept people mindful of the bomb (even if only indirectly) throughout the twentieth century, there were other daily—*direct*—reminders as well. Myron A. Marty says that "threats of nuclear war with Russia [. . . were] portrayed by some political leaders as a real possibility if not a virtual certainty" (5). He points out that black-and-yellow signs on public buildings designated as fallout shelters were continuous reminders of nuclear attack. Also, the U.S. government and popular media (like *Life* magazine) encouraged people to construct private bomb-shelters. Marty cites surveys in the 1960s and '70s that indicate both children and adults were "worried" about the likelihood of nuclear war: "This sense of 'futurelessness' [. . .] may haunt the baby boom through life, and may well be the most intense of the generation's shared experiences" (6). The measured self/apocalyptic self duality (as described by Lifton and Mitchell) may best be exemplified by the private bomb-shelter which, said *Life*, could be used for guys'-night poker games or a guest bedroom for the mother-in-law until it might be needed to save the family from nuclear warfare with the Soviet Union (5-6). Moreover, there were regular civil-defense drills in which schoolchildren were trained to crawl under their desks and cover their heads with their arms, as if these precautions would protect them in the event of an atomic blast. Lifton and Mitchell write, "[Participants in such drills] remembered being fearful, often terrified, but they also recalled a powerful demand from authorities that they overcome, suppress, numb themselves to precisely any such fears—to conceal these emotions from themselves" (334). All of these things—media images and reports, public and personal fallout shelters, school drills (not to mention other sources like songs, poems, and day-to-day conversation)—kept Americans ever mindful, consciously and subconsciously, of the bomb and of their own conflicted psyches because of it. In terms of the dynamics of cultural trauma, Neil J. Smelser points out that "once a historical memory is established as a national trauma for which the society has to be held in some way responsible, its status as trauma has to be continuously and actively sustained and reproduced in order to continue in that status" (Anderson et al. 38). Moreover, "the mechanisms at the cultural level are mainly those of social agents and contending groups" (39).

Turning now to literature in particular and an intriguing mid-century assessment of what literature had to say about Western zeitgeist, in a lecture for the BBC in 1950, which he titled "Culture, Chaos and Order," J. Isaacs asks, "What is in the background of the modern writer's mind, what is intruding continually even into the foreground? [. . .] He feels that chaos is here, that chaos is universal, that this is the apocalypse!" (106-107). Furthermore, twentieth-century man desperately wants to put chaos into order by sensing a pattern in history: "The more artistic the pattern, the more shapely and symbolical, the happier we are" (107). The twentieth-century novel, says Isaacs from mid-century, has been about imposing order on chaos. "[T]he novel helps in confronting and exploring the problems of human destiny" (115). From our twenty-first-century perspective, Isaacs was composing on the cusp of literary postmodernism, and he concerns himself with several forms that will become hallmarks of postmodern fiction, including (what we would call) the metafictional work of André Gide and Aldous Huxley, which Isaacs traces back to Laurence Sterne; and the encyclopedic fiction of Huxley and Hermann Broch. Writing on the heels of the 1940s, Isaacs describes the *current* zeitgeist: "In a world hurtling to its doom, as so many people seem to think it is, it is not surprising that the most natural preoccupation of that world should be—time" (123). He goes on to discuss novelists who are interested in "the interweaving of time and space" (125), which could be the foretastes of the coming traumatized voice of postmodernism. Or as Ihab Hassan puts it, "Postmodernism may be a response, direct or oblique, to the Unimaginable that Modernism glimpsed only in its most prophetic moments. Certainly it is not the Dehumanization of the Arts that concerns us now; it is rather the Denaturalization of the Planet and the End of Man" (39). Hassan goes on to speak of postmodernism in a way that is eerily similar to the way journalists (and others) described their world immediately after the atomic bombings, and, by the same token, Hassan seems to be referring to PTSD symptomology. He writes: "We are, I believe, inhabitants of another Time and another Space, and we no longer know what response is adequate to our reality" (39).

Hassan is asserting that postmodernism was not a random development but a specific response to a changed world which, in turn, had changed our sense of the world and of ourselves—we recall Lifton and Mitchell's statement that the Hiroshima narrative has to do "with a sense of meaning in the nuclear age, with our vision of America and our sense of ourselves." McHale, meanwhile, speaks to the close ties between postmodern fiction and science fiction (a genre that came into its own post-Hiroshima). "Science fiction and postmodernist fiction, it would appear, have advanced along parallel literary-historical tracks," writes McHale. "Occasionally these separate but parallel lines of development have produced motifs and *topoi* which are strikingly similar" (62). McHale's argument is that a distinguishing attribute of postmodern literature is the presentation of a world that reflects reality in some ways but also incorporates unreal elements (even fantastic elements). Postmodernists combine or overlap worlds, he says, a real one and a not-real one.

After Hiroshima and Nagasaki, atrocities on the global stage (not uncommonly either directed by or at least added to by the United States) continued to mount. Erich Fromm, in his book *The Anatomy of Human Destructiveness* (1973), remarks that "in the middle of the [1960s . . .] the level of violence and the fear of war had passed a certain threshold throughout the world" (1). Fromm says that psychologists, sociologists, and professionals from other fields—as well as the public in general—began to look deeply "into the nature and causes of aggression" (1). Various theories have been brought forward by which to examine the nuances of human destructiveness. Both psychologist and artists are busy at the same work, as Fromm describes it:

> Understanding [destructiveness and cruelty] does not mean condoning them. But unless we understand them, we have no way to recognize how they may be reduced, and what factors tend to increase them. [¶] Such understanding is of particular importance today [1973], when sensitivity toward destructiveness-cruelty is rapidly diminishing, and necrophilia, the attraction to what is dead, decaying, lifeless, and purely mechanical, is increasing throughout our cybernetic industrial society. (9-10)

Interestingly, Fromm sees the wars of the twentieth century as chain reactions of "blood revenge." For example, the second World War was sparked by Germans' "wish for revenge because of the loss of the war in 1914-1918 [. . . and the perceived] injustice of the Versailles peace treaty [. . .]" (272). Moreover, the Germans' anti-Semitic campaigns were a two-thousand-year-old backlash (i.e., blood revenge) against the death of Jesus, allegedly, at the hands of the Jews (273). Fromm goes on to speculate as to why human beings are naturally inclined toward revenge, and he offers the biblical story of Cain and Abel as an example of blood revenge: "Cain could not stand the fact that he was rejected while his brother was accepted. The rejection was arbitrary, and it was not in his power to change it; this fundamental injustice aroused such envy that the score could only be evened out by killing Abel" (273). Furthermore, Fromm says that the "powerlessness" human beings feel in the face of cataclysmic atrocities can have positive outcomes, like "creativity" (296). Hence the works of postmodern writers like Pynchon, Gass, Barth, and DeLillo. It is noteworthy that Fromm compares the sadistic public spectacles of ancient Rome to the current media: "Contemporary society offers similar spectacles in the form of newspaper and television reports on crime, war, [and other] atrocities [. . .]" (297). We recall that Lifton and Mitchell, among others, posit that any references to violence or, more generally, inhumane acts can remind people subconsciously of the century's ultimate violent and inhumane act: the dropping of the bombs.

The U.S. as a Posttraumatic Culture

Returning to the present, contemporary theorists have coined phrases like "posttraumatic culture" and "wound culture" to describe the United States, in particular, and all of Western culture. Lynn Worsham, describing the seamless flow of the twentieth into the twenty-first century, writes that we are in "an especially catastrophic age characterized by unprecedented historical trauma that has produced a pervasive and generalized mood corresponding to posttraumatic stress disorder" (170). She quickly qualifies her remark—in a way that is useful to my aim: "This diagnosis of our social psychology calls attention to a collective sense of profound historical shock, to a sense that we live out our individual lives, more or less consciously, in the overwhelming shadow cast by the unspeakable atrocities of war, genocide, mass murder, and terrorism." That is, even citizens who are not directly affected by these or other traumatic events, are nevertheless suffering from mass PTSD. She cites the work of Mark Seltzer, who uses "wound culture" to describe the U.S.—"a culture that is preoccupied with (if not addicted to) suffering, woundedness, and trauma, preoccupied with its own suffering and sense of injury (both physical and psychic)" (171). Worsham notes that societal trauma may be sensed as "a kind of free-floating anxiety that cannot be easily traced to a particular source or cause, whether personal or public." We recall Kai Erikson's assertion that trauma "has to be understood as resulting from a *constellation of life experiences* as well as from a discrete happening, from a *persisting condition* as well as from an acute event" (185, Erikson's italics).

Other theorists have focused on the pervasive melancholia felt by people of the United States especially. Working off of Freud, who defined melancholia as "a pathological form of mourning" in which someone is "unable to 'properly' grieve the loss of an object, a place, or an ideal," David L. Eng writes,

> The melancholic is so militant in his or her denials
> that the lost object is finally incorporated into the

80

self, turned into the shelter of the ego, and preserved as a form of ghostly identification. In this refusal to sever any attachments to the lost object, the melancholic becomes instead haunted by it. (1276)

In the twentieth century, there have been many lost objects. On a cultural level, Americans have lost their sense of themselves as a benignly democratic, peaceloving people. The most extreme national contradiction has no doubt been the nuclear attack of Japan, but there is no shortage of other examples. Worsham cites Hayden White's 1992 list of "Hitlerism, the Final Solution, total war, nuclear contamination, mass starvation, and ecological suicide"; then she adds her own "daily agonies caused by imperialism, racism, poverty, and crime that have been endured by generations of a vast number of the world's population" (170). Of mass melancholia, Anne Cheng says that it is "interminable in nature" and "denotes a condition of endless self-impoverishment" (8). Her words recall Niklas Luhmann's description of a postmodern society that we seem to have no choice but to accept, "a society that does not provide for happiness, nor for solidarity, nor for a desirable equalization of living conditions." As a culture and in varying degrees as individuals within that culture, we suffer the symptoms of posttraumatic stress disorder. Bernhard Giesen has made the psychic response of "perpetrators" his special interest, pointing out that the studies of human-caused traumatic events have almost always focused on the victims' psyches and paid little or no attention to the psychic aftermath of those who were agents of the harm. He writes, "If a community has to recognize that its members, instead of being heroes, have been perpetrators who violated the cultural premises of their own identity, the reference to the

81

past is indeed traumatic" (Alexander et al. 114). What is more, the community that recognizes its members as perpetrators is limited in how they can respond to the traumatic event: "by a collective schizophrenia, by denial, by decoupling or withdrawal."

The History of World-Destroying Technologies

It would be gross cultural egocentrism to imply that Westerners, particularly Americans, living in the Atomic Age were the first and only human beings to feel this sort of psychic rupture. While it is true that twentieth-century technologies facilitated and expedited genocidal events like the Holocaust and the bombing of Japan, every century has managed to produce world-destroying technologies that have been put in the service of world-destroying ideologies. Here I am using *world* to mean one's individual sense of the world, one's metaphorical world. It is relatively recently in human history that people have spoken of *the world* as synonymous with *the entire planet*, and very recently, mid twentieth century, that people could speak of *destroying the world* as meaning, literally, *the destruction of the entire planet*. But even before the last century, people had conceptions of their entire worlds, though in retrospect we know that they were only referencing a part of the planet. In spite of the fact that our empirical knowledge of the planet has evolved over time, the old conception of *world* remains with us, as evidenced by linguistic constructs like "Old World," "New World," "Third World," "industrialized world," and "English-speaking world"—terms which only reference part of the planet, yet a trace of the whole still lingers in their connotations.

Central to my argument is the assertion that people in other time periods sensed their impending destruction, even though their whole worlds could not have been destroyed in the literal way that we think of nuclear Armageddon. In the Christian era, apocalyptic doom has been a projection of every generation. In *The Sense of an Ending* (1966), Frank Kermode writes, "[Apocalypse] is a pattern of anxiety that we shall find recurring, with interesting differences, in different stages of modernism [i.e., the Christian era]. Its recurrence is a feature of our cultural tradition, if not ultimately our physiology [. . .]" (96). Kermode has identified variations of Apocalypse: "The apocalyptic types—empire, decadence and renovation, progress and catastrophe—are fed by history and underlie our ways of making sense of the world from where we stand, in the middest" (29). Therefore, while the scientific possibility of true world destruction has only existed for the last half century (the period associated with literary postmodernism), the belief in the possibility seems as old as humanity itself. Indeed, our most ancient recorded stories tell of the destruction of the world from flood, plague, war—across cultures, which suggests that such imaginings are a human attribute, not one limited to a specific century or geography (i.e., time and space). In short, says Kermode, "The End [that human beings] imagine will reflect their irreducibly intermediary preoccupations. They fear it, and as far as we can see have always done so" (7). Hence, *Beowulf* and numerous works from various centuries and cultures demonstrate tenets of literary postmodernism. It is worth noting that in his study of the twentieth-century, apocalyptic novel, Dewey says that "[f]or all its technological wizardry, the nuclear age had returned people to a most medieval mindset" (7). In contemplating the Apocalypse, people in every century ask the ontological questions that McHale says all postmodern literatures raises. McHale cites Dick Higgins for some of the questions and the basic idea behind the approach:

> "Which world is this? What is to be done in it? Which of my selves is to do it?" [. . .] What is a world?; What kinds of world are there, how are they constituted, and how do they differ?; What happens when different kinds of worlds are placed in confrontation, or when boundaries between worlds are violated?; What is the mode of existence of a text, and what is the mode of existence of the world (or worlds) it projects?; How is a projected world structured? (10)

It would seem that these investigations are ones that would be advanced by a traumatized people, and careful analysis of the history and culture of the specific time and place, integrated with a psycholinguistic approach to its literature, should expose the cognitive underpinnings of "postmodernism" and help to explain why "postmodern" texts can be found hundreds of years before the end of the Second World War. Moreover, such an analysis could advance our understanding of the psychic connections between cultural experience and the art that that culture produces.

1. Perhaps the height of government obfuscation was reached during the Donald J. Trump administration. According to *The Washington Post*, President Trump made 30,573 "false or misleading claims" during his four years in office.

Chapter 4

Anglo-Saxon Trauma Culture

If indeed the trauma culture that evolved in the latter half of the twentieth century was responsible in significant ways for the literary voice which became known as "postmodern," then it is reasonable to suggest that other cultures have been marked by a zeitgeist of trauma and that this pervasive mood contributed to "postmodern" texts being produced in those cultures as well. As evidence of such a culture and such text I will offer the Anglo-Saxon poem *Beowulf*, produced sometime in the last centuries of the first millennium. I will speak to specific features of the poem that illustrate its postmodern-ness within the trauma-literature paradigm I have been using throughout this study, but for now let it suffice to say that my calling *Beowulf* postmodern is not my own invention. In the preface to their *The Postmodern* Beowulf (2006), editors Eileen A. Joy and Mary K. Ramsey refer to the collection's "belated arrival" (xiii) as they characterize it as the "first-ever anthology of critical essays on *Beowulf* that represents scholarship influenced by postmodern thought [. . .]" (xiv). Moreover, in their introduction Joy and Ramsey write,

> A literary text like *Beowulf* that speaks of and points toward a traumatic and violent history—part real, part wholly unreal—so far removed from us in time that we could easily feel emotionally disconnected from it, and for which there are no recognizable memory sites [. . .], and whose composition history is fraught with so many unresolvable aporia [. . .], would seem to provide the ideal site through which to

explore the always compromised relationships between memory, history, and art. (xlix-l)

In other words, the Old English poem is nicely suited for exploring the hypothesis that cultural trauma results in the production of literature which reflects that trauma via a style we have come to call "postmodern."

Anglo-Saxon Culture

Let us then accept, provisionally, that *Beowulf* is "postmodern" and focus our attention on the Anglo-Saxon culture which produced it. At first glance it seems that it would be helpful to locate the poem's production to a specific time and place, not to mention a specific poet. After all, a great many scholars have worked long (and, to date, fruitless) hours to do just that. This preoccupation to identify as closely as possible—if not exactly—the circumstances by which *Beowulf* was produced is due at least in part to our contemporary notion of text production. Employing the work of several theorists (including Foucault, Barthes, Kristeva, and Pasternack), Mary Swan says that the "modern 'image of literature' [quoting Barthes specifically] has resulted over the last two hundred years or so in much Anglo-Saxon literary production being ignored and pushed to the margins of the canon of English Literature simply because, as it has no identifiable author, we cannot validate it as worthy of study" (73). Swan pays special attention to Foucault's influential essay "What Is an Author?" and its discussion of the "author-function." Swan's attention is justified and because of the essay's pertinence to my study, I will take a moment to look at Foucault's ideas beyond the frame provided by Swan. As we recall, Foucault examines our modern (and Western) concept of "author" as compared

86

to the concept in previous centuries (and cultures) in order to demonstrate how it affects our interpretation of the author-produced text. By linking a text to its *author*, whose *authority* as an expert/genius we readily accept, the author, says Foucault, becomes "a certain functional principle by which one impedes the free circulation, the free manipulation, the free composition, decomposition, and recomposition of fiction. [. . .] The author is therefore the ideological figure by which one marks the manner in which we fear the proliferation of meaning" (516). That is, because we know the author of a work, we default to interpreting that work via our knowledge of the author: "[T]he author provides the basis for explaining not only the presence of certain events in a work, but also their transformations, distortions, and diverse modifications (through his biography, the determination of his individual perspective, the analysis of his social position, the revelation of his basic design)" (510). In his essay, Foucault acknowledges that there is no going back, that the author-function is here to stay. However, being aware of it, we can consciously examine texts in search of other influences and thereby make other interpretations: "Perhaps it is time to study discourses not only in terms of their expressive value or formal transformations, but according to their modes of existence. The modes of circulation, valorization, attribution, and appropriation of discourses vary with each culture and are modified within each" (515).

Returning to Mary Swan and Anglo-Saxon literature, she says that Foucault's author-function contributes to our understanding of why modern readers have trouble with anonymous Old English texts: "[W]e cannot 'construct' an individual author for it, and therefore cannot use what we

87

define as significant about that author's personality to interpret the text" (73). Swan suggests that this anonymity has discouraged modern readers from considering Anglo-Saxon texts "literature" and Anglo-Saxon writers "authors" (75). However, the anonymity of the *Beowulf* poet works to my advantage. It prevents my becoming unduly focused on (and muddled in) the individual life and times of The Poet and requires the examination of Anglo-Saxon culture more broadly—which after all is my concern: *zeitgeist*, not *ennui*. Moreover, it is widely acknowledged by Anglo-Saxonists that the production, transmission, and reception of texts were much more *social* rather than *individual* functions. In modern times, we tend to think of the individual author producing text in isolation (perhaps in a lonely mountain cabin . . . or a writers' colony like Yaddo) and of the individual reader interpreting textual meaning in isolation (preferably in a leather chair, sipping a hot beverage). We know, when we consider the process, that it is not so simple. In between writer and reader there are numerous filters (editors, publishers, distributors, etc.); and readers rarely just pick up a totally unknown text and begin reading. They generally have some foreknowledge given to them by reviewers, other readers, book-jacket blurbers, Internet bloggers, or Oprah; and frequently the reading is in a decidedly social context, like a classroom or a book-club meeting. Nevertheless, our modern notion of writer-reader communion is seen informally as individualistic and even intimate.

Literacy in the Anglo-Saxon Period

During the Anglo-Saxon period, though, there tended to be very little that was individual or intimate about reading.

Obviously literacy rates were far below modern rates, but even among the literate (who tended to be members of the clergy or specially trained laypeople) reading to oneself (that is, silently) was an uncommon practice. In fact, one-on-one, writer-to-reader transmission "would have seemed incomprehensible to a medieval reader shaped by classical practices and texts as they were absorbed into Christian culture," writes Nicholas Howe. Furthermore, the "quiet and solitude" that we associate with reading today "would have disturbed a medieval reader accustomed to reading as a public, spoken act" ("The Cultural Construction of Reading" 2). Hugh Magennis concurs, pointing out that "some Old English literature was purely oral, and even that which was written down could be delivered orally to a non-literate as well as a literate audience by someone who could read" (89). By reading aloud, even to those who could read for themselves, the text could be interpreted, for the better, as a communal project. Howe writes, "What was alien, opaque, seemingly without meaning becomes familiar, transparent, and meaningful when read aloud by those initiated in the solution of such enigma" (6). What is more, Katherine O'Brien O'Keeffe suggests that methods of constructing meaning associated with orality shed light on interpretation even for the person who was reading text: "[E]arly readers of Old English verse read by applying oral techniques for the reception of a message to the decoding of a written text" (*Visible Song* 21).

For modern educators, these medieval reading practices make perfect sense. How often do educators read text aloud to students—from kindergarten to graduate school—to aid comprehension (oftentimes without even adding any gloss to the reading)? Or how often do educators encourage students to read passages aloud, especially poetry perhaps, to contribute to their overall understanding? Another contemporary example akin to Anglo-Saxon reading habits would be the numerous reading groups that are dedicated to an unusually challenging modern text, a text like *Finnegans Wake*, for which groups around the globe read the book aloud and discuss it line by line, obscure allusion by obscure allusion. The Albuquerque, New Mexico, group "tak[es] turns reading the text aloud then discussing it"; the Berkeley, California, group does "oral recitation [. . .] focusing on a page a week"; and the Dubuque, Iowa, enthusiasts "take turns reading by paragraphs"—to cite but a few examples from The Finnegans Wake Reading Society of New York. The Dubuque group in particular emphasizes that anyone is welcome, from Joyce scholar to non-literary type, in a sense mirroring the medieval textual communities that included literate, barely literate, and illiterate members.

Textual Communities and Anglo-Saxon Literature

The concept of a "textual community" (a term that Howe attributes to Brian Stock) is important to our interests here because it reflects that meaning was quite literally socially constructed; that is, the experiences and know-how of the entire reading body contributed to the assignment of textual meaning. Howe writes that "the medieval textual community [. . . was] a group bound together by the reading aloud of texts to listeners for the purpose of interpretation. In a culture unaccustomed to the written text, the act of reading would have seemed remarkably like solving a riddle" ("The Cultural Construction of Reading" 6). As such, by examining text produced in a culture that is in transitional flux between dominant orality and dominant literacy, we can glean a strong sense of group knowledge, experience, and mood. "As we read an Old English text in search of its audience, author, and context," writes R. M. Liuzza, "we must remember that woven into the very fabric of its textual identity is the voice of the entire community" (*Old English Literature* xv). In fact, the group-production aspect of Anglo-Saxon literature allows us to make inferences about a time period whose historical record is decidedly incomplete. He writes,

> Meaning is a collaboration between a text, its historical situations (both then and now), and its readers, and any and all of these elements may be complicated, compromised, conflicted, and conditioned by factors no longer entirely discernible. [. . .] Yet despite the fragmentary nature of the evidence, and all the gaps and discontinuities between medieval texts and our world [. . .] it is still possible to make the leap in imagination from one age to another through patience, sympathy, knowledge, and attention to detail. (xxxiii)

Patrizia Lendinara agrees, saying that "[Old English] texts are now studied as both product and mirror of a social reality, though far away in time" (128). Also, O'Brien O'Keeffe writes that "[s]urviving Old English verse texts, whatever the circumstances of their composition, are collaborative products whose scribes have not merely transmitted the texts but have actually taken part in shaping them" (*Visible Song* 193). What is more, "to recognize the time-bound nature of perception [. . .], even as it divides us from the past, allows us to claim kinship with it. In that moment of recognition we affirm the past's critique of the present" (194). In sum, then, the social aspect of Anglo-

Saxon textual communities allows us to determine their zeitgeists—via "patience, sympathy, knowledge, and attention to detail"—and it further allows us to not only connect the past to the present but to gain a deeper understanding of both because of that connection.

Hence, minus an "author" we gain a more dynamic sense of group consciousness in a medieval poem like *Beowulf.* In a moment I want to examine why imprecision in dating the poem and in placing its production geographically is not counterproductive to our overarching interests, but meanwhile we should devote some time to the accepted temporal and physical boundaries of its production, and to the status of the dating controversy. O'Brien O'Keeffe, in her foreword to Kevin Kiernan's controversial Beowulf *and the* Beowulf *Manuscript* (republished in 1996), points out that a 1980 conference at the University of Toronto devoted to the poem's dating yielded "an impressive range of opinion" (xii). Kiernan, who posits a very late composition date (during the reign of Cnute the Great from 1016-1035), writes that

> the origin of the poem has nearly always been restricted to the 8th century or earlier on the rough historical grounds that a poem eliciting sympathy for the Danes could not have been composed by Anglo-Saxons during the Viking Age of the 9th and 10th centuries. Historically, at least, there is a better argument for an 11th-century, post-Viking origin of the poem, since an 8th-century poem would still have to be transmitted by Anglo-Saxons through the Viking Age. (4)

O'Brien O'Keeffe applauds Kiernan's methodology (his rigorous examination of the *Beowulf* manuscript) and notes that his original publication in 1981 redirected much Anglo-Saxon scholarship toward the extant manuscripts, but her own analysis of Cotton Vitellius A. xv. refutes Kiernan's claims: "The evidence of the pointing [early form of punctuation] simply cannot sustain such a hypothesis. Rather, the relatively undeveloped punctuation [. . .] suggests a pointing of the text from a time in the tenth century [. . .]" (*Visible Song* 179). Bruce Mitchell and Fred C. Robinson, who also allude to the 1980 Toronto conference in their introduction to *"Beowulf": An Edition* (1998), "believe that the balance of linguistic and non-linguistic evidence gives some credence to a broad date for the composition of *Beowulf* which was urged as long ago as 1968: 680-800" (11-12). Liuzza, similarly, suggests that all theories about the dating of the poem, from the eighth to the eleventh century, may be *correct* in a sense. He writes, "*Beowulf* may thus reflect the interests of several different eras, its traditional materials coalescing into a rough form before being shaped by the hand of its final author; it may respond to diverse moments of cultural crisis and triumph in early and later Anglo-Saxon society [. . .]" (*Beowulf* 29). In general, it seems that the traditional view of the poem's composition in the time of Bede (c. 725) has lost devotees over the past twenty years, and many scholars are favoring a later date but not as late as Kiernan's placement. On the other hand, Mitchell and Robinson note that there are "despairing scholars" who "decline to conceive any date at all for the composition of the poem" (12).

The Mootness of the Dating Controversy
 The precise dating of the poem, in an effort to characterize the Anglo-Saxon zeitgeist that produced

Beowulf as a "postmodern" text, is unnecessary for two main reasons. One has to do with the nature of cultural trauma as discussed in detail earlier. We will recall that Freud said passing of a mood, like melancholia for example, can happen from generation to generation and from time period to time period via two pathways. One is oral communication whereby details of an event are transmitted through storytelling and mythmaking. Freud discusses this process in detail in *Moses and Monotheism* (1939). There are distortions and omissions over time, but the nucleus of the event and often its prevailing mood will endure. The other way that mood is passed down is by the psychic mechanism Freud called *archaic heritage*, or "retain[ing] an impression of the past in unconscious memory traces" (120). Important to my study, Freud asserts that "the archaic heritage of mankind includes not only dispositions, but also ideational contents, memory traces of the experiences of former generations" and indeed a region's "national character" (127). We further recall Kai Erikson's contemporary analyses which claim that "traumatic experiences" can "supply [a] prevailing mood and temper, dominate [. . .] imagery and [. . .] sense of self, govern the way [. . .] members relate to one another [. . . affecting] whole regions, even whole countries" (190). What is more, a geographic location can become so closely associated with trauma that the place itself actually generates a zeitgeist of anxiety, affecting anyone who moves into the region.

When we consider the virtual ubiquity of warfare and terror during the Anglo-Saxon period, especially the centuries during which *Beowulf* was likely composed, combined with our understanding of the ease with which trauma can transcend temporal and geographic boundaries, it is highly probable that the poet would have been suffering some level of traumatic stress. Obviously this assertion requires much more fleshing out, which I will get to momentarily. First, however, it must be underscored that our contemporary concept of memory—indeed our *power* of memory—is very different from the Anglo-Saxons', who were living for the most part in a primarily illiterate world. O'Brien O'Keeffe points out that "in those cultures which possess some literacy but experience a heavy oral residue, the dominant power of the mind is memory" (*Visible Song* 10). Moreover, she says that pondering the dominance of literacy in contemporary times "reminds us [. . .] of some things we have lost: among them the communal intimacy of spoken communication and the prodigious feats of those for whom mind was the only means for storing information" (22). Given O'Brien O'Keeffe's assessment, I suggest that, for the Anglo-Saxons, the transmission of traumatic events, from time to time and from place to place, was even more vivid and affective than it is in recent centuries because of the heightened proficiency of their memory faculties. What is more, Magennis says that one of the "central functions" of a poet like the *Beowulf* poet was "to keep alive a people's memory of its past and values and to interpret the present in terms of those values" (93). Consequently, even if the *Beowulf* poet did not experience violence and terror firsthand, trauma would have been transmitted to him (and by him!)—with *potency*—from earlier times and other places.

It would be simple enough (though time-consuming) to catalogue the violent acts of Anglo-Saxon England from, say, 700 to 1025, but I want to approach my analysis of this period in a more specialized manner. Instead of focusing on military engagements in general (and the subsequent ascensions of warlords and kings, and some queens)—which dominate the anonymously written *Anglo-Saxon Chronicle*, the primary historical text for the period—I will examine how the masses experienced such engagements; and, moreover, I will attempt to portray the psychic lives of the peasants who were forever caught in between the warlords and their rivals, both foreign and domestic. It is also worth our time to take a special look at the Christian monks of this period as it is a virtual certainty that the monasteries played a key role in the production, transmission, and preservation of texts like *Beowulf*.

Violence in Anglo-Saxon England

There is no question that violence and its aftermath were pervasive in Anglo-Saxon England. Referring to the ninth and tenth centuries in particular, Eric Linklater says that they "were not centuries of continuous war, but centuries so inundated by war that their periods of peace are like the scattered islands of an archipelago in an angry sea" (49). When so-called Viking raids escalated in 865, the English and their vast resources were "vulnerable because their coast-line was long and they had no defensive navy or an over-all military command that held in reserve the mass of manoeuvre to meet attack" (51). Sir Frank Stenton, meanwhile, writes that by the fall of that year "the whole fabric of English society was threatened by a great army [...] prepared to spend many consecutive years in the deliberate exploitation of all the opportunities for profit which England offered" (246). Stenton's characterization, that the *whole of English society* was under attack, is significant because it makes it clear that virtually no one was insulated from the invasion. He goes on to describe the modus operandi of the Danish army, which was "to seize a defensible position, fortify it, and ravage the surrounding country systematically until its inhabitants bought peace from them" (247). The phrase "surrounding country" is somewhat misleading as Stenton notes that "the Danish army might affect the life of districts eighty miles or more from its base" (251). In less than a decade of continuous hit-and-run raiding, "England itself was becoming emptied of the wealth which made fighting profitable" (252). This ten-year period is emblematic of the three centuries preceding William of Normandy's conquest of England in 1066. Urban T. Holmes, Jr., discussing the period 500 to 1000, calls warfare "a dreadful sorrow to these early people" and says that "[t]heirs was an age of super warriors. One gigantic man of great strength could dominate a battle or a campaign" (28).

The *Anglo-Saxon Chronicle*, the period's primary historical text, is fraught with language that speaks to the people's trauma. Terms like *terror*, *slaughter*, and *destruction* are common in the text. For example, for the year 823 the *Chronicle* notes that "Egbert, King of the West-Saxons, and Bernwulf, King of Mercia, fought a battle at Wilton, in which Egbert gained the victory, but there was great slaughter on both sides." It is further noted that the same year the East-Angles applied to Egbert for "peace and protection against the terror of the Mercians" (43). Frequently the chronicler speaks of an army subduing or overrunning the land or country, implying that the attacks and their effects were pervasive. In 878, for example, "the Danish army stole out to Chippenham, rode over the land of the West-Saxons; where they settled, and drove many of the people over sea; and of the rest the greatest part they rode down, and subdued to their will" (49). It is further noted, matter-of-factly, that among the "booty" that the various branches of the Danish army collected were women and children. We are told that in 894 when King Alfred's troops "routed the enemy, [and] broke down the work [fortification]," they took all the "money, women, and children and brought them to London" (52). Another way that warfare affected the peasant class was by depriving them of food. Alfred's army lay siege to the Danes at Chester, also in 894, and in "some two days took all the cattle that was thereabout, slew the men whom they could overtake without the work [outside the fortification], and all the corn they either burned or consumed with their horses every evening" (53). In 896, Alfred's army had to camp near London "whilst [the farmers] reaped their corn, that the Danes might not deprive them of the crop" (54). For the following year, the chronicler notes,

> The enemy had not, thank God, entirely destroyed the English nation; but they were much more weakened in these same years by the disease of cattle, and most of all of men; so that many of the mightiest of the king's thanes, that were in the land, died with the three years. (54)

Alfred, who died in 899, did much to develop England's national defenses, but the terror associated with warfare continued throughout the tenth century virtually unabated. The *Chronicle* says that in 918, for example, "a great naval armament [came] over hither south from the Lidwiccians [(essentially pirates who lived in their ships) . . . and] plundered in North-Wales everywhere by sea, where it then suited them." King Edward dispatched a guard to deal with the invaders, and there were numerous engagements, in which "[t]here was great slaughter each time" (58).

In all the plundering and military engagement, it is easy to lose sight of the peasant class, but it is important to keep our focus there. Stenton says that by the end of the ninth century, throughout much of England, "the free peasant formed the basis of society." Among his duties was "personal service in the fyrd, or national militia" (278). Writes Stenton, "The part played by the peasant militia of the shires is never brought out so clearly, but it was certainly not insignificant" (264). Alfred was able to establish a system for national defense that made greater military use of the peasant class than his predecessor kings had been able to manage:

> By the early part of the tenth century no village in Sussex, Surrey, and Wessex east of the Tamar was distant more than twenty miles from a fortress which formed a unit in a planned scheme for national defence. [. . .] Each fortress was kept in repair, and garrisoned when necessary, by the men of the surrounding country. (264-65)

Linklater, meanwhile, credits "a peasantry instructed in war" as one of the keys to English survival during the successive waves of Viking invasions, along with "a nobility dedicated to war" (51). The peasants obviously had a vested interest in serving the king or warlord who pressed them for military service, as they tried to avoid being murdered, starved, kidnapped and ransomed, or enslaved—they themselves or their families. In 975 King Edgar died and his son Edward, still a youth, ascended to the throne, and during the ensuing instability powerful lords snapped up as much land and wealth as they could from the monasteries and from anyone too weak to put up a defense. Stenton writes that "[l]ittle can be gathered about the character of Edward's reign beyond a vague impression of disorder" (372)—a disorder that led to Edward's being murdered in 978 "under circumstances of abominable treachery which shocked men who were ready to tolerate any crime of frank violence" (373). This instability was no doubt felt at every strata of English society.

Monastic Life in Anglo-Saxon England

The reference to the dissolution of the minsters is a good segue for spending some time looking at Anglo-Saxon monastic life and how it was affected by the successive waves of violence. Most of what we know, or can infer, of the Anglo-Saxon period comes from their written texts, and, as Michelle P. Brown tells us, "monks and nuns were undoubtedly the key generators of books." She goes on,

> With writing skills being acquired as part of a claustral education, and with humility in the undertaking of manual labour being a feature of the monastic regime (in whichever form), it would be surprising if some of the leading clerical authors of the Anglo-Saxon age did not on occasion take up the quill themselves. (102)

While some laypeople acquired reading and writing skills, "[t]he physical task of producing works in the vernacular [...]," says Brown, "probably remained in clerical circles" (114). Authorship of works like *Beowulf* is of course unknowable, but "[w]hoever their original owners or communities of readership, [the extant manuscripts] are likely to have been penned by clerics trained in the scriptorium" (115). Moreover, the scribal efforts "to stock the shelves of the monastic library" resulted in our at least having the precious few manuscripts that we do today. We know further that it was via the Church that Alfred combated ignorance and illiteracy. Stenton writes that Alfred's

> unique importance in the history of English letters comes from his conviction that a life without knowledge or reflection was unworthy of respect, and his determination to bring the thought of the past within the range of his subjects' understanding. The translations of ancient books by which he tried to reach this end form the beginning of English prose literature. (269-70)

Alfred worked alongside clerical translators to render books from Latin into the common vernacular, "and then all the free-born youth of England who could be supported at the task should be sent to school until they could at least read English writing" (270).

Yet the literary accomplishments of the monasteries were achieved in spite of the warfare that continually disrupted their work and diminished their numbers. Bede, in his invaluable *Ecclesiastical History of the English People* (written in Latin and completed in 731), recounts one of the most heinous acts directed at the Church when he describes a battle of 603 between a British warlord (Stenton identifies him as Solomon, son of Cynan [78]) and King Ethelfrid (or Æthelfrith). According to Bede, more than a thousand monks from a nearby monastery had come to pray for the Britons before the battle. Ethelfrid, learning of their purpose, directed his army against them first of all, though the monks "were assembled apart in a safer place." Bede claims that 1,200 monks were slaughtered while only fifty managed to escape with their lives (107; 2.3). Bede's inclusion of the event is noteworthy, too, because in general his *History* does not dwell on violence. D. H. Farmer says that the *History* "gives the impression of far greater tranquility" than was true because "it seems certain that Anglo-Saxon society was more violent than Bede makes out" (23). In Bede's *Life of Cuthbert* (716), he describes the travels of the seventh-century monk (later bishop and saint) and recounts how Cuthbert encountered a small band of nuns who "had fled from their own monastery for fear of the barbarian army shortly before" his arrival (84; ch. 30). Another chronicler of the Church, Eddius Stephanus (or simply Stephan) wrote the *Life of Wilfrid* (720), and he too tells of violence directed toward the clergy and Christians in general in his annals about this seventh-century monk turned bishop turned saint. In a lengthy passage, Stephan describes how Bishop Wilfrid and a small group of companions were returning from Gaul when a violent storm landed them on the coast of the South Saxons, who "intend[ed] to seize the vessel, loot it, carry off captives, and slay without more ado all who resisted." Wilfrid tries to win over "the great horde of pagans" with "soothing words" and "a large sum of money," but they were "as fierce and stubborn as Pharaoh" (121; ch. 13). Wilfrid and his clergymen prayed fervently to God, who aided the grossly outnumbered Christians in defeating the "untamed pagan host" while experiencing only five casualties themselves.

One may argue that these seventh-century events recorded by early eighth-century historians are, most likely, before the time of the *Beowulf* poet, but it is crucial to keep in mind both the residual effects of trauma (transcending generations and geographies) and the acute memories of Anglo-Saxons in general. Interestingly, both Bede and Stephan make special mention of memory. In his *History*,

Bede builds the case that a mid-fifth-century "famine [. . .] left a lasting memory of its horrors to posterity [that] distressed the Britons more and more," and as a result they were less inclined to stand up to invaders for fear of the past repeating itself (61; 1.14). Stephan, meanwhile, in his praise of Wilfrid, writes, "He laid special emphasis on prayer, fasting, and vigils, and was forever searching the scriptures and studying the canons of the Church. He had a wonderful memory for texts" (119; ch. 12). But violence against the Church continued throughout the Anglo-Saxon period, as the *Chronicle* frequently attests. For example, in 916 "the innocent Abbot Egbert [was] slain [. . .] with his companions" (57); and among the accomplishments of Abbot Athelwold recounted in 963 were his efforts to reestablish "all the minsters that heathen men had before destroyed" (69). Stenton says of the seventh century that England "was distracted by war which destroyed the peace of scholars" (177), but the characterization seems a fair one for the entire period. The main point here is that the stratum of Anglo-Saxon society that was almost certainly responsible for the production, transmission, and preservation of *Beowulf* (and virtually all literature) was often the target of violence and therefore a likely victim of trauma.

Further Documentary Evidence

Besides the Anglo-Saxon histories compiled during the period, other documentary evidence speaks to both the harshness of life and its effects on cultural mood. Alfred, perhaps the most learned of Anglo-Saxon kings, codified his country's laws, probably around 895, and included with little modification language he borrowed from Ine of Wessex, Offa of Mercia, and Æthelberht of Kent. In addition, however, writes Stenton, "[t]here are important features in his laws which are not derived from any known source and may well be original. They include provisions protecting the weaker members of society against oppression, limiting the ancient custom of the blood-feud, and emphasizing the duty of a man to his lord" (276). Each of Alfred's apparently original contributions reflects the violence of the age and, at least two of the three, could be viewed as a state-sponsored initiative to reduce the trauma associated with people's daily lives. O'Brien O'Keeffe, meanwhile, has suggested that Anglo-Saxons added a darker edge to the Latin *enigma* tradition, which consisted of a series of riddles. "The images of violence [. . .] are to the best of my knowledge an English contribution [. . .]," she writes, "and the metaphors of sad transformation, common to these *enigmata*, appear as well in the Old English riddle tradition on writing" (*Visible Song* 54). She notes in particular that "mouthless speakers, dead lifegivers, dumb knowledge-bearers, [and] clipped pinions [. . . are] all metaphors of loss." Stenton, in describing a series of early Anglo-Saxon poems that focus on the lives of common folk, says that "[t]he bulk of Old English poetry obviously reflects the conditions of the age in which it arose." Moreover, they are "the first of their kind in Germanic literature [. . .] which represent the mood of an author" (198). Using Stenton's language (though not verbatim), among the poems' subjects are *a ruined city*, *a disillusioned sailor*, *the miseries of an exile*, *estranged couples who are each in misery*, and *a woman who is distressed because of her tyrannous husband* (198-99). Stenton is just one of many scholars who have noted the overall bleak and somber tone of Anglo-Saxon literature as a whole. Liuzza, in confirmation of Peter Orton's analysis of

104

The Seafarer, writes that "[t]he elegiac mood is found at almost every turn in Old English literature, from *Beowulf* to the homilies to the short dramatic monologues now called 'elegies' found in the Exeter Book" (*Old English Literature* xxix). Of *Beowulf* in particular, Liuzza claims that "most serious readers of the poem have come to recognize that *Beowulf* is a complex product of Anglo-Saxon cultural tensions, itself a work of long gestation and mixed heritage born of melancholy and nostalgia" (*Beowulf* 9). Striking a similar chord, Mitchell and Robinson say that "it is remarkable that the dominant tone most often sensed by readers [of *Beowulf*] is one of melancholy" (29).

Living Conditions in Anglo-Saxon England

This consistent melancholic tone is even more understandable when one looks at the lives of Anglo-Saxons as reflected in their primary medical texts, namely their native-born *Leechbooks* and the *Herbarium*, a translation of a fifth-century Latin collection. The *Leechbooks*, composed in Old English probably about the year 900, comprise a three-part manuscript, which is a copy of a lost exemplar. The first two parts are known collectively as Bald's *Leechbook* (Bald being the original owner), and the third part is known simply as *Leechbook III*. The fifth-century (or even earlier) *Herbarium* was translated into Old English about the year 1000. Its first modern-English translator/editor, Oswald Cockayne, suggested in the nineteenth century that Anglo-Saxon interest in the *Herbarium* was essentially as a curiosity of antiquity as the collection was of no practical use (due mainly to the fact that many of the plants referenced in the guide did not grow in England). Contemporary scholars, however, refute Cockayne's conclusions. As Anne Van

105

Arsdall points out in *Medieval Herbal Remedies* (2002), the number of surviving copies of the *Herbarium* indicate its value to Anglo-Saxons; and, moreover, she cites several studies that argue the Anglo-Saxons would have known and been able to grow or acquire the plants referenced in the guide. Van Arsdall writes, "The philosophy behind the present [her] translation is that this was a text used to transmit information on the healing properties of plants and how to administer them. The *Old English Herbarium* is one of several key texts in understanding late classical and medieval medicine in Western Europe [. . .]" (110). Her findings are important to our interests here because it must be clear that any conclusions reached based on an analysis of the *Herbarium* are in fact about the Anglo-Saxons and not about an earlier, Continental culture.

M. L. Cameron begins his careful study, *Anglo-Saxon Medicine* (1993), by looking at the typical living conditions of people during the period. He writes,

> The contents of grave sites reveal a fairly short life expectancy, a high infant mortality, women dying young, particularly in child-birth, and a fairly high incidence of bone and joint diseases[. . . .] The Anglo-Saxon population cannot have been particularly healthy. [. . . M]ost persons lived in small, damp, dark hovels, probably one room, heated by a fire on a central hearth, with an opening in the roof through which smoke was supposed to escape. (5)

Cameron goes on to describe inadequate clothing, arduous working conditions, and poor available diet (lacking especially vitamins A and C, and iron). All of which contributed to compromised immune systems, difficulty in healing after injury, and even impeded problem-solving skills (18); and "[f]or most of these troubles not much could be done" (11). He writes, "The medieval physician was not indifferent to his patients' welfare; he simply had very little background on how living bodies behave and so his treatments were all too often of little or no use for the ailments he treated" (16). Holmes, Jr., citing the work of Russell, who analyzed data from a somewhat later period, about 1200, says that life expectancy at birth was 35.28 years, and if someone could survive to age five, life expectancy increased to 39.87 (24). In earlier centuries, longevity may have been about the same, if not somewhat less.

My interests in Anglo-Saxon medical practices are twofold. First, I want to demonstrate the prevalence of injuries that were likely caused by physical violence, especially the sort of violence one experienced in a medieval combat situation. Second (and this presents a greater challenge), I want to show that a number of practices may have been a response to traumatic stress, if not posttraumatic stress disorder itself. As we know, PTSD was not officially recognized as a clinical illness until the 1980s, but the human psyche was no different in 1980 than it was in 980 (or 980 BCE for that matter)—so Anglo-Saxons must have suffered from traumatic stress, just as modern trauma victims do. Recently, scholars in a variety of fields have been at work identifying evidence of posttraumatic stress in non-Western cultures. For example, Lynn A. Struve, in her examination of the *Yusheng lu*, a seventeenth-century memoir from China, writes that "it need not be assumed that PTSD is an affliction only of 'the modern mind.' [. . . In the memoir of Zhang Maozi] we find a virtual catalog of ways in which the violence of warfare and political upheaval are known to disintegrate what is integral to the life-spirit of human beings anywhere" (15). Meanwhile, social anthropologist Michael G. Kenny believes that "traumatic memory" (a term coined by Pierre Janet, a contemporary of Freud) has been identified as other phenomena in various cultures throughout history. One such culture would have been the Azande (or Zande) people living in what is now the Sudan Republic and the Zande's belief in witchcraft. In short, studies conducted in the mid-twentieth century showed that members of the Zande who demonstrated textbook symptoms of traumatic stress were believed to be the victims of witchcraft—and the Zande procedure for rooting out the malignant spell was very much akin to identifying and dislodging a traumatic memory. Moreover, just as PTSD sufferers are, by and large, not held accountable for their behaviors that are due to the condition, bewitched Zande were not accountable either. "Both Zande witchcraft and western traumatic memory therapy deploy a theory of causation with a framework of moral judgements," writes Kenny. "It is the perpetrator who is guilty" (Antze and Lambek 154). Kenny has also studied the phenomenon of *susto*, widely known in cultures throughout Central and South America; *susto* "in its classical form is precipitated by fright leading to soul-loss and generalized debility" (155). Kenny believes that people who develop *susto* are suffering from what Westerners would identify as PTSD. The main point here is that other scholars have been able to extrapolate a diagnosis of posttraumatic stress based on the symptomotology of peoples living in non-Western cultures and/or other centuries—and in some instances scholars have done so with no direct contact but merely documentary evidence.

Anglo-Saxon Medicine and Medical Procedures

To a contemporary reader, the ailments that must have been common for medieval people make the age seem like a never-ending trip through a house of horrors. Eye and lung problems abounded, probably due in large part to their living in smoky, unsanitary hovels with poor air circulation. All manner of intestinal ailments were frequent, too, due probably to parasites that thrived virtually unchecked. As Cameron puts it, "[m]edieval people lived in a medically dangerous and helpless world" (40). As far as injuries were concerned, there were obviously any number of ways that they could have occurred, and the Anglo-Saxon medical texts do not dispense treatment information with that sort of exactness. That is, there are numerous references to wounds but not specifically for a wound caused by a sword or battleaxe. The *Herbarium* makes several references to wounds, often differentiating between fresh and old ones. More interesting, however, are the several remedies offered for wounds caused by iron or wood. In fact, agrimony is to be used "[f]or a blow from an iron or wooden stake" (165). *For a blow* obviously suggests that the wound was gotten via some violent act. Nettle is also good for wounds and "[i]f any part of the body has been struck" (226). Comfrey is recommended "[i]f someone has an internal rupture" (175). Globe thistle could be used for "bad bruises" and "coughing up blood" (216). Gladiolus was good "[f]or a fractured skull" and "anything on the body [that] is injured" (171). Of special interest given our focus is the yarrow plant, also known as "achillea," for "fresh wounds" and to "stop the bleeding"; achillea is named for Lord Achilles, the greatest warrior in ancient literature, who "used it often to treat wounds" (225).

The frequency of these sorts of references implies that Anglo-Saxons were regularly in need of such remedies.

Cameron, meanwhile, takes special notice of a procedure in response to disembowelment mentioned in *Leechbook III*. He writes,

> Very interesting is a treatment (incomplete) for handling a wound through which the bowels came out; the physician was to replace the bowel and then to sew up the wound with a silk suture. Silk, which would dissolve as healing took place, would not need to be removed when the wound had healed. This also shows us that silk, whether from Asia Minor or from China, was an accepted surgical necessity. (39)

Cameron also notes a group of salves that could be used for cracked skulls as well as puncture wounds and dislocated limbs: "[O]ne can envisage a fight in which a man was stabbed in the belly, a blow which broke the skull, a scrimmage in which a shoulder was wrenched out of joint […] One is saddened by the futility of the remedies" (40). Furthermore, R. A. Buck points out that the first hospital appeared in England about 1070, "although places to care for particular groups of sick people certainly existed" (41). Royalty and members of the clergy would have had infirmaries of sorts on the grounds of their estates or in monasteries, "but other people in society had to manage as best they could with healing themselves or their families" (41). There were specially trained physicians, or leeches, but in all the extant writings of the Anglo-Saxon period, "only around seven" are named. She writes, "Monks, priests, and professional healers worked alongside surgeons, lay healers, midwives, and folk healers, many of whom were ordinary men and women with no formal medical training" (41).

Cameron notes that while some of the medical recipes were surprisingly effective—people had stumbled upon making antibacterial balms in ancient times even—the vast majority of medical advice, if it helped at all, did so due to its psychological impact. He writes, "Perhaps [the leech's] most useful role was to offer support to his patients in the hope that recovery was possible[. . . .] When all else failed, the Anglo-Saxon physician could resort to charms, in themselves of no effect, but probably of great psychological benefit to the patient" (23, 24).

Anglo-Saxon Posttraumatic Stress

The reference to psychological impact brings us to an important issue, but one that is difficult to verify with any degree of certainty—and that is the occurrence of traumatic stress in Anglo-Saxon England. Common sense tells us it must have been manifested in a culture that was rife with violence and extreme hardship, but some sort of evidence would be useful. It is fair to say that only a small percentage of today's population, fortunately, ever experiences the sights, smells, and sounds of medieval-type carnage. Describing mid-twelfth-century warfare based on contemporary accounts, Holmes, Jr., writes, "The odor of decayed flesh was most unpleasant, but it could be tolerated when necessary. After a conflict, dead bodies could be left *in situ* for an indefinite time [. . .] where they were chewed by dogs and by other carrion-eating beasts and birds" (44-45). Again, this is a somewhat later time than our focus, but the situation could not have been any better between 500 and 1000. We can surmise that any number of psychiatric disorders would have been experienced by the Anglo-Saxons given the common circumstances of their lives. As defined

111

by the American Psychiatric Association in its 2000 *Diagnostic and Statistical Manual of Mental Disorders, Fourth Edition, Text Revision (DSM-IV-TR)*,[1] posttraumatic stress disorder occurs when both of the following are present:

1. the person experienced, witnessed, or was confronted with an event or events that involved actual or threatened death or serious injury, or a threat to the physical integrity of self or others

2. the person's response involved intense fear, helplessness, or horror. (218-19)

The traumatic event is reexperienced via "recurrent and intrusive distressing recollections of the event, including images, thoughts, or perceptions"; "recurrent distressing dreams"; and "acting or feeling as if the traumatic event were recurring (includes a sense of reliving the experience, illusions, hallucinations, and dissociative flashback episodes" (219). Specific symptoms of PTSD include "difficulty falling asleep or staying asleep"; "irritability or outbursts of anger"; "difficulty concentrating"; "hypervigilance"; and "exaggerated startle response" (220).

It must be noted that an increasing number of psychiatric professionals feel that the APA's diagnostic description of PTSD is inadequate. Eian Newman, David S. Riggs, and Susan Roth write that "some have argued that [PTSD as defined] does not sufficiently portray the distinctive changes in affective, behavioral, and interpersonal regulation observed among those exposed to on-going repetitive traumatic stressors" (201). That is, there are a host of other serious disorders and extreme behaviors that appear directly linked to trauma that are not accounted for in the APA's definition of PTSD or even ASD (acute stress

112

disorder). The psychiatric community has been inconsistent in its attempts to label and define this variation of PTSD, but the term *complex posttraumatic stress disorder (C-PTSD)* has been gaining acceptance. According to Newman, Riggs, and Roth, C-PTSD "reflects a broader and more severe form of pathological traumatic adaptation that is likely to occur subsequent to early and repetitive trauma" (201).

Looking for indicators of traumatic stress in Anglo-Saxon culture, the most straight-forward evidence of psychiatric disorders among the Anglo-Saxons are references to insanity or lunacy. The *Herbarium* recommends sage-leaved germander, wood sage, halwort, cat-thyme, or polygermander for insanity, which it characterizes as an "evil condition" (175). On the other hand, for lunacy—which seems to vary from insanity only in that it was believed to be caused by the cycles of the moon—buttercup is prescribed, but it is to be bound "around a person's neck with a piece of red thread when the moon is on the wane in the month of April and in early October" (152). From our perspective, the remedy for lunacy relies as much on magic as on *science* (that is, on the supernatural as much as the natural), and magic or the supernatural is a subject I want to deal with in particular in a moment. In terms of actual behaviors, the fact that insanity and lunacy are virtually the same is demonstrated in the cure for "lunacy" that involves placing peony "over an insane person when he is lying down" (178). Cameron discusses suggestions in the *Leechbooks* specifically "[a]gainst a woman's mad behaviour" (40). Meanwhile, looking at other maladies that could be symptoms of trauma, digestive and excretory complaints are alluded to with great frequency in the *Herbarium*. More interesting, however, is the plant wood betony, which is the

113

first remedy listed in the *Herbarium* and is said to be "good both for one's soul and one's body [. . . as] it protects a person from dreadful nightmares and from terrifying visions and dreams" (138-39). In the APA's list of PTSD symptoms, at the very top are intrusive, upsetting memories; flashbacks; and nightmares. The APA also lists difficulty in falling or staying asleep as a symptom, and the *Herbarium* recommends white poppy for "sleeplessness" (173-74). The white poppy's juice was to be used topically, but Cameron notes, from *Leechbook III*, the use of henbane to be ingested orally, which, scientifically speaking, has a "hypnotic" effect and "induc[es] a sleep very similar to a natural one" (126).

The fact should be underscored that today, by and large, we accept—though still do not fully understand—the interrelatedness of consciousness, unconsciousness, dreaming, and physical and psychiatric health; and our comprehension of it all may be only slightly less primitive than the Anglo-Saxons', who apparently correlated peaceful sleep with soundness of both body and soul, with soul perhaps being a sort of metaphor for mental health. Among other conditions listed in the *Herbarium* that could be seen as indicators of traumatic stress are "trembling" (153), "sickl[iness]" (184), "witlessness" (unclear thinking or inability to concentrate) (192), "nerve pain" (204), and "cramps and tremors" (223). In her examination of Bald's *Leechbook*, Buck mentions "uneasiness without occasion" and "immoderately long wakings, and witless words" (46). Anglo-Saxons might also become unable to talk and suffer from "half-dead disease" (47). Moreover, Cameron says that there are thirty-six references to rue in the *Leechbooks*: "The leaves are very bitter but if chewed are said to leave a refreshing taste in the mouth and to relieve various nervous

114

conditions" (125). Cameron further points out that rue has chemical properties which make it a frequent ingredient in herb-based medicines today.

Cameron devotes much of his study to charms and potions that were used to combat any number of supernaturally caused afflictions, including "elfshot" and "witchshot," names for pains and injuries that came on without any observable cause. He writes, "There is good evidence that many ailments which appear suddenly were once thought to be caused by elves or witches shooting arrows at the sufferer" (142). I conjecture that these inexplicable aches and pains and otherwise debilitating conditions could have been, some of the time at least, symptoms of trauma, which, we know today, may not present themselves until days, weeks, months, or even years after the causal event. The afflictions are caused by the damaged psyche, which would have seemed a malignant and invisible force to the Anglo-Saxons, who then anthropomorphized their wounded psyches into troublemaking elves, witches, and other supernatural entities. (We recall Kenny's assertion, earlier in the chapter, that the Zande people of the Sudan believed traumatic memories were in fact spells cast by a witch.) By the same token, the *Herbarium* alludes several times to, simply, "evil" as a sort of disease. The abstract concept of *evil*, too, may have been a figuration of a traumatized psyche. That is to say, the Anglo-Saxon sensed something was amiss in his or her world, but that something could not be seen or smelled or touched so it was attributed to a supernatural malevolence. Nowadays we might refer to helplessness, hopelessness, depression, or despair as the same sort of malevolent force in our lives that the Anglo-Saxons assigned to "evil." Moreover, the

115

Herbarium offers assistance with "demonic possession" (152), "evil [. . .] com[ing] near you" (197), and "evil footprints coming toward" you (228). In each case, the malady suggests our contemporary notion that a traumatic event possesses or haunts its victim.

PTSD's Effects on Anglo-Saxon Culture

Now I want to consider complex PTSD and how it may have affected Anglo-Saxon culture. C-PTSD, sometimes talked about as disorders of extreme stress (DES) in psychiatric literature, tends to be suffered by those "being taken hostage, experiencing torture, or experiencing physical or sexual abuse during childhood" (Newman, Riggs, and Roth 201). We recall that the *Anglo-Saxon Chronicle* frequently refers to acts of hostage-taking and torture (as we would define it), including those directed at women and children. In a study conducted by Newman, Riggs, and Ross (published in 1997), they screened test subjects for C-PTSD by looking for exposure to "high-magnitude" traumatic episodes in their lives: "combat/military experience, physical abuse or assault, sexual abuse or assault, homicide, disaster, accident, [. . .] other life threatening life events." They also screened for "exposure to stressful life experiences" that included "financial stress, interpersonal stress, death or illness of loved one, severe illness and whether close friends or family were at risk or in danger due to [war]" (202). If we equate "financial stress" to stress associated with trying to provide basic necessities (food, shelter, clothing) for oneself and one's family, then it is reasonable to say that the typical Anglo-Saxon could have answered *yes* to virtually all of the factors that are indicators of C-PTSD. For our interests, it is significant that C-PTSD has been causally linked to violent behavior, especially of a sexual nature, including homicide and serial homicide. Bruce A. Arrigo and Catherine E. Purcell write,

> Research indicates that many individuals who engage in such behaviors experience traumatic events in their early adolescence, usually in the form of sexual or physical abuse. [. . .] For example, studies conducted on [child molesters, rapists, and lust murderers] report that offenders used paraphilia and fantasy in their conduct precipitated by childhood trauma, triggering their sadistic and/or deviant behavior or serial killing. As others have explained, the effects of such adolescent traumatization can be devastating, even producing [. . .] revenge fantasies. (9-10)

Paraphilic behaviors include *erotophonophilia* ("lust murder"), *flagellationism* ("an intense desire to beat, whip, or club someone"), and *picquerism* ("the intense desire to stab, wound, or cut the flesh of another person") (10). It seems that C-PTSD may have been a pervasive and self-perpetuating phenomenon in Anglo-Saxon England. That is, the extreme violence that was commonplace during the period, especially as it was inflicted on the young, may have generated even more extreme violence and revenge in a continuous cycle throughout the so-called Dark Ages. Indeed, advances in neuropsychology are shedding new light on the period. For example, Steven M. Southwick and his colleagues report that "[a]lterations in [the brain's level of] serotonin have been implicated in PTSD as well as in disorders of mood, impulsivity, and aggression" (Vasterling and Brewin 40). They further cite a 2000 study that suggests a pathophysiological link between PTSD and "aggressive psychiatric patients, impulsive violent men, and suicide victims who have killed themselves through violent means" (41). The hopelessness of the period may best be reflected in Arrigo and Purcell's assessment that, even with today's clinical knowledge, "the prognosis for treatment [of C-PTSD] is not good" (26).

To summarize my key points, then, if cultural trauma results in storytellers developing a "postmodern" style, then such literature must have appeared at various points in history when there was a zeitgeist of trauma—and one such historical site might well have been Anglo-Saxon England, where *Beowulf* was produced sometime between 725 and 1025. The facts that we cannot definitively date *Beowulf* or identify its author are not impediments to my study. In fact, given medieval reading practices (that texts were read and interpreted by "textual communities") we can more readily get a sense of the whole culture and not just the attitudes of a single author. What is more, the nature of trauma to transcend time and place makes knowing the precise date of composition unnecessary. The three centuries of probable production, transmission, and preservation of *Beowulf* were rife with violence and hardship, so much so that Anglo-Saxon culture must have been a "trauma culture." The monasteries, which were responsible for producing works like *Beowulf*, were often targets of extreme violence. Living conditions in Anglo-Saxon England were difficult even in the best of times, and an analysis of their chief medical books suggests that the people were often victims of violent injury. Furthermore, the medical texts may also support the contention that Anglo-Saxons suffered from traumatic stress and related psychiatric disorders. In fact, they may have attributed mysterious ailments, that we know to be related to PTSD, to a general evil in their world. Moreover, complex traumatic disturbances, affecting people at the neurochemical level, would have continuously fueled the cycle of violence throughout the age.

1. For a discussion of the revisions in the APA's *Diagnostic and Statistical Manual of Mental Disorders* (*DSM*-5) regarding trauma and PTSD, as compared to *DSM-IV*, see the Introduction.

Chapter 5

Beowulf as "Postmodern" Trauma Text

With the Anglo-Saxon epic *Beowulf* I want to demonstrate that the poem reflects a "postmodern" narrative style that has become associated with the traumatized voice. I first encountered *Beowulf* as a college freshman in 1981 taking a survey course in British literature. I read an excerpt in the course anthology that mainly consisted of the three monster fights. It must have included Unferth's challenge, too, as I recall having a class discussion about Beowulf's swimming contest with Brecca. I found it intriguing, though I did not get a lot out of the initial encounter. My academic life led me away from the poem until a little more than a decade ago when I had an opportunity to teach *Beowulf*. I read it for the first time in its entirety and became captivated by the epic, though often befuddled by Beowulf's elusive characterization and by the narrative's loops and switchbacks and flash-forwards. A year or two later, starting to get serious about a Ph.D. in English, I read Thomas Pynchon's *Gravity's Rainbow*, a novel that many consider quintessentially postmodern; and while confronting Tyrone Slothrop's elusive characterization and the narrative's loops and switchbacks and flash-forwards, I kept having *Beowulf déjà vu*. In my ignorance, I thought I was the only one seeing the Old English poem as postmodern. I soon discovered otherwise, that a growing number of scholars had begun to look at *Beowulf* as a postmodern text. What was more, numerous older texts (including works by Shakespeare, Laurence Sterne, and Herman Melville, to name but a few) were being studied as "postmodern." But what I did not

121

discover was any scholar saying *why*. That is, no one in any serious sort of way had tried to account for this phenomenon, for "postmodern" texts being produced centuries before "postmodernism." Thus my dissertation topic had sprouted an egg-tooth. Over the next few years, taking courses and reading and researching on my own when opportunities presented themselves, I came up with various hypotheses (I was enamored of chaos theory for a time) and each kind of worked but mostly did not. Then I came across the work of Cathy Caruth, Laura Di Prete, Anne Whitehead, and Lynn Worsham, and what these scholars were doing with trauma theory as it applied to literary production. Suddenly it began to make sense: If postmodern literature was born of twentieth-century trauma culture, then "postmodern" texts in other centuries may have been spawned from the same sort of traumatic zeitgeist.

Postmodern Characteristics of Beowulf

Hence in what ways, specifically, is *Beowulf* "postmodern"? Or said differently, in what ways does the poem's narrative style correspond with aspects of the traumatized voice? Let us review those aspects. Based largely on the work on Anne Whitehead, I have identified four features of postmodernism that reflect the traumatized voice: intertextuality, repetition, dispersed or fragmented voice, and a search for magical language. Intertextuality, which mirrors the traumatic event's imposing itself on and distorting the victim's sense of here-and-now reality, could take the form of various sorts of texts being synthesized together (poetry, fictional prose, mythology, folk-tales, history, testimony, ethnographic writing, scientific reporting, not to mention other sorts of "texts" like art, music . . . even human bodies), or it could be seen as historical figures and events being transplanted to different narrative frames— what Umberto Eco called a shifting *transworld identity*. Repetition, which reflects the traumatic event's coming back to the victim unbidden in flashbacks and dreams/nightmares and perhaps linguistically as "slips of the tongue," may be specific words or phrases repeated in the narrative, or the echoes of images/symbols, or that characters find themselves in emplotted loops. A dispersed or fragmented narrative voice, related to a trauma victim's inability to recount the traumatic event(s) in a whole or logical way, could manifest itself in multiple narrative voices or genres, the revelation of story in scattered bits and pieces, or narrative that is never completed. Finally, a search for magical language, having to do with a trauma victim's efforts to take control of the traumatic memory and to tell it as coherent narrative memory, may reveal itself in "postmodern" narration as a preoccupation with obscure or highly specialized language/vocabulary, or as particularly complex syntactical constructions. Each of these four aspects places the reader/audience in a similar role to the psychoanalyst as someone who is having to work at reconstructing and assimilating the narrative in order to make meaning.

As stated earlier, I am not alone in seeing *Beowulf* as a work that fits (and fits easily) into our modern technological world. Michael Swanton, for example, in the introduction to his prose translation of the poem, makes the point that the age of the Anglo-Saxons is not as far removed from ours as one might imagine:

> Early medieval society felt itself closely surrounded
> by the whole paraphernalia of common pagan fear:
> hobgoblins, trolls, elves, things that go bump in the

night, which dwelt in the wastelands, swamps and deep forests, approaching human awareness only at night, in darkness—and against which the warmth of the hall and its society offered the only security. This belief is not so naïve as it might at first seem to the average twentieth-century man—who also believes in a whole range of things he has not personally seen, from bacteria to men on the moon, and in literary terms a host of science-fiction wonders. (20)

Even more closely akin to my interests, James W. Earl talks about relating to *Beowulf* due to a near-death experience he had as a boy and then a few years later experiencing the Cuban Missile Crisis: "At school the next day [after President Kennedy's explanation of the situation on television], we all shook hands and said good-bye, not knowing if we would see each other again" (691). Speaking of Kennedy, Earl says that twenty years later he discovered JFK had read *Beowulf* while in the Senate chamber, in session. It made perfect sense to Earl, who told the person that had seen Kennedy reading the poem, "'This is the man who wrote *Profiles in Courage*, the hero of PT 109. He was studying to be a hero and a leader. *Beowulf*'s a classic on the subject'" (691-92). That is, Senator Kennedy found something in the eighth-to-eleventh-century poem that spoke to his mid-twentieth-century life—to his ambitions even. Earl claims that he himself grew up "modern, not postmodern [. . . but while] there are things in *Beowulf* that appeal strongly to this modern subjectivity of mine—its existentialism, for example—there is also much in the poem's premodernism that appeals strongly to our collective postmodernism" (692). Besides Earl's categorizing *Beowulf* as postmodern, I would also call attention to his referring to a *collective* postmodernism, that is, a worldview that is held by the culture as a whole.

The Beowulf *Poet's Intertextuality*

The *Beowulf* poet made extensive use of what we would call intertextuality. Via embedded stories in the main narrative (what used to be commonly referred to as *digressions* but I will call *substories*), the poet brings a number of texts to bear on the exploits of Beowulf in Denmark and Geatland. Some of these texts are of a folk-mythological nature. For example, at the banquet celebrating Beowulf's victory over Grendel, Hrothgar's *scop* sings of Sigemund the dragonslayer (lines 874-97). Sigemund's story was "well-known in Anglo-Saxon England," according to Swanton (193), and the allusion serves several intertextual functions, including the amplification of Beowulf's warrior status by his comparison to a legendary dragonslayer, the foreshadowing of his own dragon encounter, and the maintenance of an overarching mood of gloom (because the audience would have known that Sigemund, though successful against the dragon, was later killed due to treachery). Instead of folk-mythology, history may have provided the longest and best-known intertext in the poem: "The Fight at Finnsburh" (lines 1068-1159), which recounts a bloody run-in between the Danes and Frisians in spite of the peaceweaving marriage between the Danish princess Hildeburh and King Finn of Frisia. Again, the substory's inclusion is multifaceted within the broader framework of *Beowulf*. For one, the Finnsburh episode underscores one of the poem's central themes, that being the futility of peace-making in a culture based on the principle of the bloodfeud, an eye-for-an-eye system of order-keeping that often demanded bloody violence be repaid with equally bloody violence. The Finnsburh story also prefigures the inevitable bloodshed when war breaks out between the Danes and Heathobards in spite of the peaceweaving marriage between Hrothgar's daughter Freawaru and Prince Ingeld—predicted by Beowulf himself (2024-69). "The Fight at Finnsburh" may be a historical or quasi-historical text as one of the Danish leaders is identified as Hengest, who is referenced in the *Anglo-Saxon Chronicle* (c. 499) as being instrumental in founding a kingdom in Kent (Swanton 197). The intertextual nature of these two substories is especially clear—both visually and aurally—in Seamus Heaney's translation of *Beowulf* (2000). He writes in the introduction, "For a moment it is as if we have been channel-surfed into another poem, and at two points in this translation [the Sigemund and Finn substories] I indicate that we are in fact participating in a poem-within-our-poem not only by the use of italics but by a slight quickening of pace and shortening of metrical rein" (xiii).

While the reference to Hengest *may* be historical, there is no question that Beowulf's lord and uncle, Hygelac, is a historical figure who has a *transworld identity* in the poem. Hygelac is referenced several times; in fact, we are first introduced to Beowulf not by name but as a thane of Hygelac (*Higelaces þegn*, line 194). Later, when Beowulf returns to Geatland, Hygelac is an actual character in the poem, welcoming the young warrior home and questioning him about his adventures (1983-98). They have a lengthy exchange of information and gifts before the *Beowulf* poet jumps ahead fifty-plus years to Beowulf's ascension to the throne, and we learn the details of Hygelac's death on the battlefield in Francia, a death that has been referenced briefly on three other occasions in the poem. According to more than one reliable historical source, Hygelac was killed by the Franks in about 521—an incident that is woven into *Beowulf* (Swanton 197). In fact, the purely fictional (as far as can be determined) Beowulf was said to be at the battle in which Hygelac was killed (2490-2509). Among other things, this intertextual episode of bona fide history gives an air of credibility to an otherwise incredible tale of monsters and superhuman accomplishments.

Examples of intertextuality are copious in the poem, but they need not all be discussed for my purposes here. However, one other noteworthy example is an ekphrastic passage wherein Hrothgar reads the legend on the golden sword-hilt that Beowulf retrieved from the underwater lair of Grendel's mother (1688-98). The implication is that there is a pictographic representation of the biblical flood showing the destruction of giants. Swanton explains, "Germanic art of the kind applied to sword-hilts, jewels and so forth[,] at this period characteristically took the form of a pattern of disjected zoomorphic and anthropomorphic writhings, which could well have been interpreted as a monstrous conflict at the time the *Beowulf* poet was writing—when such art had been superseded" (199). Swanton's specific hypothesis (whether on the mark or not) underscores the point that the poet has incorporated another sort of text—a pictographic text which may in itself have been rich in allusion for the Anglo-Saxons—into his highly intertextual poem, with the decorated hilt connecting backward and forward to several incidents and details in the poem, like the legend of Cain and Abel told in the beginning of the poem to account for Grendel's ancestry, and to the giants that Beowulf claimed to have put in chains when he presents his curriculum vitae to

Hrothgar, and to the water that is associated with death and destruction throughout the epic.

Repetition in Beowulf

Repetition is another prominent feature of *Beowulf*. As with intertextuality or any of the other "postmodern" features of the poem, repetition could blossom into a book-length study of its own. However, keeping a taut tether to the subject at hand—how these features are mimetic of a traumatized voice—I will attempt to restrain my observations accordingly. Specific words and phrases are often repeated in the narrative. Many scholars, especially in the earliest decades of modern interest in *Beowulf*, have accounted for the repetition as a characteristic of oral storytelling—that is, the *scop*, who was improvising the contours of the poem during performance, used stock words and phrases because they were helpful to the audience as the story meandered over time and land and sea, and also because it assisted the *scop* as he thought ahead of himself as to how he was going to connect the various bits and pieces of the generally familiar tale. This view of composition technique can be seen in the analysis of Friedrich Klaeber, who was writing in the 1920s, during so-called high modernism. Clearly, Klaeber had affection for the poem and its anonymous poet, but he did not see *Beowulf* as a work of great literary art: "In explanation of some discrepancies and blemishes of structure and execution it may also be urged that very possibly the author had no complete plan of the poem in his head when he embarked upon his work, and perhaps did not finish it until a considerably later date" (cvi). Klaeber, who expressly states that *Beowulf* "does not rank with the few great masterpieces of epic poetry" (cxix), goes so far as to suggest passages that could be cut from the poem for aesthetic reasons (cvii), and of Beowulf and Wiglaf's dispatching of the dragon, he asks, "May not signs of [the poet's] weariness be detected in a passage like 2697 ff.?" (cvi). More contemporary scholars, however, writing in the era of postmodernism, tend to see the poem quite differently. A good example is David Wright's assertion that "[f]ar from being a rambling, incoherent affair, the poem is built up of themes, motifs, contrasts, and parallels, and is in fact as sophisticated in its construction and use of allusion as *The Waste Land* of T. S. Eliot" (125). Ironically, *The Waste Land* was published the same year, 1922, as Klaeber's *Beowulf and the Fight at Finnsburg*, but most scholars would accept that *The Waste Land* was a harbinger of postmodern style.

Andy Orchard is one contemporary scholar who views the *Beowulf* poet's use of repetition as deliberately artful. In Orchard's *Pride and Prodigies* (1995), he makes the case that the poet used linguistic repetition to imply the monstrousness of human characters and the humanity of monsters. For one example he points to the dragon's being awakened when a human thief steals a cup from his ancient treasure hoard (lines 2287-89):

> Here the stout-hearted one (*stearcheort*) is the dragon and the foe (*feond*) the human plunderer of his hoard. An exact reversal is seen in the dragon-fight itself, in which Beowulf, on the only other occasion in the poem on which the word is used, is described as 'stout-hearted' (*stearcheort*, line 2552), and the dragon is the 'foe' (*feond*, line 2706). (30)

Orchard further points out that the lairs of both Grendel's mother and the dragon are connected to Heorot, the legendary meadhall, via specific diction. Grendel's mother's subaqueous chamber is described as a "roofed hall" (*hrofsele*, 1515) and simply as a "hall" (*reced*, 1572); meanwhile, the dragon is said to live in an "earth-house" (*eorðhuse*, 2232), and "earth-hall" (*eorðsele*, 2410 and 2515; *eorðreced*, 2719). Furthermore, Orchard writes that "the same word *dryhtsele* ('noble hall'), unattested outside *Beowulf*, applies equally to Heorot (lines 485 and 767) and the dragon's lair (line 2320)" (30). To Orchard's observations, I would add the *Beowulf* poet's synecdochic use of *winter* for *year* to note the passage of time. Just three of several examples: Grendel's attacks have taken place over twelve winters/years (*twelf wintra*, 147), Beowulf's father Ecgtheow lived for many winters (*wintra worn*, 264), and Queen Hygd was wise in spite of only having been alive a few winters (*wintra lyt*, 1927).

In terms of repeated images or symbols, a well-known example is the golden necklace or torque or neck-collar that passes from Wealtheow to Beowulf to Hygd to Hygelac back to Beowulf (after Hygelac's death) to Wiglaf (just before Beowulf dies). The assumption is that these passages refer to the same necklace, but the poet does not always make this point crystal clear. In any event, if not *the* necklace, then certainly *a* necklace becomes an item of special note at various points throughout the story. A simple reading of this repeated image, the *heals-beag*, has been that it symbolizes the newly hardened bonds of allegiance between peoples, particularly the Danes and Geats. However, Tomoaki Mizuno is among scholars who have developed an alternative interpretation of what she refers to as the "magical necklace." Researching the Old Norse folk-history of the necklace, as implied by the poet upon Wealtheow's bestowal of the gift to Beowulf, Mizuno has concluded that far from being a symbol of allegiance the necklace transplants the doomed fate of the Danes to the Geats, as Beowulf returns home and presents it to Queen Hygd, for whom Beowulf harbors a romantic/sexual affection, according to Mizuno's complex reading. She offers the nucleus of her findings in the following passage:

> Wealtheow's necklace [. . .] represents her favor for Beowulf, her premonition of Hrothgar's death, and her affections for [her nephew] Hrothulf. This gift carries her psyche into the donee Hygd. That which was Danish becomes Geatish through Beowulf's role as an intermediary. Thus Hygd is driven to entertain not a little affection for Beowulf, her nephew, once she receives the necklace. And, owing to the same necklace and Heorogar's corslet, Hygelac is doomed to die, earlier than his nephew Beowulf, in Frisia, just as Hrothgar, it is implied, will die earlier than his nephew Hrothulf. (390)

Mizuno delves further into the psycho-sexual implications of the necklace, but for my purposes here it is enough to point out that she considers the repetitive nature of the necklace references to add several multifaceted layers to the narrative.

Narrative Structure and Repetition

The poet's use of emplotted loops is another form of repetition in the poem. To be sure, the repetitive nature of the episodes is a feature of the poem that caught the attention of some of its earliest modern readers. Mitchell and Robinson say that "structurally *Beowulf* is composed of static comparisons and contrasts as much as it is of linear narration. Even the repetitions induce us to compare one account with another" (22). They point to Beowulf's retelling of his Danish adventure immediately upon his return to Hygelac's court as the "most remarkable example of repetition" in the poem (21). Meanwhile, John D. Niles has offered a detailed analysis of the poem's repetitive patterns, or ring composition: "In organizing the narrative of *Beowulf*, the poet relied heavily on *ring composition*, a chiastic design in which the last element in a series in some way echoes the first, the next to last the second, and so on" ("Ring Composition" 924, Niles's emphasis). He represents the basic pattern as ABC . . . X . . . CBA. Niles terms the "X" a "kernel" or "key element" around which the details and actions of an episode "radiate" (926). For illustrations, Niles primarily focuses on the three monster fights in the poem. Here is the fight with Grendel, according to Niles's analysis (but somewhat rephrased and labeled with letters):

A. Preliminaries: Grendel's approaching, rejoicing, and devouring Hondscio

B. Grendel's wish to flee: "finger's burst"

C. Uproar in hall: Danes are panic-stricken

X. Heorot seems that it may break apart

C. Uproar in hall: Danes experience "horrible terror"

B. Grendel's "joints burst asunder": he flees the hall

A. Aftermath: Grendel's returning to mere, Beowulf's rejoicing and keeping of Grendel's arm. (diagram 3; 926)

Moreover, the poem as a whole conforms to this ring composition, with the fight with Grendel's mother functioning as the kernel around which the entire poem radiates. Here is a somewhat simplified and relabeled version of Niles's sixth diagram:

132

A. Prologue
- a. Panegyric for Scyld
- b. Scyld's funeral
- c. History of Danes before Hrothgar
- d. Hrothgar's order to build Heorot

B. First fight, beginning with Grendel's unexpected nocturnal attack

C. Interlude, featuring the great banquet at nightfall

X. Second fight, beginning with Grendel's mother's unexpected nocturnal attack

C. Interlude, featuring the banquet at nightfall

B. Third fight, beginning with the dragon's unexpected nocturnal attack

A. Epilogue
- d. Beowulf's order to build his barrow
- c. Prophecy of Geats after Beowulf
- b. Beowulf's funeral
- a. Eulogy of Beowulf. (930)

In sum, Niles writes that "[f]ar from having been an unskilled compiler of separate tales, the *Beowulf* poet appears to have been endowed with a keen (although always flexible) sense of narrative form" (931). Similarly, Mitchell and Robinson, though focusing their attention on the two-part (young Beowulf/old Beowulf) division of the poem coordinated with the three monster battles, write, "Although quite different from the order principles in most western narratives, these interlocking structural patterns—a bipartite chronological structure together with a tripartite narrative development—give the poem a coherence that leaves no doubt of the poet's artistic control over his matter" (23). Regardless, then, of how modern scholars specifically describe the structure of the poem, they tend to view its repetitive patterns as a deliberate aesthetic technique.

The Poet's Fragmented Narration

The third aspect of postmodern style that reflects the traumatized voice is a dispersed or fragmented narration. Of all the "postmodern" characteristics that are part of the poem, this is probably the most profound and most infamous one. It is the so-called narrative digressions that have perplexed and bewildered first-time readers of the poem for more than a century, but even early scholars were often left scratching their heads in befuddlement. Indeed, Klaeber's 1922 analysis of *Beowulf*'s structure—which he subtitles "Lack of Steady Advance"—seems comical in retrospect. He writes,

> The reader of the poem very soon perceives that the progress of the narrative is frequently impeded. Looseness is, in fact, one of its marked peculiarities. Digressions and episodes, general reflections in the form of speeches, an abundance of moralizing passages [. . .] interrupt the story. The author does not hesitate to wander from the subject. When he is reminded of a feature in some way related to the matter in hand, he thinks it perfectly proper to speak of it. Hence references to the past are intruded in unexpected places. [. . .] No less fond is the poet of looking forward to something that will happen in the near or distant future. (lvii)

Elsewhere Klaeber speaks of the poet's "rambling, dilatory method" and "the forward, backward, and sideward movements" of the narrative (lviii). As several scholars have since pointed out, the *problem* with *Beowulf* is that it does

134

not fit the Aristotelian paradigm that Western artists have tended to pattern their work after for more than two thousand years. Mitchell and Robinson stress that "we must remind ourselves that Aristotle and the entire classical tradition which we tend to think of as a cultural universal have nothing to do with *Beowulf*" (18). Swanton, meanwhile, writes, "This poem corresponds with none of the genres or kinds into which we are accustomed to divide modern or classical literature, and any attempt to judge it by classical criteria merely frustrates" (9). In short, then, modern scholars have come to accept that the poem's "forward, backward, and sideward movements" are a mark of the poet's sophistication, not indicators of a haphazard and ultimately failed artistic structure.

A specific manifestation of the dispersed or fragmented voice is the use of multiple voices or genres in the text. In some regards this and other issues associated with the dispersed or fragmented voice have already been discussed in that these various features tend to overlap, so I may be able to assert this point without quite as much textual elaboration. For example, it has already been noted that the poet drew from history, quasi-history, legend, and folk-mythology—though it is worth noting that these labels reflect our modern sense of genre, and the *Beowulf* poet himself would not have thought of them as we do. What is more, we have looked at the fact that Beowulf becomes his own storyteller upon his return to Geatland and recounts in greater detail his Danish adventures. In terms of fragmentation, we have seen that the story of Hygelac's military exploits (and eventual death) is given to us via backstory and flash-forwards—as is the passing of the golden necklace—so that the audience must piece together

135

these odd bits in order to see the whole picture in each instance.

Nevertheless, some further specifics regarding these issues are worthwhile. While I have tended to use Klaeber as an example of early scholarship that has since been largely rebuked, his careful analysis is still useful in several respects, with one being his remarks on the speeches in the poem— that is to say, those sections that we would call dialogue where a character speaks to others in the scene. According to Klaeber, approximately 1,300 of the poem's 3,182 lines consist of characters' speeches: "The major part of these contain digressions, episodes, descriptions, and reflections [... and] they are characterized by eloquence and ceremonial dignity" (lv). He further reports "[t]he shortest of these consists of four lines (the coast-guard's words of God-speed, 316-19), the longest extends to 160 lines (Beowulf's report to Hygelac, 2000-3027, 2155-62)." Another useful observation is that the "prominent and rather independent position of the speeches is signalized by the fact that, in contrast with the usual practice of enjambment, nearly all the speeches begin and end with the full line." This comment is especially meaningful because it adds yet another facet to the poem's linguistic variety. One other significant voice in the poem is the narrator's as he frequently speaks directly to his audience. As mentioned earlier, the narrator is how we learn of the folk-mythological pedigree of Wealtheow's golden necklace; he further declares that it is "the greatest necklace of those I have heard spoken of on earth" (lines 1195-96; Swanton's translation). More interesting still, from a postmodernist perspective, is his metapoetic statement: "At times one of the king's thanes, a man filled with high-sounding words, with a memory for stories, who remembered a multitude of all kinds of old legends, improvised a new poem linked in true metre; again the man began by his art to relate Beowulf's exploit and skillfully to tell an apt tale, varying his words" (867-73). Here the storyteller comments on the process of storytelling, a feature of postmodern metafictional texts. Regarding the use of multiple genres, it is worth underscoring Joseph Harris's 1982 study in which he declares the poem a *summa litterarium*, "a unique compilation of the oral genres of the Germanic early Middle Ages" (Bjork 390). Harris identifies at least eleven distinct genres at work in *Beowulf*.

The Magical Language of Beowulf

The last feature of the "postmodern"/traumatized voice that I need to speak to is the search for magical language. Analyzing the language of *Beowulf* has been a special interest of scholars in recent years. Orchard, in 2003, writes that "it would be no exaggeration to say that the whole issue of the precise implications of *Beowulf*'s clearly formulaic style of composition has (rightly or wrongly) dominated recent literary appreciation of the text" (*A Critical Companion* 57). Indeed, the debates over the language of *Beowulf* have been closely tied to its dating and place of origin—and have therefore been just as heatedly contested. Klaeber framed the basic question almost ninety years ago—"How can this mixture of forms, early and late, West Saxon, Northumbrian, Mercian, Kentish, Saxon patois be accounted for?" (lxxxviii)—and no wholly satisfactory answer has been accepted by the academic community to date. In 1998 Mitchell and Robinson gave Klaeber his due. Klaeber concluded that it was "perfectly safe to assert that the [extant] text was copied a number of times, and that scribes of heterogeneous dialectical habits and different individual peculiarities had a share in that work" (lxxxviii-lxxxix). Mitchell and Robinson's analysis "justifies" Klaeber's conclusion, and they write, "We believe that Klaeber's hypothesis is more credible than the view that this orthographic and dictional mélange was concocted by one person late in the Anglo-Saxon period" (17). Their statement appears a refutation of Kevin Kiernan's hypothesis that the poem was composed in Mercia during the reign of Cnut (1016-1035): "[A] literate, 11th-century Mercian poet alone could have brought about the particular mixture of forms in *Beowulf*" (50).

The language debates tend to be waged at the microlinguistic level, on issues like spellings, conjugation, and syntax. The richness of the poem's language has not been in question. Orchard, characterizing the poet's language, writes that he "uses a range of pithy, self-contained and understated phrases, often couched in proverb or other gnomic expression, more or less as marks of aural punctuation" (*A Critical Companion* 58). Moreover, Orchard tips his hat to Arthur Brodeur's "masterful analysis" in which Brodeur found 903 distinctive noun-compounds, with 518 being unique to *Beowulf*, and 578 appear only one time in the text of the poem (60). Orchard sums up *his* careful analysis of the poet's use of compound words in general by saying, "[S]uch forms are certainly frequent within the poem, and the degree to which the poet seems at pains to vary his precise choice of words is simply staggering" (70). Given the variety and complexity of language in the poem, one can imagine the *Beowulf* poet's having a similar composition mantra to William H. Gass's: . . . *the better word . . . the better word . . . the better word. . . .* That is, it seems clear that the poet was "at pains" to find the ideal language to express complex ideas to an audience that was receptive to such complexity.

The issue of orality versus literacy may be brought up at this point as one may argue that if the poet's primary medium for delivering his text was oral, by performing it for a live audience, then he could not have expected his listeners to pick up on the more sophisticated nuances of his language and language-play. As discussed in the previous chapter, the Anglo-Saxons on average surely had a better developed memory and more refined critical listening skills than modern people do (modern people who can easily turn to print and electronic material to retrieve information). Niles speaks to a closely related issue in his analysis of the poem's ring composition:

> [O]ne suspects that the patterned structure of *Beowulf* would not have been wholly without aesthetic effect. [. . . N]o event [in the poem] would be thought of as random or isolated, without antecedents or consequences. [. . .] The probability that such expectations would have been unconscious makes them no less real. (931)

Niles also offers the view of Cedric Williams, who was commenting on Homer's audience, but his statement is germane to *Beowulf*'s audience as well:

> The human mind is a strange organ, and one which perceives many things without conscious or articulate knowledge of them, and responds to them with emotions necessarily and appropriately vague. An audience hence might feel more symmetry than it could possibly analyze or describe. (931)

139

In other words, even if one posits a largely oral transmission of the poem, the poet still would have been in the business of using sophisticated form and language, and he could have counted on the audience's absorbing his meaning consciously *and* unconsciously. It must be pointed out, too, that some of the complexities of his poem may have developed without the *poet's* conscious awareness, a point I will address more fully.

The Psychic Origins of Creativity

Offering any fresh perspectives on the poem is a challenge; in fact, simply keeping abreast of *Beowulf* scholarship has become a daunting task. Speaking of just the publications dedicated to the poem, Orchard says that "the sheer number [. . .] has become somewhat bemusing" (*A Critical Companion* 3). He goes on, "Indeed, such has been the proliferation of books and articles on *Beowulf* in recent years (with a new item a week appearing on average over the last decade [c. 1993-2003]), that simply controlling the secondary material has become a near-impossible task." Nevertheless, some of the approaches associated with postmodernism—and especially those associated with psychoanalysis—have only recently been taken up by scholars interested in Anglo-Saxon literature. Eileen A. Joy and Mary K. Ramsey acknowledge that medievalists by and large have been slow to embrace poststructuralist critical models. Joy in particular writes, "Scholars working in contemporary literary studies do not often look to the field of Old English for enlightenment or direction on the subject of critical theory, and within the field of Old English itself, the resistance to theory, in general, has been strong, and occasionally mean-spirited" (xiii). However, one scholar with an interest in psycholinguistic critique is M. R. Godden, who claims that a "rich seam" has been opened in looking at "the way in which Anglo-Saxon poets present the workings of the mind" (284). Referencing the work of I. A. Richards on the correlation between a culture's language and its psychological concepts, Godden writes, "Anglo-Saxon writers have important and often novel things to say about the nature of the mind and soul, and their discussions touch significantly on the problem of continuing interest, the relationship of psychological ideas and linguistic expression" (284).

It must be said that it is impossible to know how much symbolic interaction in a creative work is due to a writer's deliberate planning and how much is due to the workings of the writer's unconscious mind. In a 2008 interview, novelist and short-story writer Adam Braver spoke to this issue in particular. Referring to his conceptual novel *Mr. Lincoln's Wars* (2003), Braver said,

> [. . .] I was giving a reading somewhere and somebody asked me a question about the link between all these stories with fathers and sons, and disappointments in fathers and so on . . . and it was really news to me. I looked at the person as though I had no idea what he was talking about. Then he went through and listed the stories [. . .] and the light went on in my head, and I couldn't argue because it was right there, but it really was something that was completely unconscious in the act of writing. (31)

But Braver also makes the point that just because the symbolic connections are unconsciously wrought, they are no less valid: "[. . .] I can say from my own experience, and from the experience of other writer friends of mine, that so

141

often [. . .] the writer can be the last person to know that he or she was doing this—which again does not mean the theme is not there, but it's working completely unconsciously." Leslie Fiedler concurs, stating, "[M]any of the things you do [as a writer] you don't know you're doing until you get somebody's response to it. [. . . T]here's meaning that comes from writers who are gifted, especially in writers who please many and please long—and it comes from levels deep within their unconsciousness" ("'Nothing'" 238-39).

In addition to unconscious symbolism, artists may deliberately choose details for reasons other than realistic logic and accuracy. Being a creative writer myself I can speak to this phenomenon, and I will offer a couple of specific anecdotes. When I have read for an audience, one of the most common sorts of questions after the reading is, *What happens next?*—Does the couple get divorced or do they save their marriage? Is the lost child reunited with her family? Does the narrator end his life? The questioners seem to believe that writers have worked out the entire histories of their characters' lives, and we are only sharing a little piece in a given story or novel. While that may be somewhat true for some writers some of the time, many, many writers have to respond to such questions the way I always do: *I have no idea*. Audience members tend to be disinclined to accept that response and seem to suspect that I am just being cagey. One may expect such skepticism from "non-English folk," but I have experienced similar responses from "English folk" too. In 2008 I read a short story titled "Communion with the Dead" at the College English Association Conference in St. Louis (the story was published that fall in *The Chariton Review*). In the story, the teenage main character sneaks into a courtyard at night and is staring at an upstairs window

142

when a man speaks to him in the dark, a man who seems to know him and his mother and their situation—but I never identify the courtyard speaker in the story. At the conference that evening, at a social function, I met a woman (a college literature instructor) who had been at my reading and claimed to like the story. We chatted for a few minutes before she told me that she had a theory about who the man in the dark was, and she wanted to know if I would confirm her theory. I told her that I had no idea who the man in the dark was—not when I wrote it, not now. She seemed taken aback by my assurances that I myself was *in the dark*. She also seemed a bit disappointed, and perhaps she thought a little less of the story and of me because I did not fully know my own creation. One more example: I wrote a sequel to Mary Shelley's *Frankenstein*, a short story titled "A Wintering Place" (published eventually in *Eleven Eleven*). One of the many places that rejected it was a British journal which published both academic and creative writing. Normally in creative writing, an author gets either a "yes" or a "no" from an editor; in academic writing the rejections tend to be much more explanatory—and it was just such a rejection I received on my story from this journal. I set the story in Russia, probably Siberia (though I mention neither by name), because when Shelley's novel ends, the creature (my narrator) is more or less in that part of the world—plus I just liked the exoticness of a maybe-Siberia location. The editor who rejected my story had several reasons for doing so, but chief among them was that he (I have always imagined the editor as a stodgy and tweedy male professor) knew that part of Russia well and I had gotten the geography all wrong. So he was reading under the assumption that I meant a specific place and that I had not done my homework in making my setting accurate. But there is nothing in the story (intentionally anyway) that is meant to identify a *specific* location; moreover, I had mountains in my story because the story wanted them, not because that part of the world really has mountains.

My point here is not that all creative writing is random or organic. Indeed, creative writers make many conscious choices, but even the conscious ones are often made for artistic reasons, rather than realistic ones. All of this would have been true for the *Beowulf* poet as well. Certainly much of the complexity of his poem is due to conscious artistic expression, but much of it is likely the machinations of his unconscious creativity as well. Yet even the conscious choices may have been for purposes of his art, not for his possible function as a historian or geographer or sociologist or folklorist. Because traumatic stress tends to reside at the unconscious level (we recall the work of twenty-first-century neuropsychologists who report that many trauma victims have no conscious recollection of the source event(s) whatsoever), it is quite possible that much of what goes on in the poem is based on the poet's unconscious thought. Furthermore, since unconscious thoughts, especially those generated by a traumatized mind, are fragmentary and connected in ways that are anything but logical, developing a fully articulated and logically organized interpretation of the poem from a trauma-theory perspective may be all but impossible. That is, metaphors in the poem are likely operating on many different levels, some only hinted at while others are drawn much more fully—*not* the way a fable operates, for example, where *the fox* fully represents *ambition* and *the grapes* fully represent *a desirable goal*. In their book *A* Beowulf *Handbook* (1997), editors Robert E.

144

Bjork and John D. Niles attempt to provide detailed summaries of all (as much as that is possible) the various approaches to reading *Beowulf*. Niles ends the book's introduction by suggesting that the multiplicity of readings may return the poem to "the guise it had a thousand years ago, when for its listeners (if my guess is correct and the poem did have listeners) it was not a document at all but rather a diaphanous fabric of words, a shimmering web of multiple significances" (9). It is in this spirit that one might pursue a reading of *Beowulf* grounded in trauma theory; such a reading could prove useful, I think, to Anglo-Saxonists as they continue to expand their critical repertoire in the new century.[1] Or, as Nicholas Howe puts it: "In the new millennium, I suspect, we will have the future we create today by writing studies that deepen and complicate our sense of the period, its culture, its persist value [. . .]" ("The New Millennium" 504).

1. See T. Morrissey, *The 'Beowulf' Poet and His Real Monsters: A Trauma-Theory Reading of the Anglo-Saxon Poem* (Mellen, 2013).

Chapter 6

Twentieth-Century
Postmodern Literature

In a writers' symposium on postmodern literature held at Brown University in 1989, Robert Coover, in his welcoming remarks, gave the impression that the writing style which became known as postmodernism sprang up in the 1950s and '60s almost by sheer coincidence. Among the symposium participants were Leslie Fiedler, John Hawkes, Stanley Elkin, William Gass, Donald Barthelme, and William Gaddis. Coover noted that other writers who certainly would have fit in but were not in attendance included John Barth, Thomas Pynchon, Angela Carter, Italo Calvino, and Gunter Grass. Coover said, "[T]his group sought out some form, some means by which to express what seemed to them new realities" ("'Nothing'" 233). However, Coover goes on to suggest a remarkably thin theory as to why so many writers, all working in relative isolation, began constructing narrative in uncannily similar styles:

> We felt we were all alone. No one was reading us, nor was anyone writing remotely like the sort of writing we were doing until, in the little magazines, we began slowly to discover one another. Few of us knew one another at the time we began writing. There was a uniform feeling among writers at that time that something had to change, something had to break, some structure had to go. And that was, I think, what most united us.

Even though the panel was intended to be a debate, and not merely a discussion, not a single writer challenged Coover's explanation for the emergence of postmodern style. At first this assessment may seem startling—that some of the keenest and best-educated minds who were at the forefront of producing and (many) critiquing literary postmodernism accepted the premise that postmodern narrative style more or less just happened; essentially that individuals writing in isolation on various continents, including North and South America, and Europe, just all happened to begin writing in the same sorts of ways, all in a narrow time span, from about 1950 to 1965. According to Coover, writers, with virtual simultaneity, decided to abandon modernist realism for something fragmented, repetitive, largely unrealistic and illogical, and highly intertextual. Joe David Bellamy, in his preface to *The New Fiction* (1974), expresses a similar notion as to the origins of postmodern narrative style. Bellamy cites an essay by Louis D. Rubin, Jr., who "described his sense that the most interesting writers (at that hour of the world [mid 1960s]) were in the process of struggling against a 'whole way of using language . . . a whole way of giving order to experience,' which had been imposed on the sensibility of the times by the great writers of the immediate past" (ix-x). Again, Bellamy appears to support the idea that *post*modern writers simply decided to rebel against *modernist* literary convention.

Trauma Theory and Postmodern Style

A more cogent explanation rests with trauma theory: The trauma of the nuclear age, which was experienced by the entirety of Western culture, affected the psyches of these writers in a way that resulted in postmodern literary style—a style, as we have seen, that reflects the traumatized voice. Here we must recall Jay Lifton and Greg Mitchell's assertions regarding twentieth-century zeitgeist as it suddenly evolved after the Second World War. One is that the "[s]truggles with the Hiroshima narrative have to do with a sense of meaning in a nuclear age, with our vision of America and our sense of ourselves" (xvi). Another is that Americans were deeply and immediately conflicted with the atomic bombings of Hiroshima and Nagasaki, that they experienced the "contradictory emotions of approval and fear the bomb evoked, a combination that has continued to disturb and confuse Americans ever since" (33). A third assertion is that "[o]rdinary people [. . .] experienced their own post-Hiroshima entrapment—mixtures of nuclearism and nuclear terror, of weapons advocacy and fearful anticipation of death and extinction" (306). And all of this internal conflict, much of which resides in the unconscious, has contributed to a "sense of the world as deeply absurd and dangerous" (335). As noted, literary critic Ihab Hassan sees a connection between the horrors of the Second World War and postmodernism: "Postmodernism may be a response, direct or oblique, to the Unimaginable that Modernism glimpsed only in its most prophetic moments. Certainly it is not the Dehumanization of the Arts that concerns us now [1987]; it is rather the Denaturalization of the Planet and the End of Man" (39).

It is quite possible that Coover and the other postmodernists at the Brown University symposium experienced the same sort of repression and dissociation that individual trauma victims frequently do. We recall that it is not uncommon for people suffering the symptomology of PTSD to have no conscious recollection whatsoever of the traumatizing event, or to have a dissociated recollection; and we recall MacCurdy's characterization that trauma can be

149

simultaneously "indelible" and "forgettable." While the symposium participants did not seem to recognize post-nuclear cultural trauma as the source of their collective postmodern style, they inadvertently came near the mark—so much so that reading their comments from here in the twenty-first century, with our growing understanding of trauma theory, one experiences a sort of dramatic irony. An example is this exchange between Fiedler and Elkin regarding the role of the unconscious in narrative production:

> Fiedler: [. . . The writer's] possessed with certain hallucinations that he would like other people to take as real and to weep over and laugh over and shiver over. [. . .] One of the marvelous things about being a writer is many of the things you do you don't know you're doing until you get somebody's response to it.
> Elkin: I don't believe that.
> Fiedler: You don't believe anything's out of control in a writer?
> Elkin: There's plenty out of control, yes. Absolutely. But I don't think there's any such thing as serendipitous meaning.
> Fiedler: Well, there's meaning that comes from writers who are gifted, especially in writers who please many and please long—and it comes from levels deep within their unconsciousness. ("'Nothing'" 238-39)

I would note Fiedler's use of the word "possessed" as we know that trauma tends to possess its victim, distorting reality in numerous ways; and "hallucinations" of course are among the symptomology of the traumatized. Also, while Fiedler and Elkin disagree on specific points, they concur that fiction is harvested in large part from the writer's unconscious mind. Moreover, Gass cited Gertrude Stein's theory of composition and applied it to Elkin's earlier statement that he imagined William Faulkner peering over his shoulder as he composed: "[Stein] wrote, she said, finally, for the human mind, which was the same in some remote, abstract sense. When Stanley [Elkin] says he's writing with Faulkner looking over his shoulder, that's the superego who's telling you that your paragraphs are lousy" (238). Stein's assessment gets at the notion of a collective *un*consciousness, that writers and their readers are able to *connect* because all are tapping into the same neuropsychic substructures. Coover, meanwhile, referenced the nuclear-age zeitgeist of the 1960s:

> I also wanted to get involved in telling stories. But we were in that period of time in the 1960s when telling stories was no longer so simple. A lot of people were telling stories, and it was getting us into wars. It didn't seem to stop the growth of nuclear armaments in the world. The stories seemed to be contributing in some way to all those activities. (242)

Coover also discussed writing as "a kind of therapy." He said, "There are things you have to work your way through. There are issues that have to be confronted[. . . .] So you work that out in fictional forms, and you do feel that Freudian answer, that kind of power over what would otherwise be your impotent life" (242). Hence Coover recognized the unsettling cultural climate of post-Hiroshima America and how it contributed to narrative style; also, his view of writing-as-therapy is consistent with trauma theorists who suggest that postmodern techniques are akin to victims' struggling to transform *traumatic* memory into *narrative* memory. Even the Rubin quote that Bellamy cites in *The*

151

New Fiction—about writers "struggling" to find a "way of giving order to experience"—sounds very much like the difficult transformation from traumatic into narrative memory.

Development of the Apocalyptic Temper

In his examination of the apocalyptic temper in the American novel, Joseph Dewey theorizes about the literary community's response to Hiroshima and Nagasaki, which he describes as "slow in coming." Citing the work of Paul Boyer, Dewey writes, "[T]he literary conscience of America did not seem ready in the 1940s and even in the 1950s to engage the menace of the mushroom cloud" (8). At first, writers, along with the rest of their culture, experienced a "psychic numbing [. . .] in the face of such catastrophe." In the '50s, notes Dewey, "the American literary community pondered the bomb only in tentative ways." He references "a glut of forgettable speculative fiction" that appeared during the decade. In the early '60s, however, "the American novel began to work with the implications of the nuclear age" (9). Dewey speculates that the Cuban Missile Crisis—"the nuclear High Noon over Cuba"—may have acted as a catalyst for writers in general to "begin to think about the unthinkable." Dewey does not approach his subject in this way, but he seems to be accounting for the dual starting point for American postmodern literary style, which some trace to the mid 1940s and others to the '60s. Nor does Dewey tend to speak in psychological terms, but he seems to be suggesting that American writers were by and large *repressing* the atomic blasts for nearly two decades, until nuclear Armageddon loomed in 1962, which caused the cultural literary psyche to begin to confront the source of its

152

trauma, if only dissociatively. The scenario that Dewey suggests corresponds with the way many individuals respond to a traumatic event. As van der Kolk and McFarlane explain,

> [p]eople's interpretations of the meaning of the trauma continue to evolve well after the trauma itself has ceased. This is well illustrated by a case of delayed PTSD reported by Kilpatrick et al. (1989): A woman who was raped did not develop PTSD symptoms until some months later, when she learned that her attacker had killed another rape victim. It was only when she received this information that she reinterpreted her rape as a life-threatening attack and developed full-blown PTSD. (6)

Perhaps the fear of nuclear Apocalypse was part of the American psyche since 1945, but it seemed unreal until 1962's standoff with Cuba and its ally the Soviet Union. It is also useful to recall that groups—entire nations even—can respond to trauma just as individuals do. In fact, Neil J. Smelser, in his work on cultural trauma in particular, notes that societies can undergo a delayed response to trauma akin to the Freudian notion of a breakdown in repression, which "only succeeded in incubating, not obliterating the threat"— though he qualifies the analogy as not being perfect (Alexander et al. 51).

The Fiction of William H. Gass

While evidence of a link between post-Hiroshima trauma and postmodern technique can be found, with greater or lesser conspicuousness, in the work of all writers who occupy the established pantheon of postmodernists, I think the connective tissue is most apparent in the fiction of

William H. Gass, one of the writers at the Brown symposium, and, interestingly, the writer Coover called "our real living biographer of the human mind" (242). In his work, which was begun in the early 1950s (when Gass was in his late twenties) but did not start to appear in print consistently until the 1960s, Gass often alludes to trauma and symptoms of posttraumatic stress disorder (though not necessarily by these labels), and he cites directly and indirectly the nuclear age as the source of widespread anxiety. It must be stated upfront that Gass's childhood was, by his own description, miserable, raised by an alcoholic mother and an agonistic father; and one could certainly point to these influences for his prose's negativity. As Stanley Fogel writes, "Directly and indirectly, Gass's outrage at his early family life filters into his writing, both fiction and nonfiction" (14). Gass also served in the U.S. Navy, an experience he "detested," according to Fogel (15). There is no question that these facts have affected Gass's writing, much of which is overtly autobiographical; however, I believe I can show that the Cold War zeitgeist had an even greater impact on his storytelling. One might even conjecture that the insecurities caused by Gass's childhood made the fear associated with that zeitgeist even more potent. The psychological community has long recognized that individuals respond differently to trauma due to a variety of factors, including their mental health when they experience the trauma, and even their genetic predisposition to dealing with traumatic stress. As Smelser puts it, "every individual has a distinctive and preferred pattern of modes in his or her individual armory" (Alexander et al. 47).

In any event, a good place to begin is Gass's well-known short story "In the Heart of the Heart of the Country," which appeared in *New American Review* and then in a collection by the same title in 1968 (though Gass says that it was written much earlier, implying the beginning of the decade [Bellamy 39]). The oddly and disjointedly segmented *story* features a disillusioned poet-teacher narrator living in a small Indiana town, called simply "B," a town which represents (it has been widely noted and in fact acknowledged by Gass) W. B. Yeats's Byzantium from the poem "Sailing to Byzantium" (1927). The short story has generated a fair amount of critical attention over the past forty years, and much of that criticism examines the psychological underpinnings of the narrative. In one of the earliest studies, in 1973, Frederick Busch writes, "[Gass's poet-narrator] is caught in the heart of the country, he is fallen. And the country he has come to is his mind. [. . .] This little story is a saga of the mind" (99, 100). Similarly, Charlotte Byrd Hadella says that the "narrator/poet is miserable, lonely, and lost in a fragmented world, much like the world of Eliot's *The Waste Land*, because he fails to participate fully in either art or life" (49). As such, "the narrator has left one world and entered another—the world of his own imagination." What is more, Hadella claims that "[w]ith the fragmented structure of his story, Gass conveys a subliminal message of isolation, loneliness, and departmentalized perception of his narrator" (50). Both critics are unwittingly keying on psychological components of the story that are mimetic of posttraumatic stress disorder—the unbidden merging of real and unreal worlds, profound feelings of disconnectedness with one's self and others. In another psychoanalytic reading, Bruce Bassoff notes a "narcissistic fear of castration [. . .] everywhere

155

diffused in 'In the Heart of the Heart of the Country'" (49)—
emblematic of a trauma victim's paranoia.

These analyses are useful to be sure, and in fact I
want to look at some of the same passages in the story that
these critics cite, but I believe even more can be gleaned
from the story via a trauma-theory paradigm. Given the
insightfulness of these critics' observations, I am struck by
an omission that they and other commentators have
committed in their readings of the narrative. No one has paid
any attention whatsoever to a passage that I see as key to
understanding the narrator's disjointed psyche. In a section
subtitled "Politics," the narrator criticizes his fellow
townspeople (and Americans in general I would say) by
stating, "I have known men [. . .] who for years have voted
squarely against their interests. Nor have I ever noticed that
their surly Christian views prevented them from urging
forward the smithereening, say, of Russia, China, Cuba, or
Korea" (197). Here the narrator makes direct reference to
using nuclear weapons against Cold War enemies—attacks
which would be squarely against American interests (as it
would provoke retaliation, including nuclear retaliation) and
which contradict the Christian morality that the majority of
Americans claim to advocate. This atomic-bombing
reference does not come out of the blue, so to speak. In an
earlier section also subtitled "Politics," the narrator alludes to
"the Russians [. . .] launching [. . .] their satellite" (186), and
in "Education" he says that at school "children will be taught
to read and warned against Communism" (187). Taking into
account these Cold War references, the narrator's disposition
and the townspeople he describes sound very much like the
divided, post-Hiroshima psyches that Lifton and Mitchell
discuss. We recall their writing that "[b]y the 1960s,

Americans were living a nuclear 'double life': aware that any moment each of us and everything around us could be suddenly annihilated, yet at the same time proceeding with our everyday, nitty-gritty lives and conducting 'business as usual'" (351). Americans, in short, were divided in two, with their *measured self* (which was interested in making a comfortable and meaningful life) being in constant conflict with their *apocalyptic self* (which accepted that the nuclear end was at hand and therefore every action was irrelevant). Hadella is noting this conflicted duality in the story when she writes that "the narrator's mood is a perpetual winter. The poet/narrator avoids thinking of spring as the season of rebirth and renewal. Thus, even when he does mention spring rain, the rain mentioned is only a memory, and it is not associated with desire or awakening to life" (51). It is as if Gass's narrator, with his measured self, desires a future (the coming of spring rains), but will not allow himself to believe it will arrive because of his apocalyptic self, the self that envisions a spring rain that causes "the trees [to] fill with ice" (181).

This post-Hiroshima futurelessness can also account for the bleak picture of B that Gass provides us. He describes, for example, Billy Holsclaw who "lives alone— how alone it is impossible to fathom" (179). He imagines Billy carrying "coal or wood to his fire [an action of his measured self] and clos[ing] his eyes, and there's simply no way of knowing how lonely and empty he is or whether he's as vacant and barren and loveless as the rest of us are—here in the heart of the country [because of our apocalyptic selves]" (180). Moreover, the entire town is colorless: "The sides of the buildings, the roofs, the limbs of the trees are gray. Streets, sidewalks, faces, feelings—they are gray"

157

(180). The poet-narrator uses personification in saying that the town's "houses are now dying like the bereaved who inhabit them; they are slowly losing their senses—deafness, blindness, forgetfulness, mumbling, an insecure gait, an uncontrollable trembling has overcome them" (181). On the surface at least, Gass's narrator is listing symptoms of old age, but given his references to the use of nuclear weapons (smithereening America's enemies) and the threat of Communism (a threat so great that schoolchildren are taught only to read and to fear Communism), and given how much propaganda Americans were exposed to regarding nuclear threats and how to respond to them in the 1950s and '60s— one can begin to see the population of B as suffering from nuclear fallout (deafness, blindness, insecure gait, trembling, etc.), just as the Japanese had been since the bombings. And in a psychological sense at least, the citizens of B were suffering from nuclear fallout. To be clear, I am not suggesting that this American-Japanese parallel was Gass's conscious choice but rather a manifestation of his unconscious creative mind.

I know this connection may seem tenuous, but there is more. Hadella's careful study is mainly concerned with Gass's use of weather imagery, especially winter. She suggests that the references to perpetual winter in the story reflect, among other things, the narrator's inability to move forward with his life, his "finding himself in a dormant winter state" (51). She also discusses his blaming the weather for "his barren, loveless predicament," especially the snow that he references several times. I think Hadella's reading is on track; as I said before, Hadella is keying on what could be described as the poet-narrator's conflicted psyche, his measured and apocalyptic selves, to use Lifton

158

and Mitchell's terms. In the context I am framing, the winter and its snow become even more psychologically significant as mimetic of a *nuclear* winter and its radioactive (or *dirty*) snow. Before looking at winter/snow references in way of support, I want to turn to the "Weather" section that describes a summer heatwave in B as Gass uses language suggestive, I think, of a nuclear blast. The passage is lengthy but well worth examining:

> In the summer light, too, the sky darkens a moment when you open your eyes. The heat is pure distraction. Steeped in our fluids, miserable in the folds of our bodies, we can scarcely think of anything but our sticky parts. Hot cyclonic winds and storms of dust crisscross the country. In many places, given an indifferent push, the wind will still coast for miles, gather resource and edge as it goes, cunning and force. [. . .] Sometimes I think the land is flat because the winds have leveled it, they blow so constantly. In any case, a gale can grow in a field of corn that's as hot as a draft from hell, and to receive it is one of the most dismaying experiences of this life, though the smart of the same wind in winter is more humiliating, and in that sense even worse. (180-81)

On the one hand, this *is* a wonderfully apt description of a Midwestern heatwave, but Gass's language as it relates to a nuclear blast cannot be easily dismissed: melting, even liquefying "bodies"; widespread devastation by "hot cyclonic winds and storms of dust" driven by "cunning and force"; a flattened landscape, "leveled" by "a draft from hell"; a "dismaying" life experience, but the "wind in winter" to follow is in a "sense even worse." Then there is the winter and its snow that are so closely linked to death.

The narrator says, "I would rather it were the weather that was to blame for what I am and what my friends and neighbors are—we who live here in the heart of the country. Better the weather, the wind, the pale dying snow . . . the snow—why not the snow?" (191). Images of winter/snow connected to death continue in this "Weather" section. He says, "Still I suspect the secret's in this snow, the secret of our sickness, if we could only diagnose it, for we are all dying like the elms in Urbana" (192). He references the snow, and then dust, covering the country "like our skin," implying of course how thoroughly the snow or dust covered the ground, but also suggestive of the skin's being covered by the snow or dust, and even encouraging an image of the skin itself covering the ground as if it has been shed. The passage ends with the narrator's assertion "what a desert we could make of ourselves—from Chicago to Cairo, from Hammond to Columbus—what beautiful Death Valleys." Again, viewed through the prism of the Cold War mentality and how the unconscious must have been affected by the sense of impending nuclear doom, it is reasonable that at some level Gass is describing atomic annihilation and the aftermath for those lucky or unlucky enough to survive the attacks.

An important aspect of the conflicted post-Hiroshima psyche is the sense of responsibility and guilt associated with bombing Japan, combined with pride in American resolve and ingenuity, and an acceptance of the "Hiroshima narrative" propaganda that claimed the attack to be necessary, even justified—and Hadella picks up on these vibes in "In the Heart of the Heart of the Country" as well. She writes, "Through the narrator's obsessive attention to weather, Gass emphasizes a controlling irony in the story:

though the narrator complains about the weather, he is the one who is responsible for the world in which he lives. His complaints suggest that he does not accept this responsibility" (51). Hadella's analysis reflects to the letter the psychological turmoil Americans found themselves grappling with, according to the research of historians Lifton and Mitchell. Many commentators have spoken to the story's oddly redundant yet lyrical title. At the most basic level, it makes a geographical reference as the setting is Indiana, in the heart or middle of the country. But *country* itself is multifaceted. Since B is a small, Midwestern town, *country* can be synonymous with *rural* and all of its associations, including honesty, stability, directness, and hardiness— associations which prove ironic in the story. *Country* also implies *nation*, that is, the United States; and with sections subtitled "Politics" and with references to other countries (e.g. Russia, Cuba), clearly Gass wants the reader mindful of American culture and ideology. The repetitive part of the title is even richer in nuance. *In the heart of the heart* suggests a compounded or doubled *entry* of the country, including a deep examination of American character (rooted in the United States' agrarian beginnings and its continued cultural sense of itself as dependable, independent, hardy, and guileless), and an examination of the American soul (as represented by its political agendas and ideologies). Moreover, I would point out that *heart* and *soul* have often been associated with the *psyche* or *inner-self*. It is this aspect of the title, as a profound examination of the American cultural psyche, that my analysis most fully supports. Busch notes a deep-seated "arrogance" in the narrator "which has caused him to be cast down, to be condemned to suffer in himself" (104-105). He quotes this sentence: "I want to rise

161

so high, I said, that when I shit I won't miss anybody" (189). This sentiment could be seen as symbolizing the United States' arrogance in creating nuclear bombs in the first place, unleashing them on non-military targets, then triggering an escalation of atomic armament that threatened (and continues to threaten) the entire planet. But, as has been noted, Americans have suffered from their own ingenuity via the guilt of having developed the weapons and the fear of becoming casualties of the technology themselves.

"In the Heart" of Postmodernism

I want to look at other Gass narratives that clearly bear the marks of cultural trauma, but first it should be said that "In the Heart of the Heart of the Country," a story which seems to reflect specifically *nuclear* anxieties, is consummately postmodern. Even though it has a central speaker, there is no *plot* per se—no easily recognizable conflict, resolution, dénouement. Rather, the conflict is internalized as the poet-narrator's search for meaningfulness in this tiny Indiana town, a search which brings him again and again to various literary texts as sort of spiritual reference books. As Hadella puts it, "[h]e shuns human connections and seeks literary ones; he hides behind an image of himself that he has fabricated from literary models" (49). The highly intertextual nature of the *story* is signaled in its opening line with its conspicuous allusion to Yeats's "Byzantium"—"So I have sailed the seas and come . . . / to B . . ." (172). Gass even breaks the opening line apart as a poet might, so in a sense "In the Heart" begins as a poem then proteanly becomes prose. But what sort of prose? "In the Heart" is sometimes tale, sometimes essay, sometimes mock-scientific report, all broken into subtitled segments whose subtitle may have little to do with the topic the reader encounters beneath it. For example, in a segment subtitled "Education," the narrator begins with a description of "[b]uses like great orange animals" transporting children to the classroom of Miss Janet Jakes, who tries to take control of the class by having children draw pictures of her (187); however, the narrator quickly transitions into abstract reflections on his own teaching career and ends with his unhappiness here in B: "I do not work on my poetry. I forget my friends, associates, my students, and their names [. . .]" (188). Such is the meanderingly fragmented narrative structure. Moreover, besides using language powerfully, Gass's narrator speaks directly to the power of language when he says of old Billy Holsclaw and his pathetic existence: "[. . .] I keep wondering whether, given time, I might not someday find a figure in our language which would serve him faithfully, and furnish his poverty and loneliness richly out" (190). That is, through his poetry, the narrator may be able to *save* Billy by transforming him into a dignified (and textualized) literary figure.

One last hallmark of postmodernism I will mention is Gass's creation of otherworldly zones. The narrator tells us that his "thoughts are not thoughts, they are dreams" (182); then he compares Midwesterners to Alice (in Wonderland) (186); and in a segment subtitled "Business" he says of a street in the business district: "Here a stair unfolds toward the street—dark, rickety, and treacherous—and I always feel, as I pass it, that if I just went carefully up and turned the corner at the landing, I would find myself out of the world" (189-90). Hadella writes that the narrator occupies "a zone of his own invention. Caught between the equal powers of life and death, he finds himself in a state of living death. [. . .]

Gass's narrator tries to enter the world of literature and thus [escape] death" (54). As we know, this paragon of postmodernism was composed in the early 1960s at the height of Cold War anxiety, very likely in the shadow of the Cuban Missile Crisis, which Dewey has suggested was some sort of psychic catalyst for American writers.

Gass's "The Pedersen Kid"

The passage in "In the Heart of the Heart of the Country" that references the *smithereening* of Russia and Cuba, etc. is a key to understanding Gass's fiction, and another very important passage is in "The Pedersen Kid," also an early story, written, the author says, in 1951 or '52. In this tale about a neighbor boy who escapes from the farm where his family is being terrorized by an intruder, the farmhand who finds the nearly dead Pedersen kid talks about the phenomenon of trauma (though not by name). Through Hans's unsophisticated voice, Gass encapsulates the impact and tenacious aftermath of a traumatic event. When the Pedersen kid is found half-frozen in the snow, Hans says that he understands what has happened to his neighbor (generally, because at this point in the narrative the details of the home invasion have not been revealed). He says,

> It's more than a make-up [imagined tale]; it's more than a dream. It's like something you see once and it hits you so hard you never forget it even if you want to; lies, dreams, pass—this *has* you; it's like something that sticks to you like burrs, burrs you try to brush off while you're doing something else, but they never brush off, they just roll a little, and the first thing you know you ain't doing what you set out to, you're just trying to get them burrs off.   I know.

164

I got things stuck to me like that. Everybody has.

Pretty soon you get tired trying to pick them off. (17)

Again we have the notion of possession expressed—"it hits you so hard you never forget . . . this *has* you." This event, "like burrs," can never be "brush[ed] off." The tenacity of the trauma totally disrupts your ability to live your life: "the first thing you know you ain't doing what you set out to." Instead, you are consumed by the trauma and trying to come to terms with it: "you're just trying to get them burrs off." Importantly, the narrator says that "[e]verybody has" experienced being traumatized, which, in my view, speaks to *cultural* trauma. Ultimately, you succumb to the trauma, and it becomes a permanent part of your psyche: "Pretty soon you get tired of trying to pick them off." *Cultural* trauma, then, becomes a permanent part of the *cultural* psyche. Furthermore, Gass, who is known for experimenting with textual appearance, uses expanded spacing (between *off.* and *I know.*, for example) to represent the speaker's difficulty in finding the right words; he pauses, hesitates—mimetic of the trauma victim's struggle to turn the traumatic memory into narrative memory.

Further Gass Fictions

While this passage from "The Pedersen Kid" may be the most thorough and most poignant description of trauma in Gass's oeuvre, allusions to trauma are common. In another early story, "Mrs. Mean," the narrator wonders why the Mean children do not try to escape the home that he imagines to be abusive, but decides that escape would be pointless because the trauma of abuse would stay with them:

My wife and I find it strange that they should all run home. It seems perverse, unnaturally sacrificial [. . .]

165

We'd run away, we affirm in our adulthood to one
another, knowing, as we make the affirmation, that
even old as we are, adult as we claim to be, we would
return to the poisonous nest as they return [. . .] We
would chew on our hurt and feel the pain again of our
beginnings. [. . .] The eldest Mean child may
someday say, confronted by a meanness that's his
own, by his own mean soul, that he was beaten as a
boy [. . .] (101-102)

Here then the "Mean" children are trapped by their
circumstances, destined to become mean themselves because
of the tenacious trauma of child abuse. We notice that the
trauma is internalized, *eaten* even, as the narrator projects the
children "chew[ing] on [their] hurt" and thus never escaping
it. Moreover, the trauma is so psychically penetrating that it
infects the Mean boy's soul. In the novella *Cartesian Sonata*,
which began to appear in excerpts in 1964, Gass offers a
different take on trauma via the clairvoyant Ella Bend Hess,
who can hear the dead: "Corpses, she knew, were eloquent,
she'd hear them speak, they were never quiet, they ran on
and on, even with the casket closed she could hear their
steady murmuring. They ran on and on until their voices
mingled with the wash and groan of burial dirt" (33). Even
though the tone of *Cartesian Sonata* tends to be more comic,
we note that the dead, a sort of personification of traumatic
experience, are relentless in imposing themselves on Ella's
"real" world. Even when the event is over ("even with the
casket closed"), it continuously repeats itself ("they ran on
and on"). We note too that the corpses' voices are
"eloquent," implying that they command Ella's attention,
and she is unable to ignore their "steady murmuring." Due to
her clairvoyance—the intrusion of an *otherworld* into the

166

real one (like a past trauma imposing itself on the present)—Ella is disconnected and profoundly unhappy. Her husband tells us, "She never joked, never saw the funny side of life; when was the last time they'd had a good ho ho together? no, she was always, what? grim? serious at any rate, intense, anxious, fearful [. . .]" (64-65). Ella's symptoms, including the sexual frigidity her husband complains of, are textbook PTSD.

Omensetter's Luck *and the Atomic Age*

Gass's two full-length novels[1]—*Omensetter's Luck* (1966, begun in 1951) and *The Tunnel* (1995, begun 1966)—also offer evidence of a post-Hiroshima zeitgeist of trauma affecting the author's unconscious, if not conscious, mind. *Omensetter's Luck*, which is told via three different narrative perspectives (Israbestis Tott's, Henry Pimber's, and Jethro Ferbur's), each the focus of his own section, is set in late nineteenth-century Ohio, and revolves around various townspeople's perception of Brackett Omensetter, a newcomer who seems to have a monopoly on luck. Tott tells us, "That was the kind of fellow Brackett Omensetter was. He knew it wasn't going to rain again [so he did not bother to cover his wagonload of belongings]. He counted on his luck" (18). It is true that Omensetter appears to have good fortune on his side, but when viewing the novel through a trauma-theory frame, one realizes that Gass—famously, or infamously, erudite—is invoking an older meaning of the word *luck*: not just "good fortune" but also "happy"—a correlation that survives in modern usage in words/expressions like *hapless* ("unlucky"), *happenstance* ("as luck would have it"), and *happy-go-lucky* ("carefree"). We recall that in *Macbeth* the second Witch tells Banquo

167

that he is "[n]ot so happy [as Macbeth], yet much happier" (1.3.64)—meaning, we discover, he is not as *lucky* as his friend as he will not become king, but *luckier* in that he will become the progenitor of the Stuart Dynasty. Thus the title of Gass's novel could be *Omensetter's Happiness*. Omensetter lives without self-reflection; indeed, he lives without reflection altogether. Ferbur is infuriated by Omensetter's "simple harmony and ease" and declares to Tott that Omensetter lives as worry-free as a cat asleep in a chair: "How pretty in a man? Is it attractive in a man to sleep away his life? take a cow's care? refuse a sparrow of responsibility?" (44).

While Ferbur rails against Omensetter's unattractive happiness, Pimber covets it. Pimber becomes traumatized by a nearly fatal bout with lockjaw, and is saved, possibly, by Omensetter's homespun remedy. Gass's description of Pimber's condition is classic posttraumatic stress disorder: "[Pimber] yearned to be hard and cold again and have no feeling, for since his sickness he'd been preyed upon by dreams, sleeping and waking, and by sudden rushes of unnaturally sharp, inhuman vision in which all things were dazzling, glorious, and terrifying" (66). We are told, moreover, that Pimber's love of Omensetter "lay somewhere in the chance of being new . . . of living lucky, and of losing Henry Pimber" (67). That is, after nearly dying, Pimber is plagued by nightmares, and waking hallucinations that dazzle and terrify him, and he longs for Omensetter's ability to be happy. Consumed by depression and hopelessness, Pimber tearfully hangs himself: "How sorry for it all he felt. How sorry for Omensetter. How sorry for Henry" (74). Richard J. Schneider, encouraged by Gass's edenic allusions, reads Omensetter's luck/happiness as prelapsarian innocence; he writes, "The Fall leads to knowledge, and knowledge leads to perception, the recognition of our own otherness, our separation from the world we inhabit. [. . .] The danger is that our perceptions may become more real to us than the things we perceive" (14). Within the trauma-theory paradigm, Schneider's interpretation could point to the Fall as analogue for the United States' atomic-bomb achievement, transforming Americans into their own enemies (their own otherness), thus splitting their measured selves from apocalyptic selves (separating them from the meaningful world they inhabit and propelling them into a nightmarish world of impending atomic annihilation); and making them susceptible to their own propaganda (their perceptions seeming more real than the things they perceive).

In the final section of the novel, Jethro Ferbur, who has been plotting Omensetter's demise by encouraging the town to believe that Pimber had in fact been murdered by Omensetter, is finally won over by Brackett's accepting nature, and the reverend confesses his plot to Omensetter, a development which greatly contributes to a "tone [. . .] something like passionate optimism," as described by interviewer Carole Spearin McCauley (Bellamy 37). However, optimism is not what Gass was feeling when he was working on the novel and its revisions throughout the 1960s. First of all, the upbeat ending was at his publisher's insistence; and Gass responded to McCauley by saying, "I have always been disenchanted, although I am probably less bitter about things now [1974] than I was when I wrote *Omensetter's Luck*" (37). What is more, he claimed that happy-go-lucky Brackett Omensetter was a nonexistent personality type: "America never had its Omensetters. There aren't any such human felines. Such creatures are part of the

169

American myth." In other words, America has no truly *happy* people; American happiness is a myth, a fiction—which certainly supports the notion of a zeitgeist born of nuclear trauma.

More than two decades later, Gass elaborated on what he was feeling while writing *Omensetter's* in the 1997 afterword for the novel's Penguin Classics re-release. The emotions were triggered by the fact that the novel's manuscript had been literally stolen from Gass's office at Purdue University, and by the fact that at the time he was still unpublished (that is, his work was being regularly rejected by editors). However, in the author's remarks we find him describing general feelings, too—and we must keep in mind that the nature of posttraumatic stress is to overreact to current stress because the unconscious connects it to the previous trauma (a very simple and straightforward example is a gunshot victim's ducking for cover when a car backfires down the street—but PTSD is rarely so simple and straightforward). In any event, Gass writes, "Woe is me. And rage: this feeling, which, with me, is frequent, is also usually diffuse, and is ordinarily aimed at human stupidity and avarice in general, rather than at particular individuals" (310). Here we note that Gass acknowledges a diffuse rage aimed at human stupidity and greed as a whole—not merely at the manuscript thief and the unwelcoming literary world. He further writes, "At the same time, depression, melancholy, gloom: what was the point, the new version would be no better received than the rest of my work. I didn't much like my life. I didn't much like my job. I didn't much like the world" (311). Again, one could attribute these sentiments to the embittered artist who cannot find a receptive audience, but other aspects of Gass's life seemed to be in order—professional, social, romantic—from what can be discerned from biographical and autobiographical accounts. Therefore, emotions like woe, rage, depression, melancholy, and gloom could be seen as overmuch. Perhaps the lost manuscript and literary rejection were psychically symbolic of catastrophic human loss and the rejection of morality on a mass scale. There is no way to say for certain, but textual evidence seems to reflect a response to cultural trauma.

Cultural Trauma and The Tunnel

Perhaps the most intriguing Gass text when viewed through the prism of cultural trauma is *The Tunnel*, a long, dense novel that was three decades in the making. Writing shortly after its publication, Susan Stewart said that it is "a work whose meaning will not become manifest until many readers have reflected upon it and shared those reflections over time" (399). Perhaps Stewart is correct, but given the novel's lukewarm reception it may be some time before *many* readers have an opportunity to contribute to the discussion. It is typical of Gass's other works in terms of its meandering plot, exuberant wordplay, and even its inventive typography and use of cartoonish illustrations—and it too bears marks of post-Hiroshima trauma. It is consummately postmodern and metafictonal; in fact, James Wolcott says that the novel "reflects the loosy-goosy period in which it was begun" (63). The narrator is an aging history professor, William Kohler, who has written a book titled *Guilt and Innocence in Hitler's Germany* that calls into question the popular American myths regarding Hitler and the Nazis being evil incarnate, the Jewish people being innocent martyrs, and the United States and the Allies being forces of liberation and justice. As a young man, Kohler did a tour with the First Army and then worked as a consultant at the Nuremberg Trials. Afterward Kohler discovers that his reputation has preceded him:

> Yes, by that time I had a certain dismal renown as the author of the Kohler thesis concerning Nazi crimes and German guilt, and this preceded me and lit my path, so that I had to suffer a certain sort of welcome too, a welcome which made me profoundly uneasy, for I was met and greeted as an equal; as, that is, a German, a German all along, and hence a refugee. (5)

Like Gass himself, Kohler has taken thirty years to complete his great work, and as the novel begins with the book's completion he finds himself as if paralyzed, sitting in his German mentor's chair, in his own basement. Perhaps also like Gass, who said that he rages against human stupidity and avarice in general, Kohler feels disconnected, even alienated from his own culture.

I want to speak specifically to Kohler's book in a moment, but first I want to look at references to trauma, posttraumatic stress, and nuclear aftermath. Regarding trauma, Kohler quotes Alexander Pope's "Essay on Man"— "Our proper bliss depends on what we blame"—then lists seven maxims about recollection. The seventh and final maxim concludes "[T]his is why memory must be trained not to fetch up a disabling image, but must be lapdogged, why history is so important to the vanity of nations" (56). The metaphor of the poorly trained dog suggests traumatic memory's tendency to intrude on the present moment (via a disabling flashback, for example) of its own accord. It would be reassuring to think that the dog-training Kohler advocates is what some psychoanalysts refer to as shifting the source event from traumatic memory to narrative memory, the difference being that narrative memory is under the speaker's control (it is lapdogged); however, the last part of the maxim prohibits that interpretation and instead advocates self-deception. As such it is especially germane to our interests: "why history is so important to the vanity of nations" refers back to Pope's line, implying that history is the practice of telling the national tale in a way that bolsters the nation's self-image and fosters cultural blissfulness. One such national tale would be the "Hiroshima narrative" that rationalizes the obliteration of two Japanese urban centers, thus *lapdogging* the catastrophic event. We know that this is only one version, and a gross oversimplification at that, as is all propaganda. This cultural *knowing* is oftentimes at the unconscious level, however. Consciously, the culture as a whole accepts the propaganda and participates in the dissemination of the one-dimensional narrative.

As is common in Gass texts (and postmodern texts generally), Kohler suffers from nightmares and feels often that he is in a waking dream—both typical symptomology of PTSD. Kohler tells us, for example, that his dreams of drowning are "old hat": "In my dream I dream of drowning; that is, I consider it; I imagine drowning, think ahead, project; and the terror of it wakes me. It's as if I were back in the army and my fall were part of my duty" (85). We are also told that "[d]aylight dreams, of course, consume [him]." Kohler further pontificates that "[e]very terror has its own terminology, and I am used to terror [. . .] in my life in a chair" (95). It is Kohler's protracted examination of Hitler's Germany and considerations of its guilt and innocence that have worn so on his psyche, but also his own actions and those around him and thus similar issues of guilt and innocence. As Stewart suggests, "Kohler is thrown back into the moral vacuum, the traumatic and opaque events out of which he began to write" (401). As such, we get a meandering mix of German atrocities (the machine-gun massacre of Jews), and Kohler's own atrocious behavior (paying a German boy on the street for a "hand job" and imagining a former lover while "screwing" his wife), but also the atrocious behaviors of myriad other characters, especially his parents (who mirror Gass's parents in painful detail). Here I would note in particular Kohler's/Gass's linking national behaviors and individual behaviors. Consciously speaking, they are not linked, not logically on the page that is; but by mixing them all together, as if in a blender, it suggests that they occupy the same psychic space and affect the psyche in complex ways that are not easily recognized and articulated. In fact, as Kohler writes "the tunnel" (that is, the book that we will know as *The Tunnel*), he hides the manuscript pages in the manuscript pages of *Guilt and Innocence in Hitler's Germany*—literally layering his own personal narrative with the German national narrative he has constructed too. This blending and blurring of national and personal histories are reflected in Michael Silverblatt's assessment of the novel:

> Our terror in reading is at finding how many places [Kohler] seems to be like us. [. . .] The problem with the character is not that he is a monster; the problem is that the monster has taken recognizable human form. [. . .] The monstrous is all around us. We feel comfortable blaming a Hitler, but in this book Hitler is just a spark that sets resentment ablaze. (124-25)

In other words, the national character *is* our cultural character *is* our individual character—making it impossible

174

for individuals to disassociate themselves, at the unconscious level at least, from the *personality* of their nation and the culture it generates.

I posit, then, that William Kohler's book that rationalizes German atrocities, especially the Holocaust, is an analogue for William Gass's book that examines the rationalizing of American atrocities, especially the atomic bombing of Japan. Kohler's search (his digging) for the impetus of Nazi extremism represents Gass's nearly thirty-year search for the impetus of the United States' nuclear ambitions, which culminated in the annihilation of nearly a quarter million Japanese citizens, half of them instantly carbonized by the bomb blasts themselves. Like in "In the Heart of the Heart of the Country," Gass gives us a description of summertime heat in Grand that calls to mind nuclear detonation and radioactive fallout. Kohler says that the summer sky would "leap with light [. . .] and the glass of the several stores would shout the sun at you, empty your head through your ears with whistling sunshine" (99). Also, the dust "slid through crevices no ant could crawl through," and it was

> a disease, this dust, a plague, a fall of evil, one of the many punishments God had placed upon the people—of which life itself, in Grand, often seemed the longest, most unremitting, and the worst. [. . .] The storms darkened the creases in faces and etched their crude graffiti of confusion, sorrow, bitterness, defeat. [. . . B]utterflies became extinct, though beetles thrived; there were no flowers, no fruit on trees or grapes in arbors. [. . .] And in the Midwest, that's where hell is, if there's any—outside the inside of its inhabitants, I mean. (99, 100)

175

We notice that the plague of dust is a punishment from God (reminiscent of Americans' fearing they would be the victims of their own horrific weapon), and that life (having to live with this fear of retribution) is a punishment in itself, and we note that people have a hell within them (the internal conflict of nuclearism and nuclear fear).

Importantly, in a long section in which Kohler discusses time spent on the family farm with his Uncle Balt when Kohler was a child (subheaded "Uncle Balt and the Nature of Being"), he describes his uncle as a "silo . . . sunk in the ground like those missiles would be" (118), a direct reference to nuclear warheads. Speaking to the broader contexts of *The Tunnel*, Stewart writes that "experience is known as a blow or wound [we recall that *trauma* comes from the Greek for "wound"]; it shapes us negatively and propels us toward false mythologies of transcendence or idealism. Adhering to such myths, we will be warped; we will no longer be able to recognize the particularity of our existence in a social frame" (403). In this broader context, the novel can be read as a study of how trauma affects the cultural psyche, which responds by projecting a false image of itself and thus loses a sense of self relative to humanity as a whole. Questions of right and wrong, good and evil, provocation and unprovocation become garbled in this falsified framework. (We recall Bernard Giesen's theory that the collective psyche of perpetrators respond by "schizophrenia, by denial, by decoupling or withdrawal." Interestingly, Giesen's main scholarly focus has been the German people after the Second World War.) Kohler, writing in mid-America, says, "[. . .] I know that men are capable of anything; that all of the things possible to men are therefore possible for me. There is no safety from oneself.

176

[...] In that sense Hitler's been the only God. But must I always live in Germany?" (103). That is to say, every country is or has the potential to be "Hitler's Germany," and Kohler/Gass feels as if he has always been living in just such a country.

The Founding Fathers of American Postmodernism

As stated earlier, my choice to focus on the fiction of William H. Gass in this section is because of all the postmodernists I have studied his work most readily and most consistently reveals the connective tissue between cultural trauma and postmodern narrative style. It is worth noting that among the Founding Fathers of American postmodernism, narratives about the Second World War are plentiful. A short list includes Thomas Pynchon's *Gravity's Rainbow* (1973), Kurt Vonnegut, Jr.'s *Mother Night* (1961) and *Slaughterhouse-Five* (1969), and Joseph Heller's *Catch-22* (1961). Interestingly, bombs and bombing play pivotal parts in nearly all of these novels: *Gravity's Rainbow* centers on the rockets that Germany is aiming toward the West, and the title itself refers to the parabolic arc of a rocket; the central event of *Slaughterhouse-Five* is the firebombing of Dresden, Germany, the site of an American POW camp; and *Catch-22* focuses on an American bomber squadron stationed in Italy, and the kernel of the narrative that is returned to again and again happens on a bomber during a mission. So it seems that these postmodernists are not only concerned with the events of the Second World War, but they are especially interested in bombs. None of the narratives mentioned deals directly with the bombings of Japan, but it is provocative that in each case Americans are harmed or even killed by the bombs. This indirect

177

engagement of nuclear threat could be a dissociative response. "Avoidance may take many different forms," write van der Kolk and McFarlane, "such as keeping away from reminders [. . .] or utilizing dissociation to keep unpleasant experiences from conscious awareness" (12). In addition to these novels, there appeared a second wave of significant postmodern novels that dealt with United States nuclearism, Cold War anxiety, and/or profound government mistrust. On that list would be books like Robert Coover's *The Public Burning* (1977), John Barth's *Sabbatical* (1982), and Don DeLillo's *Libra* (1988) and *Underworld* (1997). *The Public Burning* focuses on the Rosenberg espionage trial of 1951 in which Julius and Ethel Rosenburg were charged with selling nuclear secrets to the Soviet Union. Barth's *Sabbatical* tells the tale of an ex-CIA analyst who has retired from the agency and written a book about government subterfuge, and who also suspects a cover-up of the murder of his brother and other former colleagues at the CIA. *Libra*, meanwhile, centers on Lee Harvey Oswald and his dealings with the Soviets and Cubans leading up to the assassination of John F. Kennedy; and *Underworld* involves a government nuclear testing facility and focuses in part on one of its employees.

These are of course very cursory plot synopses, but the point is to show still more evidence of a psychic link between postmodern narrative style and the horrors of the Second World War, especially the atomic bombing of Japan, which then quickly evolved into a deep-seated fear of nuclear annihilation combined with paranoia about the United States government's motives and nuclear agenda. We recall Lifton and Mitchell's positing that the profound government obfuscation which began with the atomic program became a pattern of behavior on the part of high-ranking officials that led to events like Watergate and Iran-Contra.[2]

Literary Chaos Theory

A moment ago I used the phrase "Founding Fathers of American postmodernism," and this is a decidedly sexist label that deserves some attention—but first I want to briefly look at a latter twentieth-century trend that further supports the connection between a zeitgeist of nuclear fear and postmodern style; and that is the number of postmodernists who were attracted to chaos theory as a narrative device or motif. Myriad writers embraced the tenets of chaos theory in their works with perhaps the first published example being Pynchon's story "Entropy" (1960). It is too early to say, but William Gaddis's posthumously published novella *Agapē Agape* (2002) may prove to be the final postmodern text heavily influenced by chaos theory. Chaos theory, as the name implies, is complex, and various branches of science use the phrase to mean somewhat different things—by the same token, writers who adopted chaologic premises for their fiction brought a wide variety of principles to bear on their storytelling. Just one example is the term *entropy*, which can mean a system that has come to rest because it is depleted of energy, or it can describe a state of extreme disorganization or chaos (on a continuum, the opposite of *order*). Gordon E. Slethaug sees writers' adoption of chaos theory as perfectly understandable because "[i]t is surely chaos theory that can help to explore, if not entirely explain, the mysterious and complex in narration, culture, and life" (xv). I believe Slethaug's assertion is valid. The twentieth century can be seen as a system that was fairly orderly at its turn, still in the reassuringly conservative Victorian Age, but

179

with the First World War it began to spin out of control and the movement toward increasing chaos was relentless—some may argue that the chaotic trend is still waxing. Thus chaos theory appears an apt metaphor for the twentieth century. But I suspect there is more to it than that. I suspect that writers, the coming postmodernists, saw in chaos theory—rooted in the principles of thermodynamics and often discussed at the subatomic level—an analogue for nuclear warfare. The original Greek concept of chaos (*khaos*) had to do with the *nothingness* from which all things came to be and will ultimately return to. In that sense then the dynamic cycle of chaos→order→chaos is in essence nothingness→all things→nothingness: the process that describes nuclear Armageddon as whole cities disappear and humans are instantly carbonized back to their elemental parts. Again, I am referring to a largely unconscious connection on the part of writers.

This classical sense of *khaos* seems to be on Gass's mind in *The Tunnel* when Kohler says of his Uncle Balt, who a few pages earlier he compared to a nuclear silo (in fact, Balt *was* a nuclear silo) and who now he is trying to imagine in a blind rage: "[. . .] I try to imagine emptiness uprooted, nevertheless, air rising like drawn water, a desperate turning as one beset by many enemies might turn and whirl in self-defense—a furious energy, then, containing a calm and silent center . . . from nothing, Nothing coming like the climax of an ardent woman" (122). In this multifaceted metaphor Gass weaves together images of nuclear-like "furious energy" unleashed on "many enemies," with the *khaotic* sense of "Noth[ingness]" which transforms into *Beingness* as implied by the sexually charged simile of "an ardent woman['s] climax." A few lines later, Kohler references the summer dust that would cover everything "as though the sky had exploded." To reiterate, it seems that Gass, like many of his contemporaries (including Pynchon, Gaddis, and DeLillo), linked fundamental principles of chaos theory, in its various manifestations, to aspects of atomic annihilation. It is worth noting that Dewey links chaos theory to the post-nuclear apocalyptic temper as "visionaries puzzle out a way of setting the present crisis within a larger context [. . .] part of an order as wide as the cosmos itself, an order that points humanity toward nothing less than the finale of its history" (10).

White Males and Postmodernism

Finally, the term "Founding Fathers of American postmodernism" sounds baldly sexist, but it has long been recognized that postmodern writers have been almost exclusively white males, especially in the earliest decades of postmodernism, the 1950s and '60s. Not a single female writer was in attendance at the Brown University symposium, and the only one mentioned by Coover as someone whose absence was conspicuous was British novelist Angela Carter ("'Nothing'" 233). Similarly, Bellamy's *The New Fiction* features interviews with a dozen postmodernists and only two—Joyce Carol Oates and Susan Sontag—are female. In his preface, Bellamy lists thirty-three writers who could have been included if not for issues of time, budget, logistics, and willingness; and only one is female, American author Joy Williams (xiii-xiv). Janice McLaughlin comments on theories behind this one-gender-sidedness, not to mention, one-ethnicity-sidedness:

> [. . . Liz] Bondi and [Mona] Domosh (1992) suspect
> that postmodernism is a reaction led by the powerful

subject (Western Man) to deconstruct subjectivity in order to maintain their own power[. . . . They] note that postmodernism emerges from the writing of relatively powerful Western (mostly European) male writers, working from the comfort of American and West European prestigious universities. (7)

In addition, McLaughlin notes the work of Kate Soper who "argues postmodernism could have only come out of a world of privilege and power, a position as yet unavailable to many outside (and inside) the Western world." These theories, while logical, speak more to the effects of postmodernism and to its longevity as an aesthetic, but they shine little light on *why* postmodernism emerged in the first place. I do not believe it is coincidence that the virtual homogeneity of gender and ethnicity among postmodern writers is the same among the group who was responsible for waging the Second World War, developing atomic weapons, then deciding to unleash them on Japan. While all United States citizens would have been inclined to feel the complexity of emotions surrounding the destruction of Hiroshima and Nagasaki—the pride of achievement mixed with guilt and fear—it seems reasonable to think that white men could have felt these conflicting emotions even more profoundly than women and people of color in general, *because* white men occupied the position of dominant power. If America and indeed the world were going to be destroyed by nuclear weapons, it would be because white men had made it so. In other words, the traumatized voice that is reflected in postmodern narrative style *is* the conflicted voice of the white male—perhaps a justly deserved twist on the racist phrase "white man's burden." In Dewey's study of the apocalyptic novel, he includes the work of male writers

Coover, Walker Percy, Pynchon, Gaddis, and DeLillo, but mentions in his introduction the "utopian fictions" of Margaret Atwood, Ursula LeGuin, and Marge Piercy, whose work "imagines sweeping transformations—positive and netative" (42). Dewey does not make note of gender, but he nevertheless underscores some fundamental differences in male and female artistic temperament within the framework of nuclear Apocalypse.

What is more, we recall Freud's theories about the primal horde and the development of religion: The brothers who banded together to kill and consume their father attempted to expiate their guilt and their fear of retribution by worshipping the dead father, at first in animal form and later as an anthropomorphized deity. This tripartite structure (worshipful *love* combined with deep-seated *guilt* and *fear*) precisely mirrors Americans' complex feelings about atomic weapons, which very quickly began to be referred to collectively as *the Bomb*—seemingly deified, and even capitalized as we do the words for *God* (*Jehovah*, *Yahweh*, *Allah*). Dewey writes that "[t]here seemed born into the world a most supernatural presence, one that commanded a religious response" (5). As such, one could speculate that the prevalence of the male postmodern voice is profoundly tied to male love/guilt/fear that dwells at a psychogenetic level and is passed on via Freudian *archaic heritage*. The nuclear annihilation of Hiroshima and Nagasaki may have triggered a psychic response to the original traumatic event, resulting in the mimetically traumatized voice of literary postmodernism—an overwhelmingly male voice because it was males who had *authored* their primal father's destruction. This process is of course highly speculative, but if we accept Freud's theories on animism and the subsequent

183

evolution of culture and religion, and if we accept contemporary trauma theorists' ideas about the correlation between the traumatized voice and postmodern narrative style—then the dots begin to connect in provocatively meaningful ways.

1. As of this writing, William H. Gass has published a third novel, *Middle C* (2013), as well as a collection of novellas and stories, *Eyes* (2016). *The William H. Gass Reader* appeared posthumously in 2018. All three are from Knopf. These works could contribute significantly to the topic at hand: the correlation between trauma and postmodern narrative voice.

Chapter 7

Pedagogical Implications and Conclusions

My topic has several pedagogical implications. Literature study has obviously been a primary concern, and my methodology is applicable to the literature classroom. Beyond that—and perhaps in the true spirit of English studies—the findings of my research may have the most significant bearing on the writing classroom. In this section I will also speak to the implications of my research as it relates to the broad discipline of English studies in twenty-first-century American society at large. As noted earlier, the crosscurrents between literature study in particular and psychology are long standing; the notion that our stories reveal things about our minds is perhaps as old as storytelling itself, certainly older than Freud's psychoanalytic theories and his appropriation of literary figures (like Oedipus) to illustrate them. However, our cultural interest in trauma waxed and waned throughout the twentieth century, being renewed with each catastrophic event and then subsiding over time. Or as stated by Bessel A. van der Kolk and colleagues, "Mirroring the intrusions, confusion, and disbelief of victims whose lives are suddenly shattered by traumatic experience, the psychiatric profession has periodically been fascinated by trauma, followed by stubborn disbelief about the relevance of patients' stories" (xii). By the end of the century technologies, like neuroimaging, had been developed that allowed us to study the workings of the brain in infinitely more detail than had been possible before. In the current century, neuropsychologists especially have been advancing the study of the brain and how traumatic events affect it on multiple levels, including chemically and physiologically. Van der Kolk and colleagues write that "PTSD would be considered an information-processing disorder that interferes with the processing and integration of life experiences. [. . . Supporting] the classification of PTSD as a dissociative disorder, rather than an anxiety disorder" (x). As such, language professionals—like teachers of reading, writing, and speaking—can utilize new findings to make the communication arts classroom as effective as possible for a variety of learners.

Other Trauma Texts

In an effort to demonstrate that cultural trauma can produce postmodern writing style, I focused my attention on the Anglo-Saxon poem *Beowulf*, but this is only the proverbial tip of the iceberg. While our catalog of extant Anglo-Saxon manuscripts is not great, much more work could be done on other narratives to further substantiate the connection between trauma and postmodern techniques. For example, Peter Orton has already identified *The Seafarer* as an Old English poem that exudes an elegiac tone; a careful analysis of its narrative style would be in order to identify (or not) "postmodern" aspects. What is more, *Beowulf* is hardly the only pre-twentieth-century text that demonstrates postmodern narrative techniques. Other time periods and other cultures have produced "postmodern" narratives as well. I have alluded to works by Rabelais, Sterne, and Melville. It is worth noting that Elizabethan/Jacobean England—in fact, Europe in general—has become a site of investigation for scholars interested in the impact of cultural trauma. In an article for *College Literature* (2008), Anthony

186

DiMatteo reviews six recent book publications that assess "the trauma of empire" in early modern culture. He writes,

> Violence and trauma spread across Europe and wherever Europeans brought their divisive and self-serving claims to sovereignty across the globe. [. . .] Claiming the divine right to civilize, conquer or drive out uncooperative indigenous people of newly discovered lands in order to take possession of them, the monarch as 'dominus mundi' or 'imperator mundi' [. . .] sent out sailor-soldiers or sea-dogs in the sixteenth-century basically to 'discover,' claim, conquer, plunder, trade and/or settle in his (or her) name and to the honor and glory of the competing Catholic or Protestant God. (176, 178)

As one may imagine, the works of Shakespeare have begun to yield a plethora of material when viewed through the lens of cultural trauma as propagated by European empire-building: "Very often the legal and cultural focus on Shakespeare's works is upon the effects such institutionalized hubris and indifference of those in power has not only on deeds done (*res gesta*) but on what is said, felt and thought through the society represented" (178). New scholarship is beginning to examine how "Shakespeare explores a collective trauma and mourning haunting and motivating diverse national and religious agendas in the early modern period" (179).

Even a cursory examination of Shakespeare begins to point toward "postmodern" literary techniques. One thinks of otherworldly zones where the real and supernatural collide as in *Hamlet*, *Macbeth*, and *Julius Caesar*; or a play like *The Tempest* whose setting is an enchanted island, visited by unsuspecting characters from the real world. One thinks of emphatic intertextuality, whether it is allusions to other literary works from sources like Classical literature and the Bible; or the plays within plays featured in pieces like *Hamlet*, *The Tempest*, and *The Taming of the Shrew*, with perhaps the best example being *A Midsummer Night's Dream*, which Stephen Greenblatt describes as "a dream about watching a play about dreams" (844). One thinks of genre-blurring works like *Much Ado about Nothing* and *The Tempest*; not to mention the commonly called "history plays," which have been the most troublesome to categorize. Russ McDonald writes, "[. . .] Shakespeare's history plays were to some extent dramatic experiments, narrative plays whose dramatic kind and emotional impact, positive or negative, depended somewhat on the historical episode being staged [. . .] the play itself was almost always a hybrid, a combination of comic and tragic effects" (90). In general, says McDonald, "[a] great many of Shakespeare's plays transgress [. . .] formal boundaries" (97). In terms of further postmodern technique, one thinks of transworld identities and the mixing of historical, quasi-historical, and fictional characters as in plays like *Macbeth* and *Othello*.

Perhaps most of all, one thinks of the power of language and Shakespeare's exuberant use of antiquated, obscure, and simply made-up words. McDonald says that the plays demonstrate "the Renaissance delight in language, its taste for copiousness or elaboration, and its pleasure in verbal games. The touchstone for such matters is Shakespeare's—and his culture's—fondness for wordplay" (44). One thinks immediately of Hamlet's "mad" musings, and the verbal sparring of *Much Ado*'s Benedick and Beatrice. Again, it seems that work is only just beginning in the analysis of Shakespeare and his European contemporaries within the context of cultural trauma and a trauma-theory paradigm. Thomas P. Anderson, one scholar who is mining this rich vein, writes that "significant cultural loss alters normative modes of expression and representation"—implying an alteration to what we would think of as "postmodern" storytelling techniques. Anderson goes on: "The afterlife of the Reformation, the impact of royal death, and the violence of regicide provide compelling case studies of how the formal, textual properties of early modern historical transmission tried to give meaningful shape to the past" (3).

Classroom Practices

The task that I am suggesting here—the task of studying literature within the context of its being produced at a site of cultural trauma—is most appropriate for the graduate classroom, especially a classroom that is using an English studies model, as it would require advanced learners to bring a variety of disciplines to bear on a work of literature. Nevertheless, the foundational principle that cultural mood affects text production could be introduced to less experienced students, which could then lead to various intellectual pursuits in the classroom—in fact, too many to fully explore here. Overall, however, what students in such a classroom (be it high school, undergraduate, or graduate) would be engaged in is what Raymie E. McKerrow refers to as *critical rhetoric*: "a critical rhetoric examines the dimensions of domination and freedom as these are exercised in a relativized world [. . . it] seeks to unmask or demystify the discourse of power" (441). What McKerrow is advocating is an approach to text (literary or otherwise) that enables students to detect various power dynamics at work in the discourse, some in the service of the culture's dominant ideologies and some in opposition to them. Critical rhetoric promotes a *polysemic critique*, "one [that] uncovers a subordinate or secondary reading which contains the seeds of subversion or rejection of authority at the same time that the primary reading appears to confirm the power of the dominant cultural norms" (458). In practical application, students who are engaging *Beowulf*, for example, would be introduced to a traditional (modern) reading of the poem as a study of appropriate kingly behavior (Beowulf as leader of men and protector of community, juxtaposed with other effective and ineffective kings in the narrative), but they would also be taught to read beyond such a dominant interpretation of the poem (an interpretation which may have led to the story's popularity in Anglo-Saxon seats of power—though we have no way of knowing how *popular* the poem was in Anglo-Saxon times). What does the narrative suggest about the acquisition of power/wealth beyond its being glorious for the holder of that power/wealth? What does the narrative suggest about Anglo-Saxon attitudes toward women and children or anyone who finds himself on the fringes of cultural dominance? Bringing a trauma-culture reading to bear on the poem, what does it say about everyday life in Anglo-Saxon England? If these secondary readings are present in the poem, are they deliberate on the part of the poet, and if so what may his agenda have been? Are they present in the poem beyond the poet's conscious creative choice? Are we projecting our own contemporary ideologies onto the centuries-old poem?

Though he is critical of cultural studies as it has evolved in the American university system, this careful attention to text in an effort to read beyond the dominant

190

meaning (that is, the meaning that dominant elements in society would facilely attach to the text) is a crucial part of what Curtis White is advocating in *The Middle Mind: Why Americans Don't Think for Themselves* (2003). He suggests that "intelligent, sophisticated people on the whole [. . . don't] know how to abstract the integument of structure from a piece of narrative art in order to begin to talk about how the thing *means* (i.e., creates an ethical world)" (42, White's emphasis). To illustrate this point, White discusses his reading of the film *Saving Private Ryan* (by Steven Spielberg, 1998) versus the reading of many of his friends: "And if my intelligent, art-savvy friends didn't know how to do this, what was going on with all the blunt teenage receptors (mostly boys) that filled the theater on the evening that I first saw the movie?" (42-43). Moreover, drawing largely from the work of Russian formalist Vicktor Shklovsky, White points out the importance of art that employs *enstrangement*, which "seeks to emancipate the work from the leaden forms of the past by describing things as if seen for the first time, by telling stories from unusual points of view, or by placing things out of context" (84)—certainly postmodern narrative technique is attempting to accomplish enstrangement for its readers, though White does not make this specific point. I want to return to White's notion of the Middle Mind (in short, America's cultural mind that is easily influenced by ideologies and puts little stock in the value of creativity and originality), but for now it will suffice that White, like other theorists, advocates that students be taught to read beyond society's *accepted* meaning of text.

A Critical-Rhetoric Model

Ideally what students learn via a critical-rhetoric approach is that all text is a confluence of ideological agendas, and one must read carefully and analytically to unearth possible alternate readings that are obscured beneath the primary or traditional interpretation. This sort of multilayered reading, with its close examination of language, is appropriate for all types of texts, be they literary, journalistic, biographical, scientific, and so on. Moreover, McKerrow's approach is consistent with what Cary Nelson sees as an effective synthesis of literary and cultural studies. He writes that

> English offers cultural studies a rich tradition of close reading techniques and an exemplary model of rhetorical attentiveness and analytic care. An alliance between literary studies and cultural studies properly entails English moving radically outward from texts to contexts and partly desacralizing the field's traditional objects of study. (214)

Certainly encouraging students to read a poem life *Beowulf* in the context of its being produced amidst cultural trauma would be prodding them away from a traditional reading and in the direction of sources that generally have not been brought to bear on literary texts—like medical texts from the period and contemporary research in neuropsychology. The sorts of secondary sources that are used and the degree to which they are analyzed are obviously in relation to the experience level of the learners in the classroom. But all learners would benefit from a multicontextual approach that discourages the facile acceptance of traditional/primary interpretations—whether the texts are canonical literary texts, non-canonical literary texts, or non-literary texts altogether; or even other sorts of non-print *texts*. I think too that this multicontextual approach would be more in keeping with what White would want from cultural studies, which too often has "the tendency to flatten distinctions" (14) He writes, "[I]t seems very odd to me that the contemporary humanities, which began with deconstruction's distrust of truth-claims, moved very quickly to certainty, conviction, and even self-righteousness during the ascendancy of Cultural Studies" (15). It is important to note, however, that White does not advocate the study of art as an exercise in sorting out the various ideological forces at work on the artist—but rather the study of art's appeal to the sublimity of imagination (a concept I will engage momentarily).

Before turning my attention from the literature to the writing classroom, I want to touch on the results of my teaching internship, which had the modest goal of introducing undergraduates to basic theoretical models, especially postmodernism. I also included feminism, Marxism, and queer theory. Because of my interests in postmodernism in particular, I hoped to teach a course in twentieth-century American literature for my internship, but scheduling became an issue and I eventually modified an introductory course in women authors. The modifications largely consisted of focusing more attention on mid to late twentieth-century authors, and concluding with an examination of Shelley Jackson's highly postmodern hypertext novel *Patchwork Girl* (1995), which is a revision of Mary Shelley's *Frankenstein*, a text I used at the beginning of the semester. Though receptive to literary theory as a means to view texts from various perspectives, the freshman- and sophomore-level students had virtually no familiarity with literary theory per se. Of the models we worked with, postmodernism proved to be the most challenging—in part, I believe, because its tenets were the furthest from their frames of reference. That is, even though the students were not used to working with text via feminist theory, they were familiar with the broad concept of *feminism* and were therefore able to make the cognitive leap more effectively. The same was true with Marxism once it was connected to issues of economics with which they were already familiar. Postmodernism, on the other hand, was not a concept already in their frame of reference. This finding was not unexpected. When I have taught twentieth-century American literature previously, I discovered that students were by and large unfamiliar with postmodernism. Its relative obscureness is evidenced by the fact that in the textbook I use for the course, William E. Cain's *American Literature*, volume 2 (2004), postmodernism is not even mentioned in Cain's lengthy and otherwise thorough introduction to the period, "American Literature Since 1945, Cold War to Contemporary." Moreover, no "heavyweights" of postmodernism are included in the contents, which I have augmented by ending the course with Don DeLillo's *White Noise* (1985). I would conclude that the teacher of undergraduate literature who wants to deal with postmodernism should anticipate that students have virtually no foreknowledge, and therefore significant time should be given to framing the basic issues associated with postmodern texts.

Implications for Writing Classrooms

Returning to my research at hand, the implications for *writing* classrooms may be the most profound. Writing about personal trauma in an academic setting and the clinical use of writing as a component of therapy are activities that have been going on for at least a generation, and seem to have developed in tandem with writing-process theory. Jeff Park, who works with adult trauma victims in an informal "classroom" setting, traces writing-process theory back to the 1960s and early '70s, and he identifies James Britton as someone whose work has been foundational to his own approaches to using writing with trauma victims. Park says, "I have focused on personal writing, or what Britton (1970, 1975) called 'writing in the expressive function,' and have contextualized it within a larger theoretical structure of writing process" (15).[2] Park advocates styles of composition known as "lifewriting" and "freewrighting" that I will speak to further, but in general it is an approach that, in many ways, works against traditional academic expectations and standards for the writing classroom. Park says that his writers "value writing in ways that are different from what the academic community has usually validated" (38). In other words, the academic community has tended to stress the importance of analytical writing (that is, analysis of literature, of scientific data, of political/historical trends, etc.) and has paid very little curricular attention to a writer's *self-exploration.*

Marian Mesrobian MacCurdy is another compositionist who advocates expressive writing and who acknowledges that there are forces within the academy that oppose such an approach: "Social constructionists argue that the job of the writing teacher is to prepare students to write for the academy and the professional sector after graduation. Personal writing, they argue, is an effete genre with little utility in the post-modern world" (3). Both Park and MacCurdy, who teaches in a traditional university setting, state what anyone who has taught writing for any length of time already knows: Even if teachers do not actively encourage students to write about traumatic events in their lives, they will anyway—and writing instructors need to be prepared to deal with such personal and complex issues. "The academy has historically rejected such subjects," writes MacCurdy, "so we have little experience in dealing with such material and even less in the way of safe and effective protocols. We do not teach teachers how to encounter student references to personal trauma, and therefore we are understandably at a loss" (60).

Park, MacCurdy, and other teaching professionals who regularly have students engage in personal or expressive writing about their own traumatic experiences report great benefits for their students. On the one hand, I do not doubt the veracity of their claims, and much of what they do in the classroom is consistent with the latest research into brain function, the effects of trauma, and productive therapies. As such, I will identify aspects of their approaches that appear in league with the findings of researchers in the psychotherapeutic community—especially Park's advocacy of "lifewriting" and "freewrighting." Nevertheless, there are aspects of their approaches—several of which are rooted in trying to reconcile the needs of their traumatized writers and the demands of the academy—that are inconsistent with what we now know about trauma and its effects on mental processing, especially as it relates to linguistic expression and articulation. I believe that the correlation between postmodern literary style and characteristics of the traumatized voice could be very edifying in the field of composition studies and could suggest directions that would be of great benefit to students who are attempting to come to terms with their traumatic experiences, and to the teachers who are trying to coach them through the writing process.

It must be underscored that there are sound scientific data to support the necessity of teachers' being aware of how to deal with trauma-writing in the classroom. For one thing, trauma is pervasive in our culture, making it a virtual certainty that a number of students sitting in the classroom are suffering to a greater or lesser degree due to a traumatic experience. Bessel A. van der Kolk, Alexander C. McFarlane, and Lars Weisaeth report that "PTSD has turned out to be a very common disorder. Exposure to extreme stress is widespread, and a substantial proportion of exposed individuals become symptomatic" (5). They cite studies from the mid 1990s that indicate nearly a quarter of adolescents in the United States "had been victims of physical or sexual assaults, as well as witnesses of violence against others," with one in five developing PTSD—"suggest[ing] that approximately 1.07 million U.S. teenagers currently suffer from PTSD." Another mid-'90s study found more than three quarters of American adults report "having been exposed to extreme stress" (5). Meanwhile, the field of neuropsychology provides some explanation as to why trauma victims feel compelled to write about their experiences. Using a modified version of the "emotional Stroop task" paradigm, which measures how emotion affects cognitive function, researchers who conducted studies from 1996 to 2004 found that trauma-related language dominates the linguistic functioning of victims. Joseph I. Constans writes, "Despite motivated attempts to comply with instructions to name a color and ignore word meaning, individuals with PTSD are unable to avoid processing trauma-related words, and this inability to control either the emotional or attentional response to trauma-related stimuli leads to a disruption of ongoing cognitive processes" (Vasterling and Brewin 112). The implications for writers who suffer PTSD are that, because of the linguistic dominance of trauma-related words, they are much more inclined to process language connected to the traumatic event; in fact, the domination could be such that they have difficulty processing language that does not connect to the trauma. Thus it makes perfect sense that traumatized students, when given the opportunity to choose their own topic, will elect to write about their traumatic event—cognitively speaking, it may be akin to bi- or multilingual students electing to write in their first (or dominant) language when given a choice. In terms of cognitive hierarchy, trauma-related language overshadows all other language in the minds of the traumatized. Or as MacCurdy observes, "Invariably writers gravitate to their difficult stories, the ones that cause the most pain and confusion [. . .]" (15).

The Case for Trauma Writing

First, let us look at what seems to be working well in classrooms where teachers are having their students engage their own personal traumas. Perhaps the most basic statement to be made—but also the most important—is that writing about trauma genuinely appears to help victims get better. In other words, teachers who afford their students the opportunity to write about traumatic events are also affording them the opportunity to recover from those events—not fully, generally speaking, but the writing task may well be a significant part of an eventual recovery. MacCurdy notes that "[w]riting has been shown to alleviate stress or trauma responses for virtually all age groups" (18).

Moreover, "[w]hen writing connects the emotions with images, healing occurs" (39). The importance of writing is grounded in clinical research. Van der Kolk and his colleagues point out that "[t]reatment needs to address the twin issues of helping patients (1) regain a sense of safety in their bodies and (2) complete the unfinished past. It is likely, though not proven, that attention to these two elements of treatment will alleviate most traumatic stress sequelae" (17). By writing about the trauma, and gradually moving the event(s) from traumatic memory to narrative memory, PTSD sufferers can complete the unfinished past by gaining cognitive control over it. According to neuropsychologists, *gradually* is a key word. Brewin points out that more and more therapists "emphasize a graduated approach to trauma recall," because "arousal levels [the degree or intensity of traumatic-memory recall] must be carefully managed." He explains,

> If arousal becomes too high and the person starts to dissociate, becoming overabsorbed in the traumatic memory at the expense of contact with their immediate surroundings, frontal and hippocampal activity will again become impaired and the person will reexperience the trauma without transferring information from image-based to verbal memory. With complex or long-lasting traumas it is likely that repeated episodes of recall will be necessary, with the process being terminated each time the person dissociates to the extent that he or she is no longer able to reflect consciously on the material coming to mind. (Vasterling and Brewin 284)

It seems, then, that writing about the traumatic memory in a short essay for only part of a semester—which would tend to

199

be the norm anyway in a typical writing class—may be just what the neuropsychologist ordered, in terms of encouraging the transfer of the source event to verbal memory. Therapists are experimenting with having victims recount their traumas while performing a visuospatial skill (like knitting or model-building) that forces the brain to divide its attention between the traumatic recollection and the activity literally at hand. "These tasks should theoretically lessen the absorption by competing for resources in the image-based memory system," writes Brewin (284). Interestingly, he cites a 1999 study that he was involved in conducting which suggests that typing the trauma narrative, on a typewriter or word processor (as opposed to hand-writing it), is one such visuospatial skill, "perhaps because typing is more effortful [than writing by hand] and once again limits absorption in the trauma memory." This study is significant because nearly all teachers require students to type the drafts of their papers—trauma narratives or otherwise—and even though the fad of conducting writing classes in computer labs appears to be waning, there are still a good number of composition students who type/write in class. Research indicates, therefore, that teachers who allow trauma narratives to be written have been accidentally savvy in requiring typed drafts, and students may have been serendipitously helped toward recovery.

Both Park and MacCurdy emphasize the *process* of writing as key to helping students who are struggling with personal trauma—and rightly so—but ultimately it seems that Park's overall approach is the more useful (meaning the more aligned with current psychotherapeutic research), and MacCurdy's—which is likely the more typical—is more fraught with aspects that are counterproductive to therapeutic trauma-writing. In fairness, MacCurdy's and other educators' shortcomings are due largely to their working in traditional academic environments and therefore being bound by the academy's expectations and enforcement of long-established standards. Moreover, MacCurdy seems to recognize these shortcomings, for the most part, and she takes steps to minimize aspects of the academic environment that work against the success of her trauma-writers. Conversely, Park leads the Writers' Group, which is associated with the Canadian Mental Health Association, and members of the group participate voluntarily; what is more, the writers and their work are not *graded*. In other words, Park and his adult writers are free of traditional academic shackles. One may argue that examining the techniques of these two writing professionals is a waste of time in that each is as successful as her or his pedagogical environment allows. However, even though it is generally true that teachers must live with whatever advantages and disadvantages their setting provides, I think that successful—research-based—practices can be adopted and adapted to whatever is the inherent bureaucratic setting. What is more, if increasing numbers of educators become aware of effective, research-supported pedagogy associated with trauma-narratives, they can exert their agency within their respective institutions to modify traditional expectations and standards. That is the hope at least.

Even though MacCurdy and Park are just two writing professionals—two among thousands—it is worthwhile to focus on their philosophies and practices, and to compare them accordingly, because they are both knowledgeable, seasoned educators who operate based on a thorough understanding of the history of their profession and of the theoretical bases for common practices within that profession. Yet there are stark differences between their classroom practices—again due mostly to their very different educational circumstances and settings. MacCurdy's circumstances and setting are quite familiar to the vast, vast majority of teachers, while Park's are not. Nevertheless, all teachers—and their students!—could benefit by trying to adopt some of Park's pedagogical approaches—which, incidentally, are in harmony with what my research suggests regarding the psychic correlation of trauma and postmodern narrative technique. Early in MacCurdy's book *The Mind's Eye: Image and Memory in Writing about Trauma* (2007) she gives something of a disclaimer, the sort of statement that makes one wonder if it was at the insistence of her publisher's legal department:

> Teachers are advisers, mentors, and role models. Listening with compassion helps to fulfill those responsibilities and creates the trust needed for the student to delve into a difficult topic. [. . .] However, teachers are not therapists. While a therapist may listen and then counsel, teachers listen and, if appropriate, suggest counseling and other professional services—and then turn to elements of the text. The only occasion for me to intervene is to obey the law, which requires that I disclose any threats to health or safety. (6)

On the one hand, there is common sense expressed here—common sense that it is difficult to immediately argue against—but beneath the surface of this statement two significant problems begin to emerge. It seems comforting (especially to the publisher's attorneys) to say that teachers are not expected to be therapists, and that if teachers

202

encounter a student who is in need of professional psychiatric help, they are merely required to alert the appropriate person or agency. Unfortunately, that determination—distinguishing between a student who is having minor to moderate difficulty in coping with trauma, and one whose symptomology is so severe that he or she poses a threat to health or safety—is best made by a psychiatric professional to begin with. In other words, MacCurdy's disclaimer oversimplifies PTSD. Van der Kolk and colleagues' statement about childhood trauma puts into perspective the writing teacher's dilemma:

> Increased knowledge about traumatic stress in childhood, and recent studies implicating childhood trauma in adult personality disorders [. . .] and other complex disorders, have generated interest in the long-term implications of childhood trauma for adult personality. Complex, life-trajectory-based, developmental models, similar to those recently proposed for the study of childhood bereavement [...], are needed to guide prospective and retrospective investigations of the long-term impact of childhood traumatic stress. Such a model requires revised thinking about the complex disorders that have been found to be associated with histories of traumatic experiences. (351)

Nevertheless there is not much to be done, in a practical sense, other than to advise teachers to make their best guesses regarding the profundity of a student's traumatic stress. The other significant difficulty with MacCurdy's statement comes at the end of the quote I have highlighted, when she says that a teacher must then turn to the elements of the text. Again, it sounds common sensical, but

MacCurdy's syntax emphasizes that ultimately it is the textual *product* that receives the most attention (not to mention, a grade). For trauma-writing to be as useful, in terms of helping the writer to recover, as it might be, the product-oriented classroom is in many ways counterproductive.

Counterproductivity and Trauma Writing

This point regarding counterproductivity warrants elaboration, especially since *product-oriented* describes almost all academic classrooms. What I mean by *product-oriented* is that, even though a writing-*process* model is the dominant methodology, the overarching goal is for the students to produce a *product* that conforms to academic expectations (which are uniformly devised by institutions like the Modern Language Association—governing elements of presentation and typography) and that falls within acceptable standards of quality (which have been propagated by the profession for generations). MacCurdy's bias toward product is evident in a statement like the following:

> This is the crucial element for us as writing professionals: Healing is an ambient effect of good writing—and vice versa. In focusing on a detailed moment, the start of good writing [. . .] The very same elements that produce a therapeutic effect also improve the writing, particularly attention to detail and locating and focusing on the core element of the essay. For this reason, in simply focusing on what makes for good writing, writing teachers are encouraging their students on the path to self-discovery. (14)

204

The phrase *good writing* is vague, but one can assume in large part what she means based on standard concepts that are all but universal in the academy as well as in society in general; and these assumptions are substantiated to a degree at least by MacCurdy's alluding to "attention to detail and locating and focusing on the core element of the essay"— which implies body paragraphs containing specific and effective points, a clearly defined thesis, and a structure that consistently develops that thesis. Also inherent in her credo is the fact that the writing will be judged, and deemed good, bad, or otherwise (*A, F,* or something in between). Elsewhere MacCurdy offers seven practical points for writing teachers to follow. The list is not sequential, nor does it appear climactic; so order-of-importance is implied, and in the first point she makes it clear that "it is my job to teach writing and to grade student texts. I can offer compassion and understanding and still give an essay a low grade" (7). She further lists various elements that "are all critical to successful writing," adding that "[t]he personal essay has a long historical tradition with its own aesthetic, which can help teachers focus on text when we most need to." Elaborating on the instructor's role, MacCurdy writes, "We must remember that we do not have more insight into the student's life than the student. But we may have insight into what makes a text work and what inhibits it. We can provide feedback and ask questions about the text, but it is the writer's responsibility to make sense of it all" (72).

Among the troubling things here, given MacCurdy's focus on trauma narratives, is the concept of "successful writing" or of producing a text that "work[s]": One would assume that since the central argument of the book is that allowing students suffering from traumatic stress to write about their trauma helps them to recover from the disorder, *success* would seem to equate with *recovery*, or at least movement toward recovery. However, MacCurdy appears to be using *success* to mean something more traditional; to mean writing that is clear and concise and drives home a well-defined focus for the *average reader* who encounters the text. The statement that "it is the writer's responsibility to make sense of it all" is also troubling, in that the writing assignment appears to be adding burden to the trauma-writer's task at hand; that is, to likely be adding *stress* to the person who already may be suffering from posttraumatic *stress* disorder. MacCurdy offers several tips designed to assist the writer in recovering specific details of the traumatic event, but principally in the service of writing a *better* essay—not in the service of recovering from the posttraumatic condition.

My purpose is not to deride MacCurdy, not at all. She appears to be an enthusiastic and well-intentioned educator who bases her pedagogical approaches on research. Most of that research, however, is from the field of writing-process theory. She cites established theorists like David Bartholomae, Jeffrey Berman, Peter Elbow, and James Moffett—each of whom theorized without the traumatized student in mind. In fairness, MacCurdy also cites the work of psychologists and neuropsychologists like van der Kolk and Brewin. Nevertheless, much of what MacCurdy advocates for helping the trauma-writer is not validated by the psychotherapeutic profession as a whole. For one thing, even though statistics indicate that writing teachers are likely to have at least some traumatized students in their classes, many of those trauma victims have faulty or no recollection whatsoever of the source event(s). Van der Kolk, McFarlane,

206

and Weisaeth write, "Paradoxically, even though vivid elements of the trauma intrude insistently in the form of flashbacks and nightmares, many traumatized people have a great deal of difficulty relating precisely what happened. [...] One of the gravest symptoms of having been overwhelmed by a traumatic experience can be total amnesia" (10). Yet trauma victims are compelled by the trauma itself to write about their experiences, as discussed earlier. That in itself is not a problem, until one factors in a writing instructor's insistence on academic standards to be met in the personal essay, a form which, MacCurdy points out, "has a long historical tradition with its own aesthetic, which can help teachers focus on text when we most need to." Indeed, studies from 2001 and 2002 cited by Lisa M. Duke and Jennifer J. Vasterling suggest that "neurobiological abnormalities may become more pronounced and possibly take an increasing toll on brain integrity and associated neuropsychological functioning" (Vasterling and Brewin 17). That is, trauma victims, over time, may have increasing difficulty writing anything, leave be a well-wrought account of their source event. Turning specifically to long-established criteria for *good writing*, the field of neuropsychology offers more troublesome findings. For example, Constans reports,

> A number of clinical theories suggest that the narrative memory of the traumatic event is likely to be disorganized [. . . 1995] and omit sensory details [... 2001] in individuals who develop PTSD. This has led to the suggestion [. . .] that patients with PTSD might be particularly good at forgetting or be open to suggestion. (118)

Furthermore, Constans reviews a host of studies pertaining to autobiographical memory which tend to support each other's findings that sufferers of PTSD experience "an overgeneral memory effect" and hence produce "less specific memories" (121). Finally, Constans discusses the phenomenon of fragmented traumatic memory whereby victims recall the causal event via nonlinear, disconnected flashbacks (a hallmark of PTSD):

> One possible way of thinking about flashback is as involving a breakdown in the everyday process responsible for binding together individual sensory features to form a stable object, episodic memory, or action sequence. Insufficient binding means that objects or memories will be fragmented or incomplete. (135)

In short, many if not most trauma victims would be medically unable to meet academic standards for writing an essay, especially an essay that explores the source of their trauma and/or their traumatized condition. On the contrary, their symptomology encourages disorganization, vague or no sensory details, and fragmentation of thought; it is noteworthy, too, that victims may be open to suggestion, leading one to suspect that student writers often incorporate their teachers' suggestions for revision regardless of whether they are legitimate details of the experience. Thus, writing about the trauma in general may have the potential for helping the condition, but being compelled to strive for elements of *good writing* and then being judged as to how *good* or *successful* that writing is would seem to be only complicating the writer's condition and ultimately impeding recovery.

Teaching Practices for Trauma Writing

These conclusions are consistent with my central thesis—that cultural trauma is responsible for producing postmodern narrative style, with its tendencies toward traits like fragmentation, repetition, and overt complexity or obscurity of language. Indeed, the tenets of good writing as they are generally described in high school and college writing courses would hardly apply to postmodern works by heavyweights like William Gaddis, Thomas Pynchon, and William H. Gass, none of whose fiction has been described with adjectives like *clear, concise, focused*, and *logically organized*. Quite the opposite in fact. This all brings me to Jeff Park's approach to the trauma-writing-process, which he has the luxury to practice outside the traditional academy. In his book *Writing at the Edge: Narrative and Writing Process Theory* (2005), Park describes an instructional approach that is structured around *process*, and because his setting is not under the auspices of a university, process remains paramount over product—in fact, the process *is* the product. I shall explain in a moment. Early in his book, Park examines writing-process theory, which he says has come to dominate "curriculum guides, textbooks and academic journals in English language arts"; moreover, writing-process theory and writing workshops have become "basic assumptions and underlying frameworks" throughout North America (18-19). Yet in spite of its popularity—or because of it—writing-process theory remains largely unexamined. One of the chief issues that Park has with the writing process as it is practiced in innumerable courses and discussed in countless textbooks is its emphasis on product revision:

"[T]he common writing process practiced by many writing teachers is still focused on revisions of the product, or the future product, instead of the writing process of the individual writer" (19). He points out that it is not uncommon for teachers to take the much-publicized five-step process so much to heart that they organize their teaching around it. "Teachers usually interpret these steps to be sequential," writes Park, "and in extreme cases, use the five steps of the writing process to correspond to the five days of the school week." Such cases illustrate that the process, whose very name implies an organic cognitive approach, has become systematized to the point of mechanical rigidity in many educational settings.

Like the majority of writing instructors, Park uses a process/workshop model, but because his students attend voluntarily as part of a mental-health treatment program and because, therefore, they are not *graded* according to academic or professional standards, he has been able to shift the philosophy and foci of his classes in significant ways. In a traditional setting, on a par with the setting MacCurdy teaches in, Park writes that

> [t]he dominant culture coerces minorities to adapt the dominant values, with the schools as a controlling force. Within the context of the writing workshop, subtle forces encourage writers to conform. There is a similar force at work in university writing programs: radical or non-conforming work is often leveled out through revision and class discussion. (21)

Though he does not say so expressly, it is reasonable to assume that Park would count people suffering from cognitive disorders (like PTSD) as part of the minority population, as they in fact are in the population at large.

Also, his reference to work being "leveled out through revision and class discussion" implies the sort of instructing a more traditional teacher like MacCurdy might do in the name of academic expectations and standards. The concepts of "lifewriting" and "freewrighting," to which I earlier alluded, come into play here, but first we must consider another unique feature of Park's pedagogical philosophy, and that lies in the importance of *expressive writing*. Park has been greatly influenced by the theories of James Britton, in particular Britton's concept of the three writing functions: transactional, poetic, and expressive. Park envisions Britton's model as a continuum with transactional at one extreme, poetic at the other, and expressive in the middle. Here is a model based on Park's brief definitions:

transactional…….…....…expressive …………....…..…poetic
(performs, persuades   (uses language that   (a verbal
instructs & is projected   is "close to self")   construct,
outside of itself)   an object

                                                                made out

                                                                 of

                                                                 language)

                                                                 (22)

In academic settings, transactional writing (such as analyses and research-based reports) is by far the dominant form, with poetic or aesthetic writing (creative writing) being a distant second, and expressive writing (exploration of self) a very distant third. Park says that expressive writing "continues to be an underdeveloped mode of writing in most academic settings," and this is in spite of studies suggesting "that the development of expressivist or personal writing that is 'close to the self' leads to greater skills and abilities in other language functions" (25). Reading Park's book, I realized

211

that in approximately 255 college course hours, including a B.S. in English education, an M.A. in English, and a Ph.D. in English studies, plus an odd assortment of graduate hours in primarily journalism, creative writing, and literature, I have been assigned virtually no expressive writing tasks. Except possibly for a handful of reflective statements in my undergraduate education courses, my writing has been almost exclusively transactional, minus some poetic/aesthetic pieces in creative writing classes.

Britton believed that expressive writing was foundational in the pursuit of effective communication skills and that the other modes could grow out of expressive-writing pedagogy. Park differs somewhat on this point, believing that "[t]he shift to other writing functions is not a 'natural' progression as some educators have assumed, and exposure to other discourses, and other language structures is necessary" (25). Nevertheless, for his students, who are all dealing with traumatic stress on some level, Park concentrates on expressive writing with freewriting being the fundamental method for producing text. From freewriting—which encourages composition minus the cognitive and creative restraints of worry about grammar, spelling, syntax … or, for that matter, *sense*—Park adopted modified versions of the free-wielding process. One of the modified versions is "lifewriting," developed by Roy Bentley and Syd Butler: "Lifewriting allows writers to use personal memory and experience to generate text that has significance to them to explore a sense of self" (34). Park explains further that while lifewriting can take the conventional forms of biography and autobiography, it can also be "memoirs, portraits, reminiscences, anecdotes, family histories, dream descriptions, memories, letters, or even oral transcripts"—all in the service of helping the writer "to 'fix' the self at a specific standpoint in life." Park has also neologized "freewriting" into "freewrighting" to emphasize "a form of writing that constructs an artifact that can be later deconstructed or molded into other forms of writing" (8). It sounds like mere wordplay, but in practice there is an important distinction between freewriting and freewrighting; with the latter, the text that is produced is viewed as significant and substantial, as text that is worthy of discussion and contemplation, as text that is to be taken seriously by the writer, the instructor, and fellow workshop participants. Whereas freewriting connotes something disposable, an initial step toward a product that generates mostly useless *stuff*, from which a useful kernel may be extracted if one is lucky.

In Park's workshops, then, in opposition to more traditional set-ups, emphasis is truly on process insofar as the process and product are in essence the same: Something else *may* develop from the expressively freewrighted text, something more transactional or poetic, something meant for an audience beyond the writer and a small group of like-oriented peers (Park would count himself a like-oriented peer)—but these issues of development and audience are hardly primary. He says,

> Expressive writing is far more complex than originally perceived by most researchers. Instead of being marginalized, expressive writing becomes the focus of true transformative education. In expressive writing, the two kinds of knowing, narrative and paradigmatic, are entwined, and meaning is created both for oneself and the culture. (152)

213

For the traumatized writer, who feels compelled to explore the source event and his or her state of being, Park's approach is much more in harmony with psychotherapeutic techniques, especially as they are illuminated by the field of neuropsychology. Students are facilitated in the act of telling and sharing their narratives (and thus being validated in their traumatic disorder), but without worries regarding final form, readability in the eyes of a hypothetical audience, and being judged as having a superior or inferior story of their trauma: *Sorry about your parents dying in that car accident—D+*.

The difficulty, of course, is that in the typical high school or college composition class, Park's approach based on lifewriting, freewrighting, and ungraded expressive writing would not pass academic muster. What is needed is a course that allows students to explore issues of self, including issues of the traumatized self if need be, but without the rigid expectations and standards of the typical writing classroom. Giving her her due, MacCurdy recognizes the benefits of such a course, one that attempts to "manage the problem" created by student needs versus academic expectations, and suggests that English departments "provide an upper-level personal essay course that has as its explicit goals developing a voice and engaging that voice in discussion of personal, social, and cultural contexts" (80). Meanwhile, the personal narrative could be introduced as "a separate genre" in the first-year writing course. She warns that "writing teachers in classes at all levels must be prepared to encounter student essays on painful topics." Her suggestions have merit, but they seem to privilege the academy's needs over the writers'. Regardless of scholastic level, these courses would still encourage students toward acceptable product as an end result. While it may seem a matter of semantics to some, I think a better approach is the burgeoning genre of *creative nonfiction*—a type of writing that combines the expressive self-exploration of the personal essay with the freedom of form and less rigid standards of aesthetic writing, often incorporating styles one finds in fictional prose and even poetry. Since creative nonfiction is deemed a type of creative writing, the discipline has already validated postmodern narrative techniques that are consistent with aspects of the traumatized voice. Students could produce text that is fragmented, repetitive, erratic in the conventions of genres, obscure in language usage—and yet still be in the schema of acceptability within the wide-open expectations of the form. That is not to say that *anything goes* under an umbrella of postmodernism, but certainly much more is possible in terms of shaping message and form, giving the writer and instructor much more leeway in working with the trauma narrative. Consistent with MacCurdy's suggestions, creative nonfiction could be a separate course—in institutions whose populations would support the necessary enrollment—or it could be a form included in a variety of language-oriented courses. I grant that such a class would tend not to be as free of expectations and standards as Park's classes, but it comes much closer to the mark than courses which focus on the essay form.

Creative Nonfiction vs. the Personal Essay

What is more, trauma-writing as creative nonfiction (versus personal essay) would be in keeping with Curtis White's call for the unshackling of the imagination, which he says has become "'institutionalized' in universities and museums and the inane cultural programming of the media, as if we feared having something so mad walking the streets"

(199). True trauma-writing (when it is not burdened with the constraints of essay form and composition-class rubrics) would be the sort of imaginative work that American culture ought to be promoting. White writes,

> The notion of the sublime as I have been using the term is the assertion of a belief in things (freedom, justice, creativity) that we could not give an adequate empirical account of—in other words, that are not True—but that nonetheless provide the premises for the force of our activities in the world. [¶] Art is thus most pragmatic, and most consequential for the social, when it is most sublime, when it asserts its intuitions about what it means to be free, just, or creative. Art is most properly useful when it doesn't know exactly what it is about. (190)

In writing about trauma, however, there is the danger of succumbing to what Lynn Worsham calls "narrative fetishism" as opposed to genuine "mourning." Working with these notions as discussed by Freud, narrative fetishism occurs when a writer focuses on specific elements of the traumatic event (often, the horrific elements) without working through the event as a whole, whereas "the story that is transmitted to another in the work of mourning bears witness not to the *meaning* of the event but to *the truth of the event*—the fact that it actually happened—and to *the truth of its incomprehensibility*, to the impossibility of constructing a comprehensible story and an adequate representation of the event" (178, Worsham's emphasis). In other words, narrative fetishism reduces the trauma to something that is easily understood by someone who had not experienced the trauma firsthand, while mourning accepts that the totality of the experience can never be fully articulated in a way that someone outside of the event can grasp. It seems then that mourning is associated with the sublimity of imagination that White attaches to art, while reductive fetishism is an appeal to the Middle Mind: the media's insistence on a trauma victim's expressing how he *feels* in a ten-second sound bite, for example, or the movie-of-the-week's sensationalizing rape's brutality. Again, trauma-writing within the context of creative nonfiction, whose focus may well be on the sublime, appears more fruitful than within typical composition studies, whose striving for logically structured clarity would encourage narrative fetishism.

Pedagogical Implication
and the Call for Further Research

I believe the pedagogical implications of my study are far-reaching. The psychic correlation between cultural trauma and postmodern literature opens up the possibilities to a variety of literary pursuits—some to confirm the correlation in other time periods and other cultures, and some to explore if other sorts of zeitgeists spawn other sorts of literary style. Such projects would continue to synthesize the contributions of numerous diverse disciplines, including history, psychology, sociology, and of course all manner of fine arts. My findings could also promote the practice of critical rhetoric whereby students learn to read beyond the dominant ideology in a text, literary or otherwise. Just as significant are the implications for composition studies as we find that a large number of students are in need of converting traumatic memory to narrative memory but whose needs are typically not met in the typical writing classroom, even in the classroom of teachers who purport to facilitate writing the trauma narrative. Each of these endeavors would contribute to the cause of redefining English studies in the twenty-first century, or as Bruce Robbins puts it, "[A]ll disciplines must submit themselves to some criteria of urgency, ethical concern, general usefulness. In other words, they must render some account of their social significance" (316).

While I believe I have demonstrated a plausible link between cultural trauma and postmodern narrative style, I recognize that there is still much work to be done in this area. For example, when I began my research, my working hypothesis was that all postmodern literature after 1945 could be accounted for as a result of a zeitgeist of trauma; however, I think differently now. I suspect that the first wave of postmodern literature (by writers like Gass, Pynchon, Vonnegut, Gaddis, Coover, and Barth) was linked to the psychic rupture caused by bombing Hiroshima and Nagasaki—as these first-wave writers were old enough to have a pre-Hiroshima consciousness as well as a post-Hiroshima one. In my analysis of William H. Gass I chose not to muddy the waters by discussing the powerful strain of nostalgia in Gass's work, but other critics have noted it (see, for example, Charlotte Byrd Hadella). And nostalgia for America before the Second World War (or at least for the benumbed 1950s) seems to be present in many of the postmodernists' works, sometimes setting their narratives in pre-1960s or at least flashing-back to a seemingly simpler time. I am thinking of novels like Gass's *Omensetter's Luck* and *The Tunnel*, Vonnegut's *Slaughterhouse-Five*, Gaddis's *The Recognitions*, Barth's *The Floating-Opera* and *The End of the Road*, and Pynchon's *V.*, *Gravity's Rainbow*, and *Against the Day*. I believe Joseph Dewey is onto something important in his observation that the Cuban Missile Crisis seemed to spark postmodernism in the early 1960s—that perhaps coming to the brink of nuclear Armageddon forced American authors to face the atomic terrors that had been a part of their lives since 1945 but had been repressed or dissociated until 1962. In support of this argument, which Dewey only begins to frame, would be observations by critics (like Brian McHale) who see some of the early work of postmodern heavyweights as not being *postmodern*, in particular Barth's first novels (mentioned above) and Pynchon's *V.* Another thought-provoking avenue regarding the seeming delayed reaction of postmodernists comes from Donald Antrim in his introduction to Donald Barthelme's novel *The Dead Father* (1975, republished 2004). Antrim says that writers like Barthelme, Pynchon, Barth, Coover, and Gaddis "could be read almost as guidebooks to an America in which nothing could be trusted on appearances, and everything good was in danger of vanishing, because our fathers had let us down" (ix). Paired with the Freudian notion of the primal father and its psychological aftermath, Antrim's observation is worthy of further scrutiny.

However, after this first wave of postmodern work, I am not convinced that later "postmodernists" (who were too young to know a pre-Hiroshima world) were writing as they were because of cultural trauma. I am thinking of writers like David Foster Wallace (1962-2008) and Shelley Jackson (b. 1963). I am of this generation, born in 1962, and for us the Cold War's nuclear threat was genuine, but the Second World War and Hiroshima and Nagasaki were part of *history* (like the Revolutionary War and Civil War). I recall neighbors who had built fallout shelters, or who had deliberately outfitted their basements for Armageddon; but they were not thought of as paranoids, perhaps merely pessimists. I recall the black-and-yellow fallout shelter symbols on buildings (one can still find a few). The basement of the bank where I worked as a janitor during high school was a designated fallout shelter. The vault and the janitor's room were down there, so anyone who survived the Apocalypse would have plenty of cash and cleaning supplies. I also recall that as a child (seven or eight) I was consciously afraid that the Vietnam War would still be going on when I reached fighting age. Oddly, what sparked that fear most consistently was *Gomer Pyle, U.S.M.C.* (a television show which ran from 1964 to 1969). Even though it was a comedy and made Marine Corps life look like summer camp, I must have connected its subject matter with what was being revealed about Vietnam on the nightly news. I recall laughing at the jokes in *Gomer Pyle*, but then becoming nauseated with fear later, thinking about it all alone in bed. When I spoke to my parents about my fears, they assured me that either the war would be over or the draft would be eliminated before I got out of high school—which seemed a long way off at the time. I do not recall their assurances helping much with the fear. Nevertheless, when I discovered writers like Vonnegut and Barth when I was in high school, I was very much drawn to their narrative styles. My love affair with Vonnegut's prose continued through college and into my early twenties. My best friend was a Vonnegut fan, too, and he and I ran lines from Vonnegut novels like other generations have run lines from Adam Sandler movies and the way my eldest son and his friends quote Dane Cook to each other. One such Vonnegutism survives today in Morrissey family vernacular in a pair of lines from *Galápagos* (1985). I will say to (or text or email) one of my sons "I can remember when this hotel had *five* guests," and the appropriate response is "Those were the days." My sons (unfortunately) have never read Vonnegut, leave be *Galápagos*, but they know it means something like "Even though things just suddenly got worse, the 'good' news is that they've always been pretty bad, so we shouldn't notice much of a difference." It is a good example of the black humor that characterizes the work of Kurt Vonnegut and, for that matter, many postmodernists—perhaps a black humor born of post-Hiroshima apocalyptic zeitgeist.

In any event, it seems there is scholarship to be done regarding the "postmodern gestation" between Hiroshima and the Cuban Missile Crisis: Is there a psychic connection, or is it mere coincidence that the first wave of truly postmodern novels did not appear until the turbulent 1960s? Also, are all postmodernists postmodern for the same reason (post-Hiroshima trauma), or did later generations connect with postmodern literary technique for other reasons (including, perhaps, commercial, as some postmodernists, like Vonnegut, were highly successful in terms of selling books and having their books made into popular movies). As I have been writing my dissertation, two related occurrences took place that could be brought into the discussion: a new *Star Trek* movie (based on the original 1960s characters) was released, and the fortieth anniversary of the first moon landing was observed. Both events sparked retrospectives on the late '60s, and a common thread between them is that the world of the original *Star Trek* was one of optimism regarding humanity's ability to set aside ideological differences and work together for the common good; meanwhile, the moon landing was viewed as an event that would bring all nations together as occupants of a small and fragile planet that seemed to be very much alone in the universe. Now we know that such views were unrealistically romantic, but the effects of these events (and others) on the cultural psyche, in the wake of the Cuban Missile Crisis in particular and in the context of a zeitgeist of nuclear trauma, could be a fruitful study. An interesting starting point may be the novel and film *2001: A Space Odyssey* (by Arthur C. Clarke and Stanley Kubrick, respectively, 1968). In the novel (which has not had the long-term cultural impact that the film generated), Clarke alludes to nuclear Armageddon from the very first chapter, and when the Star-Child David Bowman returns to earth at the end of the novel, he arrives just in time to avert the nuclear war that is erupting. In Kubrick's film, there is no mention whatsoever of nuclear escalation and impending doom, and the Star-Child's enigmatic return to earth seems to suggest a rebirth for humankind. Clarke and Kubrick worked closely together on the two projects (in fact, Clarke is credited as co-writer of the film's screenplay), and they were released within a few months of each other. Why were Clarke's and Kubrick's views regarding nuclear holocaust so different (as far as can be determined from the two versions of *2001*)? Why has the film become iconic, while the novel has been slipping toward obscurity, in spite of the several sequels that Clarke published?

While I did make a few remarks regarding gender among postmodernists, there is clearly much more work to be done in this area. I suggested that perhaps the male psyche was more affected (more conflicted) by the bombings of Japan because males predominantly had/have authored conflict and mass bloodshed throughout human history, while women have had much less to do with warfare and weapons development. Is this difference in gender role biological, or has cultural evolution had the most impact on male aggression and female nurturing? Or, since postmodernism resided for the most part in university English departments, and since those departments were dominated by males (as were the publishing and entertainment industries in general), does this explain why we have substantially more men than women postmodern writers? Moreover, when I began this dissertation I planned to devote some attention to postmodern poetry as well as prose. However, I limited myself to prose for two reasons: As McHale states in the preface to his *Postmodernist Fiction*, he originally intended the book to be *Postmodernist Writing* and to include both poetry and theater—but it turned out there was quite enough to say even with limiting his study to fictional prose; I share McHale's sentiment in that regard. In addition (and more important), my research in the correlation between trauma and postmodern style suggests that narration is paramount. That is, the link seems to involve storytelling, in that trauma victims are not able to tell their stories in a logical manner, and the key to treating PTSD rests with shifting the traumatic memory to narrative memory.

While there is such an animal as *narrative poetry* of course, poetry creation in general does not seem to be as closely tied to PTSD as the creation of prose. Therefore, is "postmodern poetry" merely a convenient term, and in fact postmodern poetry has little in common, in an originary sense, with postmodern prose? Or does poetry represent a distinctly different psychic response to trauma? Could poetry writing have the same therapeutic value as prose writing for trauma victims? If so, under what conditions or in what circumstances would poetry writing be effective? If poetry writing (even narrative poetry writing) does not have the same therapeutic value as prose writing for PTSD sufferers, what does this begin to tell us about the creation of poetry versus prose at the neuropsychic level? These and many more issues are raised by my research into the link between cultural trauma and postmodern technique; and further investigation of them all, I believe, would be of value to multiple disciplines and to society as a whole.

1. For the Ph.D. in English Studies from Illinois State University. The title of my dissertation was "Zeitgeist and the Zone: The Psychic Correlation between Cultural Trauma and 'Postmodern' Literature." This bulk of this book is essentially that dissertation.
2. See "Locating Our Common Humanity through Expressive Writing" in the Readings at the end of the book, pp. 292-305.

Bibliography

The Age of Bede. Trans. J. F. Webb. Ed. D. H. Farmer. London: Penguin, 1998. Print.

Alexander, Jeffrey C., et al. *Cultural Trauma and Collective Identity.* Berkeley: U of California P, 2004. Print.

American Psychiatric Association. *Diagnostic Criteria from DSM-IV-TR.* Arlington, VA: American Psychiatric Association, 2000. Print.

Ammon, Theordore G., ed. *Conversations with William H. Gass.* Jackson: UP of Mississippi, 2003. Print.

Anderson, Thomas P. *Performing Early Modern Trauma from Shakespeare to Milton.* Hampshire, England: Ashgate, 2006. Print.

The Anglo-Saxon Chronicle. Trans. James Ingram. Middlesex, England: The Echo Library, 2007. Print.

Antrim, Donald. Introduction. *The Dead Father.* By Donald Barthelme. New York: Farrar, Straus and Giroux, 2004. vii-x. Print.

Antze, Paul, and Michael Lambek, eds. *Tense Past: Cultural Essays in Trauma and Memory.* New York: Routledge, 1996. Print.

Argyros, Alex. "Narrative and Chaos." *New Literary History* 23 (1992): 659-73. *MLA International Bibliography.* Web. Feb. 15 2007.

Arrigo, Bruce A., and Catherine E. Purcell. "Explaining Paraphilias and Lust Murder: Toward an Integrated Model." *International Journal of Offender Therapy and*

Comparative Criminology 45.1 (2001): 6-31. *MLA International Bibliography*. Web. 20 June 2009.

Bassoff, Bruce. "The Sacrificial World of William Gass: *In the Heart of the Heart of the Country*." *Critique: Studies in Modern Fiction* 18.1 (1976): 36-58. *MLA International Bibliography*. Web. 19 July 2009.

Baudrillard, Jean. *The Ecstasy of Communication*. Trans. Bernard and Caroline Schutze. New York: Seiotext(e), 1988. Print.

—. *Seduction*. Trans. Brian Singer. New York: St. Martin's, 1990. Print.

Bede. *Ecclesiastical History of the English People*. Trans. Leo Sherley-Price and R. E. Latham. London: Penguin, 1990. Print.

Bellamy, Joe David, ed. Preface. *The New Fiction: Interviews with Innovative American Writers*. Urbana: U of Illinois P, 1974. ix-xv. Print.

Beowulf. Trans. R. M. Liuzza. Preface and Introduction. Peterborough, Ontario: Broadview, 2000. 9-49. Print.

Beowulf. Trans. Bruce Mitchell and Fred C. Robinson. Introduction. Malden, MA: Blackwell, 1998. 1-38. Print.

Beowulf. Trans. Michael Swanton. Introduction. Manchester, England: Manchester UP, 1997. 1-27. Print.

Best, Steven, and Douglas Kellner. *Postmodern Theory: Critical Interrogations*. New York: Guilford, 1991. Print.

Bjork, Robert E. "Scandinavian Relations." Pulsiano and Treharne 388-99.

Bjork, Robert E., and John D. Niles, eds. *A Beowulf Handbook*. Lincoln: U of Nebraska P, 1998. Print.

Brewin, Chris R. "Encoding and Retrieval of Traumatic Memories." Vasterling and Brewin 131-50.

—. "Implications for Psychological Intervention." Vasterling and Brewin 271-91.

Brown, Michelle P. "Anglo-Saxon Manuscript Production: Issues of Making and Using." Pulsiano and Treharne 102-117.

Buck, R. A. "Women and Language in the Anglo-Saxon Leechbooks." *Women and Language* 23.2 (2000): 41-50. *MLA International Bibliography*. Web. 10 July 2009.

Busch, Frederick. "But This Is What It Is to Live in Hell: William Gass's 'In the Heart of the Heart of the Country.'" *Modern Fiction Studies* 19 (1973): 97-109. Microfilm.

Butts, Richard. "The Analogical Mere: Landscape and Terror in *Beowulf*." *English Studies: A Journal of English Language and Literature* 68.2 (1987): 113-21. *MLA International Bibliography*. Web. 6 July 2009.

Calvino, Italo. *The Uses of Literature: Essays*. Trans. Patrick Creagh. San Diego, CA: Harcourt Brace, 1986. Print.

Cameron, M. L. *Anglo-Saxon Medicine*. Cambridge: Cambridge UP, 2006. Print.

Caruth, Cathy, ed. *Trauma: Explorations in Memory*. Baltimore, MD: The Johns Hopkins UP, 1995. Print.

Caruth, Cathy. *Unclaimed Experience: Trauma, Narrative, and History*. Baltimore, MD: The Johns Hopkins UP, 1996. Print.

Cheng, Anne. *The Melancholy of Race*. Oxford: Oxford UP, 2000. Print.

Constans, Joseph I. "Information-Processing Biases in PTSD." Vasterling and Brewin 105-30.

"A Conversation with Adam Braver." *Quiddity: International Literary Journal and Public-Radio Program*. 1.2 (2008): 27-42. Print.

Derrida, Jacques. *Of Gammatology*. 1967. Trans. Gayatri Chakravorty Spivak. Baltimore, MD: The Johns Hopkins UP, 1997. Print.

Dewey, Joseph. *In a Dark Time: The Apocalyptic Temper in the American Novel of the Nuclear Age*. West Lafayette, IN: Purdue UP, 1990. Print.

DiMatteo, Anthony. "The Trauma in Shakespeare and Early Modern Culture." *College Literature* 35.1 (2008): 175-97. *MLA International Bibliography*. Web. 15 July 2009.

Di Prete, Laura. *"Foreign Bodies": Trauma, Corporeality, and Textuality in Contemporary American Culture*. New York: Routledge, 2006. Print.

Duke, Lisa M., and Jennifer J. Vasterling. "Epidemiological and Methodological Issues in Neuropsychological Research on PTSD." Vasterling and Brewin 3-24.

Earl, James W. "Reading *Beowulf* with Original Eyes." Joy and Ramsey 687-704.

Eco, Umberto. "Irony as the Defining Principle of Postmodernism." *Postmodernism*. Ed. Derek Maus. San Diego, CA: Greenhaven, 2001. 43-48. Print.

Eng, David L. "Melancholia in the Late Twentieth Century." *Signs: Journal of Women in Culture and Society*. 25.4 (2000): 1275-1281. Print.

Erikson, Kai. "Notes on Trauma and Community." Caruth 183-99.

Farmer, D. H. Introduction. *The Age of Bede*. London: Penguin, 1998. 9-39. Print.

—. Introduction. *Ecclesiastical History of the English People*. By Bede. London: Penguin, 1990. 19-35. Print.

Fawkner, H. W. "The Concept of Taste: Theory in the Postmodernist Era." *Criticism in the Twilight Zone: Postmodern Perspectives on Literature and Politics*. Ed. Danuta Zadworna-Fjellestad and Lennart Björk. Stockholm, Sweden: Almqvist & Wiskell, 1990. 101-12. Print.

Felman, Shoshana. "Education and Crisis, or the Vicissitudes of Teaching." Caruth 13-60.

The Finnegans Wake Reading Society of New York. Directory of *Finnegans Wake* Reading Groups, n.d. Web. 15 July 2009.

Fogel, Stanley. "William H. Gass." *The Review of Contemporary Fiction* 25.2 (2005): 7-44. Print.

Foucault, Michel. *The Archaeology of Knowledge and The Discourse on Language*. 1971. Trans. A. M. Sheridan Smith. New York: Pantheon, 1972. Print.

—. *The Order of Things: An Archaeology of the Human Sciences*. 1966. New York: Vintage, 1994. Print.

—. "What is an Author?" Joy and Ramsey 501-17.

Freud, Sigmund. *Civilization and Its Discontents*. Trans. and ed. James Strachey. New York: Norton, 1989. Print.

—. *Group Psychology and the Analysis of the Ego*. Trans. and ed. James Strachey. New York: Norton, 1959. Print.

—. *Moses and Monotheism*. Trans. Katherine Jones. New York: Vintage, 1967. Print.

—. *Totem and Taboo: Resemblances Between the Psychic Lives of Savages and Neurotics*. Trans. A. A. Brill. Mineola, MN: Dover, 1998. Print.

Fromm, Erich. *The Anatomy of Human Destructiveness*. New York: Holt, Rinehart and Winston, 1973. Print.

Gass, William H. *Cartesian Sonata and Other Novellas*. 1998. Champaign, IL: Dalkey Archive P, 2009. Print.

—. *In the Heart of the Heart of the Country and Other Stories*. Boston, MA: Nonpareil, 1981. Print.

—. *Omensetter's Luck*. 1966. New York: Penguin, 1997. Print.

—. *The Tunnel*. 1995. Champaign, IL: Dalkey Archive P, 2007. Print.

Geyh, Paula, Fred G. Leebron, and Andrew Levy, eds. *Postmodern American Fiction*. Introduction. New York: Norton, 1998. ix-xxx. Print.

Godden, M. R. "Anglo-Saxons on the Mind." Liuzza 284-314.

Greenblatt, Stephen. "A Midsummer Night's Dream." *The Norton Shakespeare*. Ed. Stephen Greenblatt, et al. 2nd ed. New York, Norton, 2008. 839-48. Print.

Gusterson, Hugh. *People of the Bomb: Portraits of America's Nuclear Complex*. Minneapolis: U of Minnesota P, 2004. Print.

Hadella, Charlotte Byrd. "The Winter Wasteland of William Gass's 'In the Heart of the Heart of the Country.'" *Critique* 30.1 (1998): 49-58. *MLA International Bibliography*. Web. 16 July 2009.

Hassan, Ihab. *The Postmodern Turn: Essays in Postmodern Theory and Culture*. Columbus: The Ohio State UP, 1987. Print.

Heaney, Seamus. Introduction. *Beowulf*. Trans. by Seamus Heaney. New York: Norton, 2000. ix-xxx. Print.

Holmes, Jr., Urban T. *Medieval Man: His Understanding of Himself, His Society, and His World*. Ed. Urban T.
230

Holmes, III. Chapel Hill: U of North Carolina P, 1980. Print.

Howe, Nicholas. "The Cultural Construction of Reading in Anglo-Saxon England." Liuzza 1-22.

—. "The New Millennium." Pulsiano and Treharne 496-505.

Hutcheon, Linda. *A Poetics of Postmodernism: History, Theory, Fiction*. New York: Routledge, 1999. Print.

Isaacs, J. *An Assessment of Twentieth-Century Literature*. London: Secker & Warburg, 1951. Print.

Joy, Eileen A. "After Everything, *The Postmodern 'Beowulf*.'" Preface. Joy and Ramsey xiii-xxviii.

Joy, Eileen A., and Mary K. Ramsey, eds. "Liquid *Beowulf*." Introduction. Joy and Ramsey xxix-lxvii.

—. *The Postmodern* Beowulf: *A Critical Casebook*. Morgantown: West Virginia UP, 2006. Print.

Kenny, Michael G. "Trauma, Time, Illness, and Culture: An Anthropological Approach to Traumatic Memory." Antze and Lambek 151-71.

Kermode, Frank. *The Sense of an Ending: Studies in the Theory of Fiction*. Oxford: Oxford UP, 2000. Print.

Khamsi, Stephen. "The Birth Scene: Otto Rank Revival." *Healing of Pre- & Perinatal Trauma*. Birthpsychology, n.d. Web. 16 Oct. 2009.

Kiernan, Kevin S. Beowulf *and the* Beowulf *Manuscript*. Ann Arbor: The U of Michigan P, 1999. Print.

Klaeber, Frederick, ed. Beowulf *and* The Fight at Finnsburg. 1922. Lexington, MA: Heath, 1950. Print.

Kroth, Jerry. *Omen and Oracles: Collective Psychology in the Nuclear Age*. New York: Praeger, 1992. Print.

Lacan, Jacques. *Écrits*. Trans. Bruce Fink. New York: Norton, 2002. Print.

231

—. *The Seminar of Jacques Lacan Book XI: The Four Fundamental Concepts of Psychoanalysis*. Trans. Alan Sheridan. Ed. Jacques-Alain Miller. New York: Norton, 1998. Print.

Lambek, Michael, and Paul Antze. "Forecasting Memory." Introduction. Antze and Lambek xi-xxxviii.

Lendinara, Patrizia. "The Germanic Background." Pulsiano and Treharne 121-134.

Lifton, Robert Jay, and Greg Mitchell. *Hiroshima in America: Fifty Years of Denial*. New York: Grosset/Putnam, 1995. Print.

Linklater, Eric. *The Conquest of England*. New York: Dorset, 1990. Print.

Liuzza, R. M., ed. Introduction. *Old English Literature: Critical Essays*. New Haven, CT: Yale UP, 2002. xi-xxxvi. Print.

Luhmann, Niklas. "Why Does Society Describe Itself as Postmodern?" *Cultural Critique* 30 (1995): 171-85. *MLA International Bibliography*. Web. 16 Jan. 2007.

MacCurdy, Marian Mesrodian. *The Mind's Eye: Image and Memory in Writing about Trauma*. Amherst: U of Massachusetts P, 2007. Print.

Magennis, Hugh. "Audience(s), Reception, Literacy." Pulsiano and Treharne 84-101.

Marty, Myron A. *Daily Life in the United States, 1960-1990: Decades of Discord*. Westport, CT: Greenwood P, 1997. Print.

McDonald, Russ. *The Bedford Companion to Shakespeare: An Introduction with Documents*. 2nd ed. Boston, MA: Bedford/St. Martin's, 2001. Print.

McHale, Brian. *Postmodernist Fiction*. London: Routledge, 2001. Print.

McKerrow, Raymie E. "Critical Rhetoric: Theory and *Praxis*." *Contemporary Rhetorical Theory: A Reader*. Ed. John Luis Lucaites, Celeste Michelle Condit, and Sally Caudill. New York: Guilford, 1999. 441-63. Print.

McLaughlin, Janice. "Feminist Relations with Postmodernism: Reflections on the Positive Aspects of Involvement." *Journal of Gender Studies* 6.1 (1997): 5-15. *MLA International Bibliography*. Web. 14 June 2008.

McLaughlin, Robert L., ed. "Innovations." Introduction. *An Anthology of Modern and Contemporary Fiction*. Normal, IL: Dalkey Archive P, 1998. xi-xxv. Print.

Mizuno, Tomoaki. "The Magical Necklace and the Fatal Corslet in *Beowulf*." *English Studies: A Journal of English Language and Literature* 80.5 (1999): 377-97. *MLA International Bibliography*. Web. 10 July 2009.

Nelson, Cary. "The Linguisticality of Cultural Studies: Rhetoric, Close Reading, and Contextualization." *At the Intersection: Cultural Studies and Rhetorical Studies*. Ed. Thomas Rosteck. New York: Guilford, 1999. 211-25. Print.

Newman, Eiana, David S. Riggs, and Susan Roth. "Thematic Resolution, PTSD, and Complex PTSD: The Relationship Between Meaning and Trauma-Related Diagnoses." *Journal of Traumatic Stress* 10.2 (1997): 197-213. *MLA International Bibliography*. Web. 20 June 2009.

Niles, John D. "Introduction: *Beowulf*, Truth, and Meaning." Bjork and Niles 1-12.

—. "Myth and History." Bjork and Niles 213-32.

—. "Ring Composition and the Structure of *Beowulf*." *PMLA* 94.5 (1979): 924-35. Print.

"'Nothing but Darkness and Talk?': Writers' Symposium on Traditional Values and Iconoclastic Fiction." *Critique* 31.4 (1990): 233-55. *MLA International Bibliography*. Web. 19 June 2009.

O'Brien O'Keeffe, Katherine. Foreword. Beowulf *and the* Beowulf *Manuscript*. By Kevin S. Kiernan. Ann Arbor: The U of Michigan P, 1999. ix-xiii. Print.

—. *Visible Song: Transitional Literacy in Old English Verse*. Cambridge: Cambridge UP, 1990. Print.

Orchard, Andy. *A Critical Companion to* Beowulf. Cambridge, England: D. S. Brewer, 2007. Print.

—. *Pride and Prodigies: Studies in the Monsters of the* Beowulf-*Manuscript*. Toronto: U of Toronto P, 1995. Print.

Orton, Peter. "The Form and Structure of *The Seafarer*." Liuzza 353-380.

Park, Jeff. *Writing at the Edge: Narrative and Writing Process Theory*. New York: Peter Lang, 2005. Print.

Pulsiano, Phillip, and Elaine Treharne, eds. *A Companion to Anglo-Saxon Literature*. Malden, MA: Blackwell, 2008. Print.

Robbins, Bruce. "Epilogue: The Scholar in Society." *Introduction to Scholarship in Modern Languages and Literatures*. Ed. David G. Nicholls. New York: MLA, 2007. 312-30. Print.

Schneider, Richard J. "The Fortunate Fall in William Gass's *Omensetter's Luck*." *Critique: Studies in Modern Fiction* 18.1 (1976): 5-20. *MLA International Bibliography*. Web. 19 July 2009.

Silverblatt, Michael. "*The Tunnel*: A Small Apartment in Hell." *Review of Contemporary Fiction*. 24.3 (2004): 117-21. Print.

Slethaug, Gordon E. Preface. *Beautiful Chaos: Chaos Theory and Metachaotics in Recent American Fiction*. Albany: State U of New York P, 2000. iii-xxix. Print.

Sontag, Susan. *Regarding the Pain of Others*. New York: Farrar, Straus and Giroux, 2003. Print.

Southwick, Steven M., et al. "Neurobiological and Neurocognitive Alterations in PTSD: A Focus on Norepinephrine, Serotonin, and the Hypothalamic-Pituitary-Adrenal Axis." Vasterling and Brewin 27-58.

Stenton, Frank. *Anglo-Saxon England*. 3rd ed. Oxford: Oxford UP, 2001. Print.

Stewart, Susan. "An American Faust." *American Literature* 69.2 (1997): 399-416. *MLA International Bibliography*. Web. 18 June 2009.

Struve, Lynn A. "Confucian PTSD: Reading Trauma in a Chinese Memoir of 1653." *History & Memory: Studies in Representations of the Past* 16.2 (2004): 14-31. *MLA International Bibliography*. Web. 17 July 2009.

Swan, Mary. "Authorship and Anonymity." Pulsiano and Treharne 71-83.

Van Arsdall, Anne. *Medieval Herbal Remedies: The* Old English Herbarium *and Anglo-Saxon Medicine*. New York: Routledge, 2002. Print.

Van der Kolk, Bessel A., Alexander C. McFarlane, and Lars Weisaeth, eds. *Traumatic Stress: The Effects of*

Overwhelming Experience on Mind, Body, and Society. New York: Guilford, 2007. Print.

Van der Kolk, Bessel A., and Alexander C. McFarlane. "The Black Hole of Trauma." Van der Kolk, McFarlane, and Weisaeth 3-23.

Van der Kolk, Bessel A., and Onno van der Hart. "The Intrusive Past: The Flexibility of Memory and the Engraving of Trauma." Caruth 158-82.

Vasterling, Jennifer J., and Chris R. Brewin, eds. *Neuropsychology of PTSD: Biological, Cognitive, and Clinical Perspectives*. New York: Guilford, 2005. Print.

White, Curtis. *The Middle Mind: Why Americans Don't Think for Themselves*. San Francisco: HarperSanFrancisco, 2003. Print.

Whitehead, Anne. *Trauma Fiction*. Edinburgh: Edinburgh UP, 2004. Print.

"William H. Gass." Bellamy 32-44.

Wolcott, James. "Gass Attack." *The New Criterion* 13.6 (1995): 63-67. *MLA International Bibliography*. Web. 12 July 2009.

Worsham, Lynn. "Composing (Identity) in a Posttraumatic Age." *Identity Papers: Literacy and Power in Higher Education*. Ed. Bronwyn T. Williams. Logan, UT: Utah State UP, 2006. 170-95. Print.

Wright, David. "The Digressions in *Beowulf*." *Readings in Beowulf*. Ed. Stephen P. Thompson. San Diego, CA: Greenhaven, 1998. 125-33. Print.

Index

chaos theory, 8, 19, 122, 179, 180, 181

Chapman, John Watkins, 35

The Chariton Review, 142

Chauvin, Rémy, 22

Cheng, Anne, 81

Chernobyl, 26

Civilization and Its Discontents (Freud), 9, 14, 15

Clarke, Arthur C., 222

Clinton administration, 65, 69

Cnute the Great, 92

Cockayne, Oswald, 105

Cold War, 38, 66, 68, 69, 154, 156, 160, 164, 178, 194, 219

collective trauma (Erikson), 25, 26, 187

College Literature, 186

"Communion with the Dead" (Morrissey), 142

Communism, 156, 158

complex posttraumatic stress disorder (C-PTSD), 113, 118; *see also* posttraumatic stress disorder (PTSD)

Constans, Joseph I., 197, 207, 208

Cooper, James Fennimore, 46

Coover, Robert, 147, 148, 149, 151, 154, 178, 181, 183, 218, 219

Cotton Vitellius A. xv., 93; *see also Beowulf* manuscript

creative nonfiction, 215, 216

critical rhetoric, 189, 190, 192, 217

Cuban Missile Crisis, 124, 152, 164, 218, 221, 222

Culbertson, Roberta, 55

cultural mood, 27, 103, 189

Cultural Trauma and Collective Identity (Alexander et al.), 4

"Culture, Chaos and Order" (Isaacs), 76

Cuthbert, 102

The Dead Father (Barthelme), 219

Death (destruction), 9, 16, 20-21, 65, 128, 149

DeKoven, Marianne, 38

DeLillo, Don, 10, 79, 178, 181, 183, 194

Derrida, Jacques, 52, 53, 54

Dewey, Joseph, 70, 71, 83, 152, 153, 164, 181, 182, 183, 218, 219

Diagnostic and Statistical Manual of Mental Disorders (DSM), 61, 112

digressions (in *Beowulf*), 125, 134, 136; *see also* substory or substories

Di Prete, Laura, 41, 55, 122

DiMatteo, Anthony, 186-187

The Discourse on Language (Foucault), 54

dispersed (narrative) voice, *see* fragmented voice

239

freewrighting (Park), 195, 196, 211, 213, 214
Freud, Sigmund, 2, 3, 4, 5, 6, 7, 8, 9, 10, 11, 12, 13, 14, 15, 16, 17, 18, 19, 20, 21, 22, 23, 25, 26, 40, 44, 50, 52, 54, 56, 60, 67, 68, 71, 80, 94, 108, 151, 153, 183, 185, 216, 219; Freudian psychoanalysis, 1
Fromm, Erich, 78, 79
Fukuyama, Francis, 69

Gaddis, William, 10, 147, 179, 181, 183, 209, 218, 219
Galápagos (Vonnegut), 220
Gass, William H., 2, 10, 58, 79, 138, 147, 151, 154, 155, 157, 158, 159, 160, 161, 162, 163, 164, 165, 166, 167, 168, 169, 170, 171, 172, 173, 174, 175, 177, 180, 181, 185, 209, 218; at Brown University symposium, 147, 149, 154, 181; *Cartesian Sonata*, 166; *Eyes*, 185; "In the Heart of the Heart of the Country," 154, 156, 160, 162, 164, 175; *In the Heart of the Heart of the Country and Other Stories*, 58; *Middle C*, 185; *Omensetter's Luck*, 167, 169, 170, 218;

"The Pedersen Kid," 164, 165; *The Tunnel*, 167, 171, 174, 176, 180, 218; "Uncle Balt and the Nature of Being," 176
Geyh, Paula, 38, 51
Gide, André, 76
Giesen, Bernhard, 81, 176
Godden, M. R., 141
Gomer Pyle, U.S.M.C., 220
Granofsky, Ronald, 41
Grass, Gunter, 147
Gravity's Rainbow (Pynchon), 58, 121, 177, 218
Greenblatt, Stephen, 188
Grendel (fictional character), 125, 127, 129, 130, 132, 133
Grendel's mother (fictional character), 127, 129, 132, 133
Group Psychology and the Analysis of Ego (Freud), 11, 12
Guilt and Innocence in Hitler's Germany (fictional book), 171, 174
Gusterson, Hugh, 66, 68, 69

Hadella, Charlotte Byrd, 155, 157, 158, 160, 161, 162, 163, 218
Hamlet (Shakespeare), 187, 188
Harris, Joseph, 137
Hassan, Ihab, 57, 77, 149
Hawkes, John, 147
Heaney, Seamus, 126
Hengest, 126

241

243

244

245

247

Readings

In order to demonstrate how trauma theory can be used to analyze literary texts, I have provided three readings, comprised of a collection of conference papers I have delivered on the work of William H. Gass. You will note that there is some overlap with material discussed in the main text of the book, especially regarding the first two of the three papers, whereas the third (focused on the novella "The Pedersen Kid") draws heavily on material not appearing in the book. I have also included a fourth reading that speaks to trauma writing from a pedagogical perspective. The paper does draw from the book, especially Chapter 7. The three papers focused on the work of William H. Gass were delivered at The Louisville Conference on Literature and Culture Since 1900, University of Louisville, in 2010, 2012, and 2013, respectively; the paper dealing with trauma writing was the introductory keynote address at the Fifth International Conference on Language, Society and Culture in Asian Contexts, held in Hue, Vietnam, in 2018. Please note that these supplemental readings are not reflected in the index.

The readings are the following:

- In the Heart of the Heart of the Cold War (pp. 253-268)

- William H. Gass's "Very Cold Winter" (pp. 269-281)

- The Trauma of Alcohol Abuse (pp. 282-293)

- Locating Our Common Humanity through Expressive Writing (pp. 294-308)

In the Heart of the Heart of the Cold War:
Cultural Trauma and the Fiction of William H. Gass

In a writers' symposium on postmodern literature held at Brown University in 1989, Robert Coover, in his welcoming remarks, gave the impression that the writing style which became known as postmodernism sprang up in the 1950s and '60s almost by sheer coincidence. Among the symposium participants were Leslie Fiedler, John Hawkes, Stanley Elkin, William Gass, Donald Barthelme, and William Gaddis. Coover said, "[T]his group sought out some form, some means by which to express what seemed to them new realities" ("'Nothing'" 233). However, Coover goes on to suggest a remarkably thin theory as to why so many writers, all working in relative isolation, began constructing narrative in uncannily similar styles:

> We felt we were all alone. No one was reading us, nor was anyone writing remotely like the sort of writing we were doing until, in the little magazines, we began slowly to discover one another. Few of us knew one another at the time we began writing. There was a uniform feeling among writers at that time that something had to change, something had to break, some structure had to go. And that was, I think, what most united us.

Even though the panel was intended to be a debate, and not merely a discussion, not a single writer challenged Coover's explanation for the emergence of postmodern style. At first this assessment may seem startling—that some of the keenest and best-educated minds who were at the forefront of producing and (many) critiquing literary postmodernism accepted the premise that postmodern

253

narrative style more or less just happened; essentially that individuals writing in isolation on various continents, including North and South America, and Europe, just all happened to begin writing in the same sorts of ways, all in a narrow time span, from about 1950 to 1965. According to Coover, writers, with virtual simultaneity, decided to abandon modernist realism for something fragmented, repetitive, largely unrealistic and illogical, and highly intertextual.

A more cogent explanation, I believe, rests with trauma theory: The trauma of the nuclear age, which was experienced by the entirety of Western culture (not to mention Eastern), affected the psyches of these writers in a way that resulted in postmodern literary style—a style, according to theorists like Anne Whitehead, Cathy Caruth, and Laura Di Prete, that reflects the traumatized voice. Meanwhile, historians Jay Lifton and Greg Mitchell have made several provocative assertions regarding twentieth-century zeitgeist as it suddenly evolved after the Second World War. One is that the "[s]truggles with the Hiroshima narrative have to do with a sense of meaning in a nuclear age, with our vision of America and our sense of ourselves" (xvi). Another is that Americans were deeply and immediately conflicted with the atomic bombings of Hiroshima and Nagasaki, that they experienced the "contradictory emotions of approval and fear the bomb evoked, a combination that has continued to disturb and confuse Americans ever since" (33). A third assertion is that "[o]dinary people [. . .] experienced their own post-Hiroshima entrapment—mixtures of nuclearism and nuclear terror, of weapons advocacy and fearful anticipation of death and extinction" (306). And all of this internal conflict, much

254

of which resides in the unconscious, has contributed to a "sense of the world as deeply absurd and dangerous" (335).

It is quite possible that Coover and the other postmodernists at the Brown University symposium experienced the same sort of repression and dissociation that individual trauma victims frequently do. It is not uncommon for people suffering the symptomology of posttraumatic stress disorder to have no conscious recollection whatsoever of the traumatizing event, or to have a dissociated recollection. Coover also discussed writing as "a kind of therapy." He said, "There are things you have to work your way through. There are issues that have to be confronted[. …] So you work that out in fictional forms, and you do feel that Freudian answer, that kind of power over what would otherwise be your impotent life" (242). Hence Coover recognized the unsettling cultural climate of post-Hiroshima America and how it contributed to narrative style; also, his view of writing-as-therapy is consistent with trauma theorists who suggest that postmodern techniques are akin to victims' struggling to transform *traumatic* memory into *narrative* memory.

In his examination of the apocalyptic temper in the American novel, Joseph Dewey theorizes about the literary community's response to Hiroshima and Nagasaki, which he describes as "slow in coming." Dewey writes, "[T]he literary conscience of America did not seem ready in the 1940s and even in the 1950s to engage the menace of the mushroom cloud" (8). At first, writers, along with the rest of their culture, experienced a "psychic numbing [. . .] in the face of such catastrophe." In the '50s, notes Dewey, "the American literary community pondered the bomb only in tentative ways." He references "a glut of forgettable

255

speculative fiction" that appeared during the decade. In the early '60s, however, "the American novel began to work with the implications of the nuclear age" (9). Dewey speculates that the Cuban Missile Crisis—"the nuclear High Noon over Cuba"—may have acted as a catalyst for writers in general to "begin to think about the unthinkable." Dewey does not approach his subject in this way, but he seems to be accounting for the dual starting point for American postmodern literary style, which some trace to the mid 1940s and others to the '60s. Nor does Dewey tend to speak in psychological terms, but he seems to be suggesting that American writers were by and large *repressing* the atomic blasts for nearly two decades, until nuclear Armageddon loomed in 1962, which caused the cultural literary psyche to begin to confront the source of its trauma, if only dissociatively. The scenario that Dewey suggests corresponds with the way many individuals respond to a traumatic event. Perhaps the fear of nuclear Apocalypse was part of the American psyche since 1945, but it seemed unreal until 1962's standoff with Cuba and its ally the Soviet Union. It is also useful to recall that groups—entire nations even—can respond to trauma just as individuals do. In fact, Neil J. Smelser, in his work on cultural trauma in particular, notes that societies can undergo a delayed response to trauma akin to the Freudian notion of a breakdown in repression, which "only succeeded in incubating, not obliterating the threat"—though he qualifies the analogy as not being perfect (Alexander et al. 51).

While evidence of a link between post-Hiroshima trauma and postmodern technique can be found, with greater or lesser conspicuousness, in the work of all writers who occupy the established pantheon of postmodernists, I think the connective tissue is most apparent in the fiction of William H. Gass, one of the writers at the Brown symposium, and, interestingly, the writer Coover called "our real living biographer of the human mind" (242). In his work, which was begun in the mid 1940s (when Gass was in his twenties) but did not start to appear in print consistently until the 1960s, Gass often alludes to trauma and symptoms of posttraumatic stress disorder (though not specifically by these labels), and he cites directly and indirectly the nuclear age as the source of widespread anxiety. It must be stated upfront that Gass's childhood was, by his own description, miserable, raised by an alcoholic mother and an agonistic father; and one could certainly point to these influences for his prose's negativity. There is no question that these facts have affected Gass's writing, much of which is overtly autobiographical; however, I believe that the Cold War zeitgeist had an even greater impact on his storytelling. One might even conjecture that the insecurities caused by Gass's childhood made the fear associated with that zeitgeist even more potent. The psychological community has long recognized that individuals respond differently to trauma due to a variety of factors, including their mental health when they experience the trauma, and even their genetic predisposition to dealing with traumatic stress.

In any event, a good place to begin is Gass's well-known short story "In the Heart of the Heart of the Country," which appeared in *New American Review* and then in a collection by the same title in 1968 (though Gass says that it was written much earlier, implying the beginning of the decade (Bellamy 39)). The oddly and disjointedly segmented *story* features a disillusioned poet-teacher narrator living in a small Indiana town, called simply "B," a town which represents (it has been widely noted and in fact acknowledged by Gass) W. B. Yeats's Byzantium from the poem "Sailing to Byzantium" (1927). The short story has generated a fair amount of critical attention over the past forty years, and much of that criticism examines the psychological underpinnings of the narrative. In one of the earliest studies, in 1973, Frederick Busch writes, "[Gass's poet-narrator] is caught in the heart of the country, he is fallen. And the country he has come to is his mind. [. . .] This little story is a saga of the mind" (99, 100). Similarly, Charlotte Byrd Hadella says that the "narrator/poet is miserable, lonely, and lost in a fragmented world, much like the world of Eliot's *The Waste Land*, because he fails to participate fully in either art or life" (49). As such, "the narrator has left one world and entered another—the world of his own imagination." What is more, Hadella claims that "[w]ith the fragmented structure of his story, Gass conveys a subliminal message of isolation, loneliness, and departmentalized perception of his narrator" (50). Both critics are unwittingly keying on psychological components of the story that are mimetic of posttraumatic stress disorder—the unbidden merging of real and unreal worlds, profound feelings of disconnectedness with one's self and others.

These analyses are useful to be sure, and in fact I want to look at some of the same passages in the story that these critics cite, but I believe even more can be gleaned from the story via a trauma-theory paradigm. Given the insightfulness of these critics' observations, I am struck by an omission that they and other commentators have committed in their readings of the narrative. No one has paid any attention whatsoever to a passage that I see as key

258

to understanding the narrator's disjointed psyche. In a section subtitled "Politics," the narrator criticizes his fellow townspeople (and Americans in general I would say) by stating, "I have known men [. . .] who for years have voted squarely against their interests. Nor have I ever noticed that their surly Christian views prevented them from urging forward the smithereening, say, of Russia, China, Cuba, or Korea" (197). Here the narrator makes direct reference to using nuclear weapons against Cold War enemies—attacks which would be squarely against American interests (as it would provoke retaliation, including nuclear retaliation) and which contradict the Christian morality that the majority of Americans claim to advocate. This atomic-bombing reference does not come out of the blue, so to speak. In an earlier section also subtitled "Politics," the narrator alludes to "the Russians [. . .] launching [. . .] their satellite" (186), and in "Education" he says that at school "children will be taught to read and warned against Communism" (187). Taking into account these Cold War references, the narrator's disposition and the townspeople he describes sound very much like the divided, post-Hiroshima psyches that Lifton and Mitchell discuss: "By the 1960s, Americans were living a nuclear 'double life': aware that any moment each of us and everything around us could be suddenly annihilated, yet at the same time proceeding with our everyday, nitty-gritty lives and conducting 'business as usual'" (351).

Americans, in short, were divided in two, with their *measured self* (which was interested in making a comfortable and meaningful life) being in constant conflict with their *apocalyptic self* (which accepted that the nuclear end was at hand and therefore every action was irrelevant). Hadella is noting this conflicted duality in the story when she writes that "the narrator's mood is a perpetual winter. The poet/narrator avoids thinking of spring as the season of rebirth and renewal. Thus, even when he does mention spring rain, the rain mentioned is only a memory, and it is not associated with desire or awakening to life" (51). It is as if Gass's narrator, with his measured self, desires a future (the coming of spring rains), but will not allow himself to believe it will arrive because of his apocalyptic self, the self that envisions a spring rain that causes "the trees [to] fill with ice" (181).

Hadella's careful study is mainly concerned with Gass's use of weather imagery, especially winter. In the context I am framing, the winter and its snow become even more psychologically significant as mimetic of a *nuclear* winter and its radioactive (or *dirty*) snow. Before looking at winter/snow references in way of support, I want to turn to the "Weather" section that describes a summer heatwave in B as Gass uses language suggestive, I think, of a nuclear blast. The passage is lengthy but well worth examining:

> In the summer light, too, the sky darkens a moment when you open your eyes. The heat is pure distraction. Steeped in our fluids, miserable in the folds of our bodies, we can scarcely think of anything but our sticky parts. Hot cyclonic winds and storms of dust crisscross the country. In many places, given an indifferent push, the wind will still coast for miles, gather resource and edge as it goes, cunning and force. [. . .] Sometimes I think the land is flat because the winds have leveled it, they blow so constantly. In any case, a gale can grow in a field of corn that's as hot as a draft from hell, and to receive

260

it is one of the most dismaying experiences of this life, though the smart of the same wind in winter is more humiliating, and in that sense even worse. (180-81)

On the one hand, this *is* a wonderfully apt description of a Midwestern heatwave, but Gass's language as it relates to a nuclear blast cannot be easily dismissed: melting, even liquefying "bodies"; widespread devastation by "hot cyclonic winds and storms of dust" driven by "cunning and force"; a flattened landscape, "leveled" by "a draft from hell"; a "dismaying" life experience, but the "wind in winter" to follow is in a "sense even worse." Then there is the winter and its snow that are so closely linked to death. The narrator says, "I would rather it were the weather that was to blame for what I am and what my friends and neighbors are—we who live here in the heart of the country. Better the weather, the wind, the pale dying snow . . . the snow—why not the snow?" (191). Images of winter/snow connected to death continue in this "Weather" section. He says, "Still I suspect the secret's in this snow, the secret of our sickness, if we could only diagnose it, for we are all dying like the elms in Urbana" (192). The passage ends with the narrator's assertion "[. . .] what a desert we could make of ourselves—from Chicago to Cairo, from Hammond to Columbus—what beautiful Death Valleys." Again, viewed through the prism of the Cold War mentality and how the unconscious must have been affected by the sense of impending nuclear doom, it is reasonable that at some level Gass is describing atomic annihilation and the aftermath for those lucky or unlucky enough to survive the attacks.

An important aspect of the conflicted post-Hiroshima psyche is the sense of responsibility and guilt associated with

261

bombing Japan, combined with pride in American resolve and ingenuity, and an acceptance of the "Hiroshima narrative" propaganda that claimed the attack to be necessary, even justified—and Hadella picks up on these vibes in "In the Heart of the Heart of the Country" as well. She writes, "Through the narrator's obsessive attention to weather, Gass emphasizes a controlling irony in the story: though the narrator complains about the weather, he is the one who is responsible for the world in which he lives. His complaints suggest that he does not accept this responsibility" (51). Hadella's analysis reflects to the letter the psychological turmoil Americans found themselves grappling with, according to the research of historians Lifton and Mitchell.

There is much more that could be said of "In the Heart of the Heart of the Country" (indeed, all of Gass's work) via a trauma-theory paradigm, but in the interest of time I want to shift my focus to the author's masterwork, the long and difficult novel *The Tunnel*, published in 1995 but begun in 1966. The plot of the novel, in a nutshell, involves the narrator, history professor William Kohler, sitting down to write the introduction to *his* masterwork, a book titled *Guilt and Innocence in Hitler's Germany*, but instead writing a memoir about his unhappy childhood, mediocre career, and loveless marriage. He writes in his basement and at some point, for reasons that are never crystal clear, decides to start digging a tunnel beneath his house to make a surreptitious and superfluous escape. The novel is especially intriguing when viewed through the lens of trauma theory, but in the interest of brevity I'll focus mainly on a section of *The Tunnel* that appeared as a stand-alone piece in *The Kenyon Review* in 1979, titled "The Old Folks"; it was retitled "The Ghost Folks" in a section of the novel (on pages 128-142, Dalkey Archive edition) with few, but significant, changes. Kohler and his wife, Marty/Martha, along with their two sons visit his parents, returning to his childhood home and all of its unpleasant memories and associations. Kohler's mother is an alcoholic and his father a quarrelsome racist.

The story is set in approximately 1950, and Kohler says that the emotion he feels when he sets foot in his childhood home is rage. When his boys act up, for which he can't blame them, he says, "[W]hat I need is total obliteration, now—now that we have the bomb, we can all be blown back into our original pieces with one clean disintegration, instead of being pulled apart slowly with dental pliers" (161; 130 in the novel). He goes on to speak of the inevitability of nuclear annihilation, saying that when a child, "I believed in doom in those days. Now, when the world ends, I doubt it will even whimper" (167; 135). Interestingly, the latter sentence, expressing the inevitability of annihilation, is deleted from the novel, which may reflect Gass's, as well as the country's, waning certainty that nuclear war with the Soviets was just a matter of time. In fact, direct references to the Second World War, to Japan, to Hiroshima, to the bomb, and so forth are frequent in the first half or so of the novel, and virtually nonexistent in the last half. I am attempting to determine the stages of development of the book, but it seems, at this point, that the overall structure of *The Tunnel* does follow, by and large, the chronology of Gass's composing it. This study is aided by the fact that several parts of the book appeared in print as stand-alone pieces over the decades. Also, in a 1971

263

interview, Gass claimed to have written 300 manuscript pages of *The Tunnel* (McCauley 11).

The idea of responsibility, especially shared responsibility, for a ruined future (or perhaps no future at all) is expressed in various ways in "The Old Folks." As Kohler and Marty are traveling with their children to his parents' home, he says that the children "cannot realize to what profound degree the adults are conspiring against them" (159; 128). Specifically, Kohler is referring to himself and his wife, but much of the story deals with human history on a broad scale, as Kohler mixes in sparring theoretical conversations he's had with his colleagues in the history department, so there is a sense that humanity in the twentieth century has conspired against itself. Twice in the story, including its opening words, Kohler asks, rhetorically, "Who is not in league?" (159, 172; 128, 139). On the most superficial level, Kohler is suggesting in the first reference that he and his wife are in league against their unsuspecting children. But given the facts that the question is repeated in connection with a conversation between Kohler's history department colleagues and that Gass's attention to linguistic nuance is second to none, the iteration is especially provocative. The word *league* of course means, among other definitions, conspiring with others for questionable purposes; but in the context of the story, *league* may be suggestive of the League of Nations, formed in 1920 in an effort to strive for world peace. Even though Woodrow Wilson put forward the initial idea, the United States never officially joined the League. So one way of interpreting Kohler's question may be "Who is not working toward world peace?" and one legitimate answer would be "the United States." This reading is bolstered by the fact that immediately after the repetition of the question Kohler morbidly describes his colleagues as mere "skulls [whose shadows] drifted across the opaque glass" (172; 139).

My final point concerns the image of the atomic mushroom cloud, which Joseph Dewey calls a representation of "the last crisis in human history," as "humans [. . . rather than God] would plot, construct, and then execute their own demise" (7). Gass seems to dissociate the mushroom-cloud shape as tornadic rather than atomic, meaning that he often writes of tornadoes, cyclones, and whirlwinds, and of their destructive abilities. Kohler refers frequently to a childhood episode when a tornado passed so near the house that it blew the shattered windows inward. In "The Old Folks," Kohler refers to himself and his wife as "whirlwinds" who have taken their children from a place of happiness and contentment to set them down here in his parents' cheerless home (161; 130). More interesting, still, is Kohler's discussion of a reoccurring nightmare in which he is falling toward the sea, anticipating his own painful death. In the novel, Kohler visually represents his falling—bomb-like— via text that takes the shape of a tornado, or a mushroom cloud:

it was like falling into the sea
to pass that open door
a wind like cold water
space a cold glass
flights of fish
surprise
my nose
my ah!
breath
goes

265

f

a

s

s

s

t

and all this has happened before (86)

The "terror" of the dream "wakes" Kohler, who feels "as if I were back in the army and my fall were a part of my duty" (85). It seems significant that Kohler connects the image to the military, the arm of the government most associated with the use of atomic weapons. There is no time to develop the idea further, but this tornado/mushroom-cloud shape also seems to represent the process of moving from chaos (life) to entropic order (death) that Kohler alludes to throughout, directly or indirectly, and it also suggests the overall shape of the novel's narrative structure, as we move from broad, global, historical issues toward an ending section that focuses quite concretely on Kohler's tunneling project in his basement, and his wife's discovery of what he's been doing these many months behind her back.

To bring this to a close, I will remind us that the first-wave of postmodern writers seemed preoccupied with bombs and the act of bombing. A few examples would be Pynchon's *V.* and *Gravity's Rainbow*; Vonnegut's *Slaughterhouse-Five* and *Mother Night*; Heller's *Catch-22*; and DeLillo's *Underworld*. These and other postmodernists may have been responding to their culture's traumatized psyche—a psyche that was conflicted between nuclearism and nuclear terror, a psyche that was attempting to move the Hiroshima narrative from traumatic memory to narrative memory, and thus come to terms with what the United States

266

had unleashed on the world . . . and on itself. Kohler seems to conclude that the most optimistic thing that could be said about the bomb is that it "will probably bring neither extermination nor peace, but prolong the life and use of conventional arms" (515)—an idea that he sums up in the limerick:

> There was a professor of history
> who explained to his class every misery
> of our human state:
> 1 war is man's fate;
> 2 hate pays for hate;
> 3 all help comes too late;
> 4 our lives don't relate;
> but why this is so stays a mystery. (535)

Works Cited

Bellamy, Joe David, ed. *The New Fiction: Interviews with Innovative American Writers*. Urbana: U of Illinois P, 1974. Print.

Busch, Frederick. "But This Is What It Is to Live in Hell: William Gass's 'In the Heart of the Heart of the Country.'" *Modern Fiction Studies* 19 (1973): 97-109. Microfilm.

Dewey, Joseph. *In a Dark Time: The Apocalyptic Temper in the American Novel of the Nuclear Age*. West Lafayette, IN: Purdue UP, 1990. Print.

Gass, William H. *In the Heart of the Heart of the Country and Other Stories*. 1968. Boston, MA: Godine, 1981. Print.

—. "The Old Folks." *The Best American Short Stories of 1980*. Ed. Stanley Elkin. New York: Houghton Mifflin. Print.

—. *The Tunnel*. 1995. Champaign, IL: Dalkey Archive P, 2007. Print.

Hadella, Charlotte Byrd. "The Winter Wasteland of William Gass's 'In the Heart of the Heart of the Country.'" *Critique* 30.1 (1998): 49-58. Print.

Lifton, Robert Jay, and Greg Mitchell. *Hiroshima in America: Fifty Years of Denial*. New York: Grosset/Putnam, 1995. Print.

McCauley, Carole Spearin. "William H. Gass." *Conversations with William H. Gass*. Ed. Theodore G. Ammon. Jackson: UP of Mississippi, 2003. Print.

"'Nothing but Darkness and Talk?': Writers' Symposium on Traditional Values and Iconoclastic Fiction." *Critique* 31.4 (1990): 235-55. Print.

Smelser, Neil J. "Psychological Trauma and Cultural Trauma." *Cultural Trauma and Collective Identity*. Ed. Jeffrey C. Alexander et al. Berkeley: U of California P, 2004. 31-59. Print.

William H. Gass's "Very Cold Winter":
The Trauma of the Fallout Shelter Frenzy
as Expressed in *The Tunnel*

William H. Gass's long and densely postmodern novel *The Tunnel*, which won the American Book Award in 1996, has perplexed both casual readers and literary critics, whose reactions and readings have varied widely, to say the least. Indeed, H. L. Hix, author of *Understanding William H. Gass*, writes that the "early responses [of which there were many] ranged from wildly enthusiastic to contemptuous" (77). Moreover, not only is *The Tunnel* an odd novel—bringing together just about every postmodern trope ("cram[med] together like [rush-hour] commuters," Gass has said [Ziegler 14])—but its writing and publishing history is equally strange in the saga of American letters as Gass worked on the project for nearly thirty years, publishing excerpts from it in literary journals, commercial periodicals, and with boutique presses on nineteen occasions from 1969 to 1988. Regardless of whether their opinion fell on the "wildly enthusiastic" or the "contemptuous" end of the spectrum, most critics agreed that *The Tunnel* warranted multiple readings and extensive excavation. When that work has been undertaken, Irving Malin has conjectured that Gass's magnum opus will be hailed, along with Nabokov's *Pale Fire*, as "the most significant novel written since World War II" (11).

Hence, with pick and shovel in hand, I arrive bearing some finds from the dig—a dig, by the way, which has not been especially extensive thus far: A review of the MLA International Database yielded only 30 articles dealing with *The Tunnel* since its publication, and the majority were

269

generated by the same handful of Gass devotees. What's more, apparently there have been no scholarly publications on *The Tunnel* in nearly seven years. Perhaps because Gass himself has been so concerned with language (especially metaphor, the subject of his doctoral dissertation, completed at Cornell in 1954), the readings of his work have often focused on its textual complexities, and only a very few have treated *The Tunnel*, especially, as an expression of trauma. And if traumatic experience is cited as a wellspring of Gass's writing, it is generally his well-known miserable childhood that is named as the culprit. In fact, Hix's essential *understanding* of Gass is that he "writes to get even for his childhood, his resentment for which he has clearly stated" (1). However, no one seems to have noticed that Gass's writing career falls perfectly in line with the extreme anxiety caused in Western culture by the United States' unleashing of atomic weapons and the initiation of the Cold War—events about which Gass has written directly numerous times. What is more, no one that I've read has made the, what I consider, obvious connection between the fact that Gass began writing *The Tunnel* at the height of the U.S.'s fallout shelter frenzy, which was initiated, according to Kenneth D. Rose, in 1961 by John F. Kennedy's Berlin speech, wherein the President called for an aggressive shelter-building program in response to the Soviet Union's threats that there would be war if the West did not withdraw from the German capital. Kennedy's response to Khrushchev was "Then let there be war, Mr. Chairman. It's going to be a very cold winter" (2).

Given the publishing history of the *The Tunnel*, not to mention the brevity of this presentation, I'm going to focus my analysis on the first two sections of the novel to appear in print—"We Have Not Lived the Right Life" in *New American Review* in 1969, and "Why Windows Are Important To Me" in *TriQuarterly* in 1971—and I'm also going to draw from a paper I presented at the conference in 2010 which provides my study's trauma-theory underpinnings. [See "In the Heart of the Cold War" above.]

First, however, it's necessary to reflect on the fallout shelter phenomenon and its myriad effects on the American people's psyches—effects that I believe often manifest themselves in Gass's narrative in which the first-person protagonist, history professor William Kohler, goes to his basement to write the final piece of his masterwork on Nazi Germany, thirty years in the making, but instead begins a meandering autobiography of his painful childhood, lackluster career, and loveless marriage; and, meanwhile, for reasons that are never quite clear, Kohler starts digging a surreptitious and superfluous tunnel behind his basement furnace. While Kennedy's 1961 speech may mark the beginning of the United States' frenzy over fallout shelter-building, it was the previous administration, under Eisenhower, that first broached the topic. For about a decade after the bombings of Hiroshima and Nagasaki, the U.S. government and consequently its people were able to convince themselves that nuclear warfare wasn't all that different from more traditional forms of warfare; however, atomic tests in the mid-fifties demonstrated just how catastrophic a nuclear attack could be on the United States. Ralph Lapp, civil defense editor of the *Bulletin of the Atomic Scientists*, wrote in 1954 that "the new peril from radioactive fall-out is more than just a threat to civil defense—it is a peril to humanity" (Rose 25-26). In the following issue of the *Bulletin*, Val Peterson, Eisenhower's chief civil defense

271

administrator, was quoted as saying that life after a nuclear war would "be stark, elemental, brutal, filthy, and miserable [… a] kind of hell" that no one was prepared for (26).

At first, the Eisenhower administration promoted the idea of a government-led program to build fallout shelters in cities throughout the country, but when the estimated costs proved astronomical and the logistics all but impossible, they shifted their emphasis to home-based shelter projects undertaken by private citizens. In spite of efforts to publicize the dangers of nuclear fallout and to cast home shelter-building as an act of patriotism, a 1960 Senate subcommittee study concluded that "few shelters of any description have been constructed in the United States" (Rose 35). However, Kennedy's Berlin speech a year later dramatically changed national sentiment as it "was made in an atmosphere of crisis and produced an immediate public clamoring for information on how citizens could protect themselves and their families" (37). Responding to this public sentiment, a tidal wave of published material (both factual and fictive, and some a confusing hybrid of each) kept the topics of nuclear annihilation and fallout shelter-building fresh in the American psyche for years to come. As Rose puts it, of possibly "great[est] significance were the numerous nuclear apocalyptic scenarios that appeared in the mainstream magazines and newspapers, often incorporated as part of a feature story on the fallout shelter controversy [. . . as] these descriptions would reach a very wide swath of the public" (40).

The controversy as it quickly emerged was multifaceted, to put it lightly, but in brief it consisted of questions like the following: How would a typical homeowner go about building and supplying a fallout shelter for his family? Could a well-built shelter truly protect a family from the initial bombing *and* from radioactive fallout? Would a homeowner be prepared to use deadly force against ill-prepared friends and neighbors wanting inside his shelter at the moment of crisis? Would a postapocalyptic life be worth living even if one did survive in the shelter? Was building a shelter courageously patriotic or was it a cowardly act in direct opposition to the American fighting spirit? How would a community that had survived essentially intact respond to homeless and desperate refugees arriving from neighboring towns and cities? Were the shelter-building and -supplying businessmen who suddenly appeared on the landscape genuine professionals who had their clients' best interests at heart, or were they conmen out to make a quick dollar off of people's fears and confusion (many swimming-pool builders, for example, recast themselves as fallout-shelter experts)?

Before looking at Gass's narrative in more detail, let me draw upon my earlier work for a brief discussion of literary trauma theory. In a writers' symposium on postmodern literature held at Brown University in 1989, Robert Coover, in his welcoming remarks, gave the impression that the writing style which became known as postmodernism sprang up in the 1950s and '60s almost by sheer coincidence; essentially that individuals writing in isolation on various continents just all happened to begin writing in the same sorts of ways, all in a narrow time span of about fifteen years. According to Coover, writers, with virtual simultaneity, decided to abandon modernist realism for something fragmented, repetitive, largely unrealistic and illogical, and highly intertextual.

273

A more cogent explanation, I believe, rests with trauma theory: The trauma of the nuclear age, which was experienced by the entirety of Western culture (not to mention Eastern), affected the psyches of these writers in a way that resulted in postmodern literary style—a style, according to theorists like Anne Whitehead, Cathy Caruth, and Laura Di Prete, that reflects the traumatized voice. Meanwhile, historians Jay Lifton and Greg Mitchell have made several provocative assertions regarding twentieth-century zeitgeist as it suddenly evolved after the Second World War. For example, Americans were deeply and immediately conflicted with the atomic bombings of Hiroshima and Nagasaki; that is, they experienced the "contradictory emotions of approval and fear the bomb evoked, a combination that has continued to disturb and confuse Americans ever since" (33). And all of this internal conflict, much of which resides in the unconscious, has contributed to a "sense of the world as deeply absurd and dangerous" (335).

In not recognizing the emergence of postmodern literary style as being connected to the nuclear age, it is quite possible that Coover and the other postmodernists at the Brown University symposium experienced the same sort of repression and dissociation that individual trauma victims frequently do. It is not uncommon for people suffering the symptomology of posttraumatic stress disorder to have no conscious recollection whatsoever of the traumatizing event, or to have a dissociated recollection. Coover also discussed writing as "a kind of therapy." He said, "There are things you have to work your way through. There are issues that have to be confronted[. . . .] So you work that out in fictional forms, and you do feel that Freudian answer, that

274

kind of power over what would otherwise be your impotent life" ("'Nothing'" 242). Hence Coover recognized the unsettling cultural climate of post-Hiroshima America and how it contributed to narrative style; also, his view of writing-as-therapy is consistent with trauma theorists who suggest that postmodern techniques are akin to victims' struggling to transform *traumatic* memory into *narrative* memory.

In his examination of the apocalyptic temper in the American novel, Joseph Dewey theorizes about the literary community's response to Hiroshima and Nagasaki, which he describes as "slow in coming." Dewey writes, "[T]he literary conscience of America did not seem ready in the 1940s and even in the 1950s to engage the menace of the mushroom cloud" (8). At first, writers, along with the rest of their culture, experienced a "psychic numbing [. . .] in the face of such catastrophe." In the '50s, notes Dewey, "the American literary community pondered the bomb only in tentative ways." He references "a glut of forgettable speculative fiction" that appeared during the decade. In the early '60s, however, "the American novel began to work with the implications of the nuclear age" (9). Dewey speculates that the Cuban Missile Crisis—"the nuclear High Noon over Cuba"—may have acted as a catalyst for writers in general to "begin to think about the unthinkable." Dewey does not approach his subject in this way, but he seems to be accounting for the dual starting point for American postmodern literary style, which some trace to the mid-1940s and others to the '60s. Nor does Dewey tend to speak in psychological terms, but he seems to be suggesting that American writers were by and large *repressing* the atomic blasts for nearly two decades, until nuclear Armageddon loomed in 1962, which caused the cultural literary psyche to begin to confront the source of its trauma, if only dissociatively. The scenario that Dewey suggests corresponds with the way many individuals respond to a traumatic event. Perhaps the fear of nuclear Apocalypse was part of the American psyche since 1945, but it seemed unreal until 1962's standoff with Cuba and its ally the Soviet Union. It is also useful to note that groups—entire nations even—can respond to trauma just as individuals do. In fact, Neil J. Smelser, in his work on cultural trauma in particular, notes that societies can undergo a delayed response to trauma akin to the Freudian notion of a breakdown in repression, which "only succeeded in incubating, not obliterating the threat"—though he qualifies the analogy as not being perfect (Alexander et al. 51).

I'll note that while Rose and Dewey are offering different years, 1961 versus 1962, as the catalytic year for American culture's traumatic response to atomic annihilation, they are both citing the same source: the sudden heating up of the Cold War.

While evidence of a link between post-Hiroshima trauma and postmodern technique can be found, with greater or lesser conspicuousness, in the work of all writers who occupy the established pantheon of postmodernists, I think the connective tissue is most apparent in the fiction of William H. Gass, one of the writers at the Brown symposium, and, interestingly, the writer Coover called "our real living biographer of the human mind" (242). In his work, which was begun in the mid 1940s (when Gass was in his twenties) but did not start to appear in print consistently until the 1960s, Gass often alludes to trauma and symptoms of posttraumatic stress disorder (though not specifically by

276

these labels), and he cites directly and indirectly the nuclear age as the source of widespread anxiety. As noted earlier, Gass's childhood was, by his own description, miserable, raised by an alcoholic mother and an agonistic father; and one could certainly point to these influences for his prose's negativity. There is no question that these facts have affected Gass's writing, much of which is overtly autobiographical; however, I believe that the Cold War zeitgeist had an even greater impact on his storytelling. One might even conjecture that the insecurities caused by Gass's childhood made the fear associated with that zeitgeist even more potent. The psychological community has long recognized that individuals respond differently to trauma due to a variety of factors, including their mental health when they experience the trauma, and even their genetic predisposition to dealing with traumatic stress.

Now, to look at some of Gass's text. The paper that I presented in 2010 deals with apocalyptic images in Gass—mushroom-cloud shapes, cyclones, extreme heat, deadly winds, and in general destruction raining down from above—and such images are certainly abundant in early excerpts from *The Tunnel*. To bring my discussion from above to below ground, I'll draw attention to a snatch of song lyric that is frequently repeated in 1969's "We Have Not Lived the Right Life" in which a crow represents death. The narrator, William Kohler ("Kohler," by the way, is German for "charcoal burner"), recalls the song from his youth, and the line goes, "Crow—O crow— / don't cross my path, / so my life lasts / a little longer" (8 et al.). This notion of extending life "a little longer" was central to the fallout shelter issue: Would a shelter merely extend life for a few weeks or months as survivors of atomic attack would eventually have to come above ground, only to die from residual radiation or starvation? The song continues, "Crow—O crow— / each time you pass, / my sickness grows / a little stronger" (10, 12). The song continues with images of protracted and painful death. There are references to enclosure throughout this early published excerpt, especially enclosure within one's own or another's body, but the imagery becomes most concentrated late in the piece when Kohler contemplates his sitting in his basement day after day pondering and writing about his wasted life. He says, "I know there are worse ways of living—deeper, darker, damper dungeons—than my own. [. . .] And yet I hold my head and groan and wish these books had fallen in upon me years ago" (30). Furthermore, he posits that "a man who brings his own walls with him is in prison"—perhaps reflective on some level of the fact that the United States has brought this dilemma upon itself with its creation of and unleashing of atomic weapons. This reading is bolstered by other elements in the text that I don't have space to discuss here.

Instead, I'd like to look at "Why Windows Are Important to Me," published in 1971, which is even thicker with images of enclosure and the complex psychology associated with becoming hidden. In this excerpt, Kohler discusses his obsession with "trenches, castles, dugouts, outposts, [and] graves" (58), relating several episodes from his childhood and early adult years in which he either created hiding places or discovered such places behind walls and inside maintenance shafts. Kohler describes "that powerful out of the world feeling" (61) he experienced whenever he hid away because, when not hiding, the world of "out there" made him "an ordinary mortal" and "erod[ed him] like rain"

(60). Here is a lengthy passage about the "bliss" of hiding that is especially rich in ambiguity when examined closely:

> [To hide is t]o enter yourself so completely that you're like a peeled-off glove; to become to the world invisible, entirely out of touch, no longer defined by the eyes of others, unanswering to anyone; to go away with such utterness behind a curtain or beneath a tented table, in the unfamiliar angles of an attic or the menace of a basement; to be swallowed by a chest or hamper as the whale-god swallowed Jonah, and then to find yourself alive, and even well, in the belly of your own being—in a barn loft, under a porch, anywhere out of the mob's middle distance like a Stuart Little, a Tom Thumb, or a Tinker Bell— unnoticed and therefore all the more noticing [. . .] to go supremely away like this was to re-enter through another atmosphere [. . .] (57)

Here we get the joy of hiding and surviving, and even the sense of superiority that those who hide feel over those who are not hidden, characterized as a "mob." To hide is a kind of mystical experience by which one comes to fully understand oneself. Yet there is also present in the passage a sense of extreme isolation and alienation from the world, and there is the frightful image of being swallowed; moreover, we note that of all the hiding places mentioned the only underground one, the basement, is also the only one overtly described as negative, as menacing in fact. It is also interesting that when Kohler hides he feels tiny—like Stuart Little, Tom Thumb, Tinker Bell—perhaps suggestive of the cowardliness that many associated with shelter-building. Finally, I'll point out the idea of transcendence, that via hiding one seems to enter an entirely new realm: maybe the difference between the pre- and post-apocalyptic worlds shelter-builders would experience. In fact, the word *bliss* itself carries with it the notion of transcendence in addition to simply being joyful—but of course to transcend into bliss, one must die.

In this paper I have only begun to scratch the surface of a rich vein in William H. Gass's writing—indeed a vein that runs throughout American postmodern literature. In my way of thinking, it's no coincidence that the vogue of postmodernism fizzled with the end of the Cold War. That is to say, the reading public and publishers in general seemed to suddenly change their tastes, and stopped being attracted to the tropes of postmodern literary style when the threat of nuclear Armageddon no longer seemed imminent. Giants of postmodernism, like Gass and Pynchon, have continued to write as they did in the sixties, seventies and eighties—but honors and accolades, once so numerous, have been far fewer with slumping book sales and contemporary critics who often find them out of step, and perhaps something like curious relics of the Cold War.

Works Cited

Dewey, Joseph. *In a Dark Time: The Apocalyptic Temper in the American Novel of the Nuclear Age.* West Lafayette, IN: Purdue UP, 1990. Print.

Gass, William H. "We Have Not Lived the Right Life." *New American Review* 6 (1969): 7-32. Print.

—. "Why Windows Are Important to Me." *The Best of TriQuarterly.* Ed. Jonathan Brent. New York: Washington Square P, 1982. 49-69. Print.

Hix, H. L. *Understanding William H. Gass.* Columbia: U of South Carolina P, 2002. Print.

Lifton, Robert Jay, and Greg Mitchell. *Hiroshima in America: Fifty Years of Denial*. New York: Grosset/Putnam, 1995. Print.

Malin, Irving. "Anti-Introduction." *Into* The Tunnel: *Readings of Gass's Novel*. Ed. Steven G. Kellman and Irving Malin. Newark: U of Deleware P, 1998. 11. Print.

"'Nothing but Darkness and Talk?': Writers' Symposium on Traditional Values and Iconoclastic Fiction." *Critique* 31.4 (1990): 235-55. Print.

Rose, Kenneth D. *One Nation Underground: The Fallout Shelter in American Culture*. New York: New York UP, 2001. Print.

Smelser, Neil J. "Psychological Trauma and Cultural Trauma." *Cultural Trauma and Collective Identity*. Ed. Jeffrey C. Alexander et al. Berkeley: U of California P, 2004. 31-59. Print.

The Trauma of Alcohol Abuse:
The True Intruder in
William H. Gass's "The Pedersen Kid"

Though written in 1951 and therefore constituting William H. Gass's first work of fiction, the novella "The Pedersen Kid" did not appear in print until a full decade later in John Gardner's journal *MSS*. This paper is based specifically on the version of the novella that appeared in Gass's seminal collection *In the Heart of the Heart of the Country* in 1968. The title story of that collection and Gass's long, dense novel *The Tunnel* (which appeared in 1995) have received the lion's share of critical attention over the decades, while discussion of "The Pedersen Kid" has been meager to put it mildly. Some writers have noted the connection between Gass's well-known miserable childhood—made miserable by Gass's alcoholic mother and hateful bigot of a father—and the fact that the novella's first-person protagonist is leading his own miserable life thanks mainly to his abusive and alcoholic "Pa"; but they have failed to go much beyond that obvious surface connection.

The purpose of this paper is to suggest that understanding the trauma of alcohol abuse within the context of a family is key to more fully understanding the enigmatic novella, whose final section in particular has left both casual readers and critics scratching their heads in puzzlement for more than forty years. In fact, Arthur M. Saltzman said that attempting to gain a clear view of the plot is "self-defeating" because "Gass steers us into cul-de-sacs, lets loose ends dangle, and plunges without warning into subjective distortions," thereby leaving the two most suspenseful narrative questions unresolved and unrelieved (60).

282

Set in mid twentieth-century North Dakota, at the conclusion of a terrible blizzard, the novella begins with the farmhand Big Hans finding the boy from the neighboring Pedersen farm in the yard unconscious and nearly frozen to death as he apparently walked there through the previous night's storm. Later, partially revived, the boy tells Big Hans (allegedly) that an intruder broke into their house and forced his parents into the frigid root-cellar, but somehow the boy escaped and managed to make it on foot all the way to the Segren farm in spite of the blizzard. Most of the novella centers around the three males of the Segren family—Big Hans, Pa Segren, and the young narrator (12 or 13?), Jorge Segren—making their way to the Pedersen farm through the frozen landscape to see if the boy's story is true, though the act is more about Pa's punishing Hans and Jorge than trying to do a neighbor a good turn; in fact, Pa seems to hate Pedersen even more than he hates everyone else around him, referring to him as a "cock," a "bastard," a "fool," and a "shit"; and blaming Pedersen for every bad turn of events, including the previous summer's grasshopper infestation and even the previous day's blizzard.

At the root of Pa's punishment, in addition to his natural mean-spiritedness, is the fact that some of his precious whiskey was found in what he thought was a secure hiding place and used to resuscitate the Pedersen kid without Pa's permission. That seems to be the reason he keeps driving them forward, toward the Pedersen farm and its possible danger, in a horse-drawn wagon that can barely make it through the all but impassable roads and fields. The motivation is freshened part way there, when they are all so miserable with cold they are thinking of turning back, Pa's whiskey bottle falls out of the wagon and is eventually

283

broken by a wagon wheel. Even though he had nothing to do with breaking the bottle, Hans apologizes but to no avail: "Pa squinted at the snow [. . . and] drove" (44).

There have been several theories put forward to explain the novella, which at first suggests a distinct and straightforward narrative arc—namely answering the questions "Did an intruder break into the Pedersen house?" and "Are the Pedersens alive or dead?"—but which disintegrates by the end into ambiguity and downright confusion. Saltzman says it well: "Relentlessly convoluted in design, as though the all-compassing blizzard in the story were rendering all perception hesitant and indistinct, 'The Pedersen Kid' is replete with allegorical options for the discerning reader and is equally accommodating to Freudian, Christian, and heraldic archetypes" (59). Also well put, Patricia Kane writes, "One can locate several points in the story at which Jorge may have hallucinated the rest. Such alternatives provide semi-rational explanations, but the story remains enigmatic and fails to lend itself to neat exegesis" (90).

In a moment, I will put forward a theory based on the findings of professionals who work with families coping with the trauma of alcohol abuse—families which must have resembled Gass's own growing up—and it is a theory that can account for some of the novella's eccentricities, especially its seemingly unresolved resolution. First, though, it is worth looking at how the Segren family exhibits many of the characteristics of families traumatized by alcohol abuse, which adds credence to my use of the substance-abuse theory to examine this work of literary art. Even though alcohol abuse no doubt began almost as soon as the process of fermentation was discovered, culture by culture, seeing it

284

as a "family disease" has been a common practice for only the last twenty to thirty years. In 1985, Stephanie Brown defined alcohol addiction as a family disease "with all family members suffering the consequences of one member's alcoholism and all seen to play a role in maintaining the destructive interactional patterns that result from alcoholism" (qtd. in Brooks and Rice 92). Indeed, these destructive interactional patterns could easily account for Gass's "miserable and damaging" childhood, as characterized by H. L. Hix, who quotes Gass as saying, "For a long time I was simply emotionally unable to handle my parents' illnesses. […] I just fled. [. . .] All along one principal motivation behind my writing has been to be other than the person I am. To cancel the consequences of the past" (2).

G. Harold Smith and his colleagues discuss various types of family structures that form around alcoholic parents, and we can see aspects of these structures in the Segren family. The "enmeshed family," for example, seems especially applicable as it is extremely isolated and wants little to do with outsiders: "Within these highly self-involved families, children's needs may be ignored because the family's attention is focused on the parent who is abusing substances" (Smith et al. 47). The Segren family, of course, is isolated by the very fact they live on a farm in North Dakota, but Pa's attitude toward the Pedersens suggests that the two families have been kept apart, thus exacerbating the geography's tendency toward isolation. In spite of the tragic nature of the occurrence (the Pedersen kid nearly died in the blizzard and may die yet), the mother, Hed Segren, seems excited at the possibility of having company, wanting to put out coffee and fresh biscuits with elderberry jelly for Mr.

Pedersen and his eldest son when they come to collect the kid. Pa, of course, ridicules her for her intentions.

However, an even more tragic trait of the enmeshed family is the alcoholic's tendency toward violence. Smith and his colleagues write, "Often that parent's behavior has to be monitored carefully to avoid negative consequences. For example, much family effort may be expended to avoid provoking a violent reaction from a parent who is intoxicated" (47). Clearly, all three members of Pa Segren's household are afraid of him, and several instances of his cruel and violent nature are recounted at various points in the story, including references to his emptying a chamber-pot filled with diarrhea on Hans's head and his destroying Jorge's favorite picture book and dropping the pieces of torn paper in the privy. In our very first view of Pa in the novella, Jorge is struck in the neck for waking his father to inquire where there is some whiskey with which to try to revive the nearly frozen Pedersen kid. And poor Hed Segren is as skittish and defeated as an abused wife can be; she may even have turned to drinking, too, to cope with her miserable existence.

Because of the enmeshed family's preoccupation with the alcohol abuser, children are often neglected and fall prey to all sorts of deprivations and depravations. Smith and his colleagues report that sexual abuse is "common" in households where substances are abused by one or both parents (48). In "The Pedersen Kid," sexual abuse is not obvious, but Big Hans's relationship with Jorge is questionable and even highly suspicious at times, showing him pornographic magazines, telling him stories about Japanese prostitutes, and even measuring the length of Jorge's penis. As Ripatrazone puts it, "Jorge stops short of claiming physical abuse, but the actions are grossly inappropriate, perhaps the reason why 'pa took a dislike to Hans.'" However, Gass may imply that Jorge—our omnisciently very limited, first-person narrator—is repressing more than he is telling as he seems fixated on penises: the Pedersen kid's, his father's, his own; and he imagines the intruder's assault on his mother as more of a sexual assault as the stranger "wav[es his gun barrel] up and down in front of ma's face real slow and quiet" (19).

There isn't time to go further into detail here, but there are numerous other elements of the novella that seem to reflect the experiences of someone growing up in a household traumatically affected by alcohol abuse. For example, the creation of the narrative about the Pedersen family's intruder, which is pulled together from mere scraps of details, may suggest a family's inclination to invent an alternate narrative about their traumatized existence to fit into their community more easily. Also, there are several spaces brought up in the story that have a duality about them, usually coldness versus warmth, which may suggest the duality of an alcoholic's home that is supposed to provide familial warmth and comfort (and may even do so at times), but that also breeds hostility, mistrust, and often emotional and physical abuse.

Throughout my paper I refer to the *trauma* of alcohol abuse, but trauma is a subjective term. At what point, in other words, does a *really terrible* situation become a genuinely *traumatic* one? From the Greek for "wound," *trauma* originally meant a physical wound. Over time, and especially with the horrors of the First World War, our sense of trauma was extended to include a wound of the mind or psyche as well. Even more recently, the definition of trauma has been expanded to include being subjected to an oppressive and reoccurring situation, like being married to an abusive or potentially abusive spouse, who may have never actually become violent, but whose constant threat of violence creates a traumatic environment. Certainly being a member of a family with a parent who abuses alcohol or other substances constitutes a traumatic situation, and in "The Pedersen Kid" William Gass gives us one of the most poignantly accurate extended metaphors of trauma in American literature:

> It's more than a make-up; it's more than a dream. It's like something you see once and it hits you so hard you never forget it even if you want to; lies, dreams, pass—this has you; it's like something that sticks to you like burrs, burrs you try to brush off while you're doing something else, but they never brush off, they just roll a little, and the first thing you know you ain't doing what you set out to, you're just trying to get them burrs off.   I know.   I got things stuck to me like that. Everybody has.
> Pretty soon you get tired of trying to pick them off. (17)

This passage illustrates the intrusive and haunting nature of trauma, its tenaciousness, its ability to disrupt your concentration, and ultimately your life—and the fact that from Hans's perspective, everyone is traumatized, which makes sense since the novella implies that Hans is a veteran of the First World War. Moreover, this passage suggests that Pa's drinking has, indeed, traumatized the Segren family, and perhaps especially Jorge, who has grown up with his father's capricious personality due to the whiskey that is

288

ubiquitous in the novella, from nearly the first page to the last.

Now for that substance-abuse theory that seems to help us to understand "The Pedersen Kid," especially the ambiguities of its final section.

In 1979, Sharon Wegscheider identified four roles that are often played by children of alcoholics, and it seems that Jorge has assumed each of these roles at some point in "The Pedersen Kid," with the final one casting light on the novella's enigmatic ending. The roles identified by Wegscheider are *family hero*, *scapegoat*, *lost child*, and *mascot* (Ackerman 52-53). The *family hero* "displays behaviors that are extremely mature" (53), and this role is manifested when Jorge is given the responsibility of making sure the Pedersen kid is still alive before they begin their journey to the Pedersen farm, and especially when Jorge is given Hans's .45-caliber pistol to load, which he then carries in his belt, even though "the gun felt like a chunk of ice against [his] belly and the barrel dug" (34). Because of the adventure they are about to embark on, Jorge thinks, "It was like I was setting out to do something special and big—like a knight setting out—worth remembering" (32-33). Later, Jorge wants a drink of Pa's whiskey to warm him, claiming that he has drunk whiskey before; but the request only provokes his father's sarcasm: "Ain't you growed up—a man—since yesterday!" (38). In a truly heroic vein, Jorge dreams about confronting the Pedersens' intruder, wrestling him to the ground and "beating the stocking cap off his head with the barrel of the gun" (33).

An only child, like Gass, Jorge also embodies the family *scapegoat*, who is often the target of "frustrations and confusions" and as a result may "outwardly [display …]

289

negative behavior" (Ackerman 53). Jorge is often ridiculed by both Pa and Hans; examples are copious in the novella. In the scene mentioned earlier, when the whiskey bottle falls from the wagon, Jorge is forced to search for the bottle in the snow in spite of his being painfully cold already. Frustrated at Jorge's not finding the bottle, Pa calls him a "smart-talking snot" and threatens to hold him down under the snow until he drowns (37). Meanwhile, Jorge's negative behaviors are varied, and perhaps his most negative behavior comes in the hallucinatory final section and may or may not happen. An example in the beginning of the story, though, is Jorge's resentment of the attention being paid to the half-frozen Pedersen kid, especially by his mother. Jorge imagines the boy is actually dead and not just near death, consequently dropping him so that his head hits the kitchen table hard (10). In the final section of the novella, however, it seems that Pa is shot dead just outside the Pedersen house. It may have been the intruder who shot Pa, or it may have been Jorge paying Pa back for years of cruelty and abuse. Patricia Kane seems to learn toward the latter interpretation, thinking that Jorge has become mad by the end of the novella (90); while Nick Ripatrzone, writing in *The Quarterly Conversation*, believes that Jorge only wishes his father dead and does not actually shoot him.

Jorge also resembles the *lost child*, who suffers "the most role inconsistency" in the family of an alcoholic (Ackerman 53). At times, Jorge tries to shield his mother from Pa's abuse, but she also scolds Hans for "pester[ing] the boy" (19)—so when it comes to his mother, he is both a mature protector and a child who needs protection. Even still, he imagines his mother coming to harm, and her fantasized death completes his sense of freedom from his oppressively abusive family. But it is via metaphor that we can see Jorge's lost child status most clearly. In the beginning of the novella, it is, quite literally, the Pedersen kid who is lost. In fact, the Segrens entertain the idea that the kid merely wandered off in the blizzard of his own accord, and the Pedersens will come looking for him now that the blizzard has stopped. By the end, however, Jorge, now occupying the Pedersen farmhouse by himself, believes that he and the Pedersen kid have "been exchanged, and we were both in our new lands" (73). And by the very end, Jorge and the Pedersen kid are more than exchanged; it is as if they are living parallel lives in their new lands. Thus, Jorge has in essence become the novella's original *lost boy*.

It is also via this exchange that we can see Jorge as the *mascot*, the child who "may be overly protected from the family problems" (Ackerman 53). After Pa has been killed, Jorge takes refuge in the Pedersens' root-cellar, waiting to be killed himself by the intruder (assuming the version of the story that there *is* an intruder who has killed the Pedersens and now Pa too). After what seems a long time, the intruder stops waiting for Jorge and leaves the Pedersen house with a slam of the front door (66). So, from this perspective, both Jorge and the Pedersen kid have been spared by the intruder, and in fact Jorge has been protected in a sense because the source of his misery—his alcoholic father—has been permanently removed from his life.

Throughout the novella, the intruder is a vague but ominous figure, with only a handful of descriptors attached to him which are repeated again and again (the black stocking cap, the yellow gloves, the green mackinaw, the gun), just as the whiskey is an object known chiefly by its fecal color, its omnipresence, and its desirability as all the

Segrens (even the mother) seem to thirst for it, or at least for the power it lends tyrannical Pa. Thus in my reading of "The Pedersen Kid" the true intruder, the true menace is the whiskey-induced alcoholism. We note that it is en route to the Pedersen farm that whiskey, as an object, disappears from the narrative as Horse Simon shatters Pa's bottle, which had fallen from the wagon, into the snow. Its destruction propels Pa toward his own demise, empowering or at least enabling Jorge to overcome him in the end. The intruder (whiskey) and his minion (Pa) destroyed, Jorge is overjoyed at the end of the novella; he is "burning up, inside and out with joy," and *joy* is, in fact, the novella's final word (79).

In addition to Wegscheider's four roles, Norman Garmezy also coined the category of *invulnerables*: "These are the children, that despite all the family problems, have not only survived, but also have grown into healthy adults" (Ackerman 53). Garmezy estimated that about ten percent of children in homes with an alcoholic parent prove to be *invulnerable*. It seems that perhaps Gass himself fits this category in that he managed to take his miserable childhood and create from it an illustrious writing and teaching career.

Works Cited

Ackerman, Robert J. *Children of Alcoholics: A Guidebook for Educators, Therapists, and Parents.* 2nd ed. Holmes Beach, FL: Learning Publications, 1983. Print.

Brooks, Carolyn Seval, and Kathleen Fitzgerald Rice. *Families in Recovery: Coming Full Circle.* Baltimore, MD: Paul H. Brookes, 1997. Print.

Gass, William H. "The Pedersen Kid." 1961. *In the Heart of the Heart of the Country and Other Stories*. Boston, MA: Nonpareil, 1981. Print. 1-79.

Hix, H. L. *Understanding William H. Gass*. Columbia: U of South Carolina P, 2002. Print.

Kane, Patricia. "The Sun Burned on the Snow: Gass's 'The Pedersen Kid.'" *Critique* 14.2 (1972): 89-96. Print.

Ripatrazone, Nick. "Let Me Make a Snowman: John Gardner, William Gass, and 'The Pedersen Kid.'" *The Quarterly Conversation*. Web. 15 Feb. 2013.

Saltzman, Arthur M. *The Fiction of William Gass: The Consolation of Language*. Carbondale: Southern Illinois UP, 1986. Print.

Smith, G. Harold, et al. *Children, Families, and Substance Abuse: Challenges for Changing Educational and Social Outcomes*. Baltimore, MD: Paul. H. Brookes, 1995. Print.

Locating Our Common Humanity
Through Expressive Writing

When the conference committee graciously invited me to speak to you, my first response was to go to the conference's website and read about its overarching objective, which, I discovered, has to do with breaking down cultural barriers between nations. Even though I do not regularly travel between nations, it is an idea with which I am profoundly familiar. In the United States, the election of our current president has dramatized the theory that we have within our borders two distinct cultures, two dominant ideologies, two divisive world views which threaten to tear us into two separate nations. Or perhaps a better way of contextualizing the situation is to say that the wound caused by our Civil War which nearly broke us in two 150 years ago has never actually healed—and the current administration has merely made us painfully aware of what has always been true.

One can despair when one considers the seeming hopelessness of bridging political, ideological and cultural divides. Emotions run deep, and people are quick to anger and to become defensive when their worldview, when their belief system is challenged. In my classroom, I encourage my students to engage in discussions of the issues that divide them: gun control, immigration, gay rights, reproductive rights, among many others. I daresay that little progress appears to be made in convincing either side to alter their perceptions.

However, when my students access other aspects of their lives—when they move away from issues related to ideologies—they instantly have things in common. In fact, I would assert, they have *everything* in common. When I ask them to access their emotions—their joys, their disappointments, their frustrations, their achievements—they speak the same language, regardless of whether they are conservative or liberal, straight or gay, gun-owning or gun-controlling, gendered or gender-neutral, Pro-Life or Pro-Choice. That is to say, when they are asked to communicate expressively, students, above all else, are *human*.

Which brings me at long last to my thesis: Through expressive writing, we can locate our common humanity. In other words, what divides us tends to be the product of intellect, while what unites us is our emotional responses to the world.

Allow me to take a moment to define some terms, especially to define them as I am using them in this presentation. The key term, obviously, is "expressive" writing, by which I mean writing that explores and communicates one's emotional reaction to a given situation, generally a situation that one has experienced personally. I am adopting and somewhat adapting concepts discussed by James Britton, who identified three writing functions: transactional, expressive, and poetic. Briefly, "transactional" writing aims to inform and/or persuade the audience through the manipulation of primary- and secondary-source material (i.e. "research"), and in this transactional mode the writer's *self* all but disappears. Transactional writing, in academic settings, takes the form of analyses and research-based reports, wherein personal experience, even in the form of anecdotal evidence, is frowned upon almost to the point of nonexistence, especially in the sciences but even in the humanities.

As Jeff Park remarks in his book *Writing at the Edge*, transactional writing is by far the dominant mode in the academy, while expressive writing "continues to be underdeveloped" (25). Returning to James Britton's terms, the other modes besides "transactional" are "expressive" and "poetic." Here things can become confusing. By "poetic," Britton means something made out of language for language's own sake but having little to do with writers' expressing their feelings on the subject. Riddles, puns, acrostics, limericks may be examples of poetic language use in the way that Britton is defining the term.

Generally, though, *poetry* refers to writing that is highly personal and expressive. Therefore, when I use the phrase "expressive writing" I am using it as synonymous with what, in the U.S., we most often term "creative writing," which includes fiction, poetry, and creative nonfiction (or the personal essay). Adding to the confusion is the fact that writers can certainly create stories, novels, poems, and essays that are not especially expressive of their emotions. They may be trying to entertain, to titillate, or to expound on some subject, but they are not trying to communicate a personal experience and how it affected them on an emotional level. Here, today, I am specifically advocating *expressive* writing as a means to breaking down or *through* cultural barriers.

Educators have long advocated *reading* as a key to developing empathy in students, including empathy for people of other cultures. I certainly agree that reading about other sorts of people can spark interest and understanding, which can in turn lead to empathy. More often that not in the U.S., however, reading literature is the *sole* means of encouraging empathy in the humanities. Empathy development is not bolstered routinely with expressive writing, and that, I believe, is a mistake. We *should* be having our students write expressively—and, importantly, sharing their writing through some means of publication (more on this in a moment).

While literary study may be only one component of fostering empathy, it is through literary study that we can most vividly see evidence of our common humanity, which is so often obscured by our politics and competing ideologies. I do not want to get too sidetracked here, but I am referring to the concept of archetypal narratives which seem to spring from a common past that transcends geography and culture. I give as just one example, in brief, the narrative of the woebegone sailor who, driven off course, finds himself and his men trapped inside the dwelling of a man-eating giant. Through his cleverness and courage, the sailor manages to blind the giant and escape the dwelling by hiding amongst the giant's grazing flock. Whether one recognizes this as the story of Odysseus, or of Sinbad, or of the Man with No Legs depends on whether one is familiar with a Greek, Persian, or Korean literary tradition.

In essence, then, the tale of the woebegone sailor is foundational in Western, Middle Eastern, and Eastern cultures (to use Western distinctions)—a tale so ancient no one can cite its precise origin. These parts of the world are sharply divided when it comes to religions and political ideologies, yet the tale of the woebegone sailor must speak to us all: the disorientation and frustration of being lost, the primal fear of being trapped by a predator of superior power, the exhilaration of resourcefulness, and the joy of our life-preserving escape: all peoples, everywhere, can relate to these emotional registers in the common story.

Through expressive writing—that is, writing that accesses and communicates our emotions rather than our ideologies—students from diverse backgrounds can locate their common humanity, and see there is as much that unites us as there is that divides us.

297

This topic is obviously complex, and I can only begin, here, to outline some of its component parts, but I will touch on the following areas: the theories which underpin the effectiveness of expressive writing for fostering empathy; the likelihood of students engaging in traumatic writing when given the opportunity to express themselves; some of the side benefits of expressive writing; the importance of publishing, and not just creating, the results of expressive writing; and some concrete classroom practices if one is inclined to use expressive writing in their curriculum.

Theories about expressive writing & empathy

First, then, how does expressive (or creative) writing create a connection between writer and reader that goes beyond, that goes deeper than other sorts of modes of communication? To respond, I turn to the work of Marcelle Freiman, who is especially interested in the cognitive connections between creative writers and their readers. Building on the work of cognitive scientists like Gerrig, Oatley and Djikic, Freiman asserts that "human long-term memory" is not only "'based on memory'" but also "'actively generates meaning'" (133). Thus, the act of writing helps writers to organize their thoughts and reconstruct memories—including all the associations those memories evoke—and it creates "an extended, externalised mental model" which readers are invited to enter. A well-wrought narrative can make a reader experience the story as if they had direct involvement in it. I am referring to the phenomenon of *being lost in a story*, to which nearly everyone can relate.

Freiman theorizes that the phenomenon is caused by the reader in essence "'writing' the text (in the mind) while reading" (134). Here she quotes Hawkes directly: "[Writers] thus involve us in the dangerous, exhilarating activity of creating our worlds *now*, together with the author, as we go along" (135, emphasis in the original). Freiman is suggesting that the relationship between writer and reader goes beyond being complementary into the realm of genuine partnership; the writer and reader are literally working together to create meaning. This process of shared responsibility in the text is true of all writing, says Freiman, but it has an enhanced dynamic when it comes to expressive writing: "This capacity for the writing of the creative or literary text occurs, perhaps, even more vividly 'as experience' because now the process involves imagination, including experiential representations of referents such as perceptions and emotions, in the language that writes what is imaginatively construed, to be read by a reader" (135). I want to underscore the words *perceptions and emotions* as these are key elements in an act of empathy. Understanding how others perceive their world and the emotions their perceptions elicit is absolutely vital to seeing people as *people* and not merely avatars for the ideologies they appear to represent.

Likelihood of students writing about trauma

Let me move on to the question, why are students likely to write about trauma when given the opportunity to write expressively? When left to choose their own subject, many students will, of course, elect to write about happy things, which is valid. Writing about successes, about favorite memories, about the love of family and friends are all legitimate responses to an open-ended task to compose; and others can relate to positive experiences. But many, many students will choose to write about a traumatic experience in their lives, and it is due to the nature of trauma. The term "trauma" is slippery, and it is used to describe a vast array of life experiences; thus, depending on how widely or how narrowly one defines what constitutes "trauma," the number of people who are suffering from some level of traumatic stress fluctuates up and down. Various studies identify between a quarter and three-quarters of the U.S. population as having had some kind of traumatic experience.[1] People who have been traumatized tend to want to write about the experience, either explicitly or implicitly. Studies in the field of neuropsychology have suggested that trauma-related language dominates the linguistic functioning of victims.[2] As MacCurdy observes, "Invariably writers gravitate to their difficult stories, the ones that cause the most pain and confusion . . ." (15).

Because the academy does not privilege expressive writing, relatively few educators are trained to facilitate it, and, consequently, to respond to students' writing about their traumatic experiences. When students elect to write about traumatic episodes in their lives, the complexities of the writing classroom multiply exponentially. The most immediate question educators must ask themselves is "Which is more important: the student's acquisition of writing skills, or the student's emotional welfare, which may be improved by engaging the traumatic event?" Before responding to my own question, I should say that communicating one's trauma is a standard practice in therapy, either through one-on-one discussions with one's therapist, in a group-therapy setting, or through writing (or some combination of these basic approaches). Once a teacher encourages students to engage their trauma in the classroom, the distinction between teacher and therapist can become murky. MacCurdy attempts to draw a distinction when she writes, "Teachers are advisers, mentors, and role models. Listening with compassion helps to fulfill those responsibilities and creates the trust needed for the student to delve into a difficult topic. . . . . However, teachers are not therapists. While a therapist may listen and then counsel, teachers listen and, if appropriate, suggest counseling and other professional services" (6).

I find no fault with MacCurdy's assessment other than to say that she makes it plain why teaching—and perhaps especially teaching *writing*—is more art than science. Knowing when and how to respond to students' work relies almost entirely on professional judgment; there are no clear-cut guidelines to follow, as much as we may wish at times there were.[3]

Benefits of expressive writing

So, writing about trauma can have therapeutic benefits for students. If one looks at that aspect of trauma writing—potential emotional benefits—certain pedagogical difficulties emerge regarding the sort of work students produce (in essence, how fragmentary or how complete it may be or must be), the ways in which it should be assessed (according to traditional guidelines for written work or by some other kind of rubric), and whether or not it should be shared with others (that is, published). How one responds to each of these issues may depend in large part on the end goal. If the end goal is for students to produce something that is most definitely going to be shared with others (versus something mainly for their own experiencing of the process), then the pedagogy must shift accordingly.

Again, we are in the realm of art more than of science. The difference between students writing something only for themselves and students writing something which will be shared with others may lie in how the teacher contextualizes

301

the act of writing and the possible benefits of sharing highly personal experiences. Allow me to say what may be needless to say: The best writing—the best art—is generally rooted in the highly personal experience. In order to create texts that are meaningful, and emotionally and intellectually engaging for readers, writers must be willing to reveal their most personal and their most private experiences and ideas. Marguerite MacRobert recommends that writers use techniques similar to those employed by method actors (à la Stanislavski). She says, "Writers are often spoken of as observers, and many writing workshops hone observation skills, but what Stanislavski says of acting could be emphasised in writing too: openness to experience as it occurs and being able to access emotional memories are crucial writing abilities. . . ." (353).

I will add anecdotally that when I took fiction writing workshops with the novelist Kent Haruf, in the opening class session Kent would always ask us to share something personal about ourselves that we had never shared with anyone else. The point of his exercise was that to be effective fiction writers we must be willing and able to share our most personal thoughts and experiences with our readers. Holding back leads to writing that is less than it could be. This sort of openness may seem like a tall order to expect of young students, but recall that traumatized students generally *want* to write about their traumatic experiences. In fact, they *need* to write about them. The pedagogical trick is not to get them to write personally, but to be willing to share their personal writing with others: to instill them with confidence, and to teach them that their sharing can benefit others, namely their readers.

Given our setting and the conference's overarching mission it is vital to note that expressive writing can transcend language barriers, and in fact can benefit from them. That is, students writing in languages other than their primary language (in English for instance) can be beneficial to the expressive-writing process in several ways. Here I will turn to the work of Owens and Brien, who developed a project in which international students attending universities in Australia wrote expressively in English with the goal of producing a published journal. Too often, international students' language skills are viewed as a weakness or an obstacle to be overcome; however, Owens and Brien, among others (I included), advocate seeing these students' language skills as a strength and an opportunity. They write, "[P]erceptions about the English skills of [Learners of English as an Alternative (or Additional) Language] have serious implications for large numbers of students, teachers, employers and, more broadly, the higher education industry. . . . [R]ecognising these learners as linguistically complex (rather than deficient) and finding new and enhanced methods to support their language needs . . . could transform both university practices and the students' experience of those practices" (361-362). In particular, Owens and Brien advocate the use of creative writing as a way to foster these learners' acquisition of alternative languages and to ease their assimilation into unfamiliar environments.

In Owens and Brien's project, they found that international students were drawn to writing about the difficulties associated with cultural assimilation. While writing in a language other than their mother tongue did present some challenges, there were also numerous benefits. They write, "[Alternative Language speakers] have both less (English) and more (languages other than English) lexical-syntactic-semantic knowledge than monolingual English speakers. They rely on a more restricted English resource but have alternative language options available to express meaning. . . . So, whilst mother

303

tongue speakers may use their language creatively in response to situational characteristics, Alternative Language speakers may use English more creatively . . ." (362). What is more, the way Alternative Language speakers approach language may lead to particularly poetic constructions, say Owens and Brien. As someone who has taught Alternative Language speakers in creative writing workshops (especially speakers of Asian languages and, most often, speakers of Chinese), I can attest that even beginning creative writers can compose some startlingly beautiful phrases and images in English *because* of their knowledge of multiple languages, not *in spite* of it.

Importance of sharing & publishing

It definitely goes without saying that if expressive writing is going to help break down cultural barriers, it must be shared across borders (both geographic and ideologic), which is where publication enters the discussion. Though discussing their project in the microcosm of their university settings, Owens and Brien found that Alternative Language students writing expressively benefited both the writers themselves and their audience: "It allows readers, such as academic staff as well as other students, to gain insight into the cross-cultural experience and develop greater empathy for the cultural sojourner" (369). Moreover, "the act of authoring such texts" can be "empowering" on multiple levels: "Promoting the creative and unique English language capacities of [Alternative Language students] . . . across English speaking host-communities, can help . . . build empathy, understanding and appreciation in a language context where they are conventionally de-valued" (369). Moreover, Jess-Cooke believes that students' producing "a completed piece of work is

304

a significant part of building self-esteem, and therefore contributes to wellbeing" (254).

Fortunately, we live in a time when sharing writing (or video or audio) across the globe is relatively simple. Material can be posted to the Web of course. Texts can be made available to download to various sorts of e-readers (Kindle, etc.), and print-on-demand options make physically published anthologies readily and cheaply available via outlets like Amazon among many others. Speaking as a publisher and author, the challenge is not to make students' writing available across cultural boundaries, but rather how to help others realize it is available in the flood of material that is published, one way or another, every day. Some estimates put the number of new book titles alone released each year in the neighborhood of a million. On any given day, several thousand new titles may become available. Unfortunately I have not solved this conundrum. I would say, as with any project, the way to begin, at least, is to start small. That is, micro-target specific audiences, perhaps via university networking opportunities, as afforded via conferences like this one. Work with colleagues in other countries to produce expressive writing and share it beyond physical borders. Perhaps combine the work of students from several countries in a single anthology to be shared and distributed amongst the project participants. Students' texts could be captured via audio recordings and video performances, adding additional contextual layers to the communicated experiences.

Concrete classroom practices

I would like to end with a practical suggestion for a writing prompt. I have found that students respond quite effectively to what I call "A Moment of Clarity" narrative essay.

I ask them to write about a time when they came to understand something about themselves or about their world due to a specific event in their lives. (I have provided the specific assignment and pre-drafting activity as an <u>appendix</u> to this presentation.) Some students write about positive things in their lives: learning the importance of teamwork or dedication, discovering what they want to do with their lives, embracing their spiritual selves, accepting their true sexuality, and so on. More students, though, tend to write about traumatic, life-transforming experiences: the death of a loved one, a near-death experience of their own, the separation of their parents, the crushing loss of a best friend or first girlfriend or boyfriend.

Allow me to share some brief excerpts of papers my students wrote this past year as a response to the "Moment of Clarity" prompt (the students have granted their permission, and I have obscured their identities):

From a student whose boyfriend was driving recklessly and lost control of his car: "The convertible Mustang [car] flipped, pinning me underneath the vehicle. The only thing that kept me from getting my head smashed was the headrest that held it up just enough. I needed to stay calm. I couldn't focus on anything else but the sound of the blood dripping on the ground. I tried to move my right arm and couldn't."

From a student who struggled with the death of her grandmother after a long illness: "Now I understand that death occurs in everyone's life and everyone is affected by it differently. She was in pain because of the cancer and all of the medicine she was taking. Seeing her in the casket was different because she looked peaceful and beautiful compared to the cancer's effect on her. I have to let her go because I love her and she would not want me to be afraid or sad. She would want me to strive and achieve my goals and to live my life."

From a student who attempted suicide: "I spent my teenage years begging myself at night not to give up, not to kill myself. My first attempt at suicide was in 2015. I remember sitting in my room and the feeling rushed upon me. 'You're not good enough . . . you don't deserve to live . . . just do it.' I felt numb in that moment. I didn't feel like a person. I got up and grabbed the bottle of pills. I begged myself to get help and go get my mother, but all I could think about was swallowing the pills and not being here anymore."

From a student who has given up her Christian faith: "I think how many Native Americans think. How we're all connected and that you should put out what you want in return. I feel life is sacred, but so is the afterlife. The two worlds co-exist with one another. Death doesn't mean the end of life, it's just the beginning."

These narratives were written by young people living in a small town in the heart of the United States, but I daresay they express feelings and concerns and issues that young people—that all people—face daily, no matter their culture, no matter their country, no matter their ideology.

Notes

1. See Bessel A. Van der Kolk, Alexander C. McFarlane, and Lars Weisaeth, editors. *Traumatic Stress: The Effects of Overwhelming Experience on Mind, Body, and Society*. Guilford, 2007, p. 5.

2. See Jennifer J. Vasterling, and Chris R. Brewin, editors. *Neuropsychology of PTSD: Biiological, Cognitive, and Clinical Perspectives*, Guilford, 2005. In particular see Joseph I. Constans. "Information-Processing Biases in PTSD," Vasterling and Brewin, pp. 105-130.

3. See Chapter 7, "Pedagogical Implications and Conclusions," pp. 185-224.

Works Cited

Freiman, Marcelle. "A 'Cognitive Turn' in Creative Writing — Cognition, Body and Imagination." *New Writing: International Journal for the Practice and Theory of Creative Writing*, vol. 12, no. 2, 2015, pp. 127-142.

Jess-Cooke, Carolyn. "Should Creative Writing Courses Teach Ways of Building Resilience?" *New Writing: International Journal for the Practice and Theory of Creative Writing*, vol. 12, no. 2, 2015, pp. 249-259.

MacCurdy, Marian Mesrodian. *The Mind's Eye: Image and Memory in Writing about Trauma.* U of Massachusetts P, 2007.

MacRobert, Marguerite. "Exploring an Acting Method to Contain the Potential Madness of the Creative Process: Mental Health and Writing with Emotion." *International Journal for the Practice and Theory of Creative Writing*, vol. 9, no. 3, 2012, pp. 349-360.

Owens, Alison R., and Donna L. Brien. "Writing Themselves: Using Creative Writing to Facilitate International Student Accounts of Their Intercultural Experience." *New Writing: International Journal for the Practice and Theory of Creative Writing*, vol. 11, no. 3, 2014, pp. 359-374.

Park, Jeff. *Writing at the Edge: Narrative and Writing Process Theory.* Peter Lang, 2005.

About the Author

Ted Morrissey was educated at Southern Illinois University in Carbondale and Illinois State University, where he completed the Ph.D. in English Studies in 2010. His books include *A Concise Summary and Analysis of The Mueller Report*, and *The 'Beowulf' Poet and His Real Monsters*, which won Edwin Mellen's D. Simon Evans Prize for Distinguished Scholarship. His most recent novels are *The Artist Spoke*, *Mrs Saville* (winner of the Manhattan Book Award), and *Crowsong for the Stricken* (International Book Award and American Fiction Award). The collection *First Kings and Other Stories* appeared in 2020. He has taught at University of Illinois and Benedictine University, and since 2016 he has been a lecturer in Lindenwood University's MFA in Writing program. He lives with his wife Melissa, also an educator and author, near Springfield, Illinois.

tedmorrissey.com – @t_morrissey – *FB* jtedmorrissey

www.ingramcontent.com/pod-product-compliance
Lightning Source LLC
Chambersburg PA
CBHW081416090426
42738CB00017B/3386